Maaike de Haardt, Anne-Marie Korte (eds.)

Common Bodies

Theologische Frauenforschung in Europa

herausgegeben von

Prof. Dr. Hedwig Meyer-Wilmes
(Nijmegen)

und

Prof. Dr. Marie-Theres Wacker
(Münster)

Band 6

LIT

Maaike de Haardt, Anne-Marie Korte (eds.)

COMMON BODIES
Everyday Practices, Gender and Religion

LIT

Umschlagbild: Foto einer Keramikskulptur
der Künstlerin Mieke van den Hoogen

Die Deutsche Bibliothek – CIP-Einheitsaufnahme

Common Bodies : Everyday Practices, Gender and Religion / Maaike de Haardt,
Anne-Marie Korte (eds.) . – Münster : LIT, 2002
   (Theologische Frauenforschung in Europa ; 6)
   ISBN 3-8258-5578-3

© **LIT** VERLAG Münster – Hamburg – London
   Grevener Str. 179   48159 Münster   Tel. 0251-23 50 91   Fax 0251-23 19 72
   e-Mail: lit@lit-verlag.de   http://www.lit-verlag.de

Distributed in North America by:

Transaction Publishers
New Brunswick (U.S.A.) and London (U.K.)

Transaction Publishers   Tel.: (732) 445 - 2280
Rutgers University   Fax: (732) 445 - 3138
35 Berrue Circle   for orders (U. S. only):
Piscataway, NJ 08854   toll free (888) 999 - 6778

Acknowledgements

This anthology is the second to be published in what we hope will be an ongoing series, initiated by the Dutch Research Programme in Religion and Gender. The programme brought together the authors of this volume. They participate in the regular meetings of the research group in which we discuss our work, our common projects, and new developments in the field of gender and religion; the fact hat we can have these regular meetings is one of the advantages of living in a small country. Therefore, we wish to express our gratitude not only to the authors for their contributions, but also to the other scholars of this Dutch research group for sharing their creativity and insights during the ongoing discussions on the Common Bodies project. We also thank the OPP, the research-group of the Women's Network for Feminism and Theology in the Netherlands, for sustaining and nourishing the Religion and Gender Research Programme.

The Netherlands Advanced School for Theology and Religious Studies (NOSTER) provides the institutional context for our Research Programme, has given the programme its own position within the structures of the school, and has also provided us with financial support to organize our meetings. Although the integration of the gender perspective does not seem to be a matter of foremost importance for most members of NOSTER, the integration of the Religion and Gender Programme in the school is a considerable step and also an important sign of recognition of the group of researchers committed to gender studies in religion in the Netherlands. We express our gratitude to the board of NOSTER for their support.

The production of a book like this needs funding in order to realize its publication. We are grateful for the financial support received from the Catharina Halkes Foundation. We thank the Sormani Foundation for their generous and substantial support; the Radboud Foundation for their donation; the Porticus Foundation for their mediation in acquiring financial support and the Faculty of Theology of the Catholic University of Nijmegen for providing us with the last financial means that made ends meet.

Living in a small country with its own language also has its disadvantages. We have chosen to present the results of our studies in English and in German, which implied that, apart from the last editing, we needed a special translation-editing and a firm last copy control. We want to thank all the persons who have helped us through this final stage. We could not have succeeded without the ongoing assistance of Willien van Wieringen, Rosaliene Israel, Meghan T. Sweeney, Diny de Jong and Magda Misset-van de Weg. We are very grateful for the invaluable help they provided in preparing the manuscripts for publication.

Finally, we thank the editors of the series 'Theologische Frauenforschung in Europa' from LIT-Verlag in Münster, Hedwig Meyer-Wilmes and Marie-Theres Wacker, for including this volume in their series and thereby giving us the opportunity to present the work of the Dutch Research Programme on Religion and Gender as part of a growing body of European feminist theological explorations.

Maaike de Haardt
Anne-Marie Korte

Nijmegen/Utrecht,
Spring 2002

Contents

Vorwort — v
    Hedwig Meyer-Wilmes

The Creativity of Corporeal Practices — 1
Introduction
    Maaike de Haardt and Anne-Marie Korte

'A Way of Being-in-the-World' — 11
Traces of Divinity in Everday Life
    Maaike de Haardt

Of Love, Life and Belief: The Story of Mary of Bethany — 27
(John 12:1-8)
    Magda Misset-van de Weg

'The Pearl Lay Hidden in the Dung' — 43
Reaching for God in *Devotio Moderna* Sisterbooks
    Mathilde van Dijk

Lebendiges Wasser — 59
Die Geschichte der samaritanischen Frau (Johannes 4) aus Rembrandts
Perspektive gelesen
    Anne Marijke Spijkerboer

Kinship of Soul — 77
Lisa Moren's *la_alma* Interactive Video Book
    Inez van der Spek

The Need for 'Another World' 93
Women's Everyday Life and the Embrace of Pain
Kune Biezeveld

A Mixed Blessing 109
Differently Abled Women and Experiences of Transcendence
Jacqueline Kool

"I Have Only One Body!" 125
The Conflict between 'Love' and Integrity in Everyday Practices
Riet Bons-Storm

Reciprocity and Grace in the Golden Rule 141
Proverbial Wisdom as Source for Intercultural Dialogue and
Moral Theology
Grietje Dresen

Zu dritt, oder: Das Gebet als eine utopische Erinnerung 157
Susanne Hennecke

Authors 177

Vorwort

Hedwig Meyer-Wilmes

Das vorliegende Buch verdankt sich einem interfakultären Forschungszusammenhang über Körper, Religion und Gender unter der koordinierenden Leitung von Maaike de Haardt und Anne-Marie Korte. In *Common Bodies. Everyday Practices, Gender and Religion* bringen zehn Beiträge unterschiedlicher disziplinärer Herkunft (Pastoral-, Fundamentaltheologie, Exegese, Kirchengeschichte, Dogmatik) ihre jeweilige Perspektive auf den Körper in der alltäglichen Praxis des Betens, Schauens (Rembrandt), des Schmerzes, Älterwerdens und der Erfahrung des Göttlichen ein.

Die Herausgeberinnen der Reihe 'Theologische Frauenforschung in Europa' möchten mit diesem Band einen Einblick in einen nationalen Diskurs geben, in diesem Fall dem niederländischen. Gleichzeitig bedanken wir uns beim Verlag für den Mut einer zum grössten Teil englisch-sprachigen Publikation, die der Internationalität der Debatte gerecht wird und damit nicht nur dem deutschen Sprachraum zugänglich.

Wenn Pascal in seinem 'Memorial' immer wieder den Unterschied zwischen dem Gott der rein argumentierenden Vernunft, also dem Gott der Philosophen und dem erzählten Gott Abrahams, Isaaks und Jakobs markiert, dann gelingt es dem vorliegenden Buch aufzuzeigen, dass der christliche Gott im ganz alltäglichen Leben (Everyday Practices) zu verorten ist, dass die Inkarnation des Göttlichen in ganz gewöhnlichen Körpern (Common Bodies) nicht ignoriert werden kann. Man findet sie, sucht nach ihm, verzweifelt an ihm beim Essen, Handeln, in Angst und Hingabe. (Gender and Religion). Widerständig und loyal werden eine Reihe der Grundkonzepte theologischen Denkens auf ihre Alltagstauglichkeit hin überprüft und neu formuliert. Körper sind in der feministischen Debatte Orte der Konstruktion einer symbolischen Ordnung, im theologischen Diskurs gilt es, diese Orte über die Askese und Fruchtbarkeit hinaus zurückzugewinnen. Der vorliegende Band bietet Schritte zu einer Theologie des Alltags, der Körper als Ort kultureller Praxis, Medium, heuristische Brille oder aber materiale Ausgangsbasis dient.

The Creativity of Corporeal Practices

Introduction

Maaike de Haardt and Anne-Marie Korte

Poignant insights in the relationship among corporeality, gender, and religion have been formulated during the last few decades by scholars like Mary Douglas, Michel Foucault, Julia Kristeva, Elaine Scarry, Peter Brown, Caroline Walker Bynum, Luce Irigaray and many others. They have incited the project of turning body into subject and subject into body onto the field of theology and religious studies, generating new insights and new questions that affect the key issues of these studies, including the concepts of faith, religious experience, religious community, God-talk, and the divine.

Common Bodies. Everyday Practices, Gender and Religion deals with the theological consequences of rethinking the relationship among corporeality, gender, and religion. This anthology continues the explorations in this field that members of the Dutch Research Programme for Religion and Gender started in their previous volume *Begin With the Body. Corporeality, Religion and Gender* (Peeters 1998). In the latter we attempted to reframe and redirect theological reflection by focusing on human bodies and corporeality problematized to an increasing degree within gender studies. Informed by secular feminist discourses on gender, language, and subjectivity on the one hand, and by feminist theological debates on anthropology, incarnation, and embodiment on the other, we tried to shape a style of feminist theological reflection that "escapes the Scylla and Charybdis of essentialism and constructivism" and that envisages the human, gendered body as "a site of pain and pleasure, transience and transcendence, continuity and change".[1]

In this publication we continue our enquiries, building on several interesting outcomes of our first anthology. An important outgrowth of our previous volume lies in the attempt to deconstruct classic theological distinctions and dualisms in which corporeality, and especially human materiality, plays an important but often unacknowledged role, as we tried to demonstrate by focusing on transcendence and immanence, infinity and finitude, God and 'the idols', life and death, spirituality and materiality, and autonomy and submission. By unraveling the intertwinement of these theological distinctions with 'natural' and 'biological' assumptions about gender and corporeality, this approach paves the way for theological reflection that is no longer captivated by these concepts and dualisms and is capable of creating

---

[1] J. Bekkenkamp & M. de Haardt, "Introduction", in J. Bekkenkamp & M. de Haardt (eds.), *Begin with the Body. Corporeality Religion and Gender* (Leuven: Peeters, 1998), 4.

alternative terms of designation. In this second anthology we attempt to pursue this project.

Another interesting result of the first volume that we take up here concerns the attentive recognition of the paradoxes and ambivalences that bodily existence evokes, as they come to the fore particularly in situations of pain, illness and death, love and violence, sexuality and procreation, and artistic performance. By addressing these ambivalences we have constituted a particular hermeneutical starting point to discuss the relevance and meaning of faith and religion in light of feminist as well as contemporary concerns. To develop this hermeneutical stance, the definitions of 'religion' and 'theology' also come into debate, as the essays in this book again will show.

In the articles that we are presenting here, we investigate 'corporeal practices' and the ways they induce, contest, and transform religious meaning. In particular we concentrate on the gendered body in its common, everyday activities and references. Recognizing the highly abstract and often 'disembodied' character of contemporary theological and philosophical debate on the body in relation to gender, subjectivity and discourse, we want to start our enquiries at a more mundane level by studying 'common bodies': human bodies and bodily practices in daily situations of (domestic) work and care, of love, sex, illness, death, and violence. From this angle of 'corporeal agency' as executed and experienced in day to day life, we discuss the meaning of religion, religiosity, transcendence, and the divine.

We have chosen this topic of enquiry for several reasons. In the first place, we aim to develop reflection on corporeality, gender, and religion, and approaches of religion and theology in close connection with social and cultural contexts and the actual living conditions of today. By focusing on 'everyday practices' we hope to stay close to what really matters in daily life, realizing that recognition hereof is often hard to detect - or to hold onto - in western academic theological debate. Secondly, and as a sequel to this aim, we strive to discuss the theological questions summoned by 'thinking the body' not only in terms of theological and gender discourse and their inner, mainly intellectual, dynamics, but also in terms of individual agency, social interaction, and concrete issues of conflict, as well as struggle for power over more or less 'common' bodies. Thirdly, our preference for studying corporeal practices is prompted by postcolonial and non-western feminist contributions to the debate on religion and theology, which call for exploring diversity in the most concrete ways and to engage with 'heterodox' and non-hegemonic religious practices. And last but not least, we want to try out processes and styles of feminist theological reflection suitable for here and now by attempting to adhere to, and not to escape, 'that daily chaos called life', as novelist Jeanette Winterson has put it.

The central questions that are worked on by the authors of this book are: When, how and why do bodily practices get religious meaning and relevance? How do corporeal practices mediate and instill religious meaning? And (how) do corporeal practices - including our own - contest, negotiate, and transform religious meaning? However, when it comes to the elaboration of 'corporeal practices', the authors' approaches and conceptualizations differ considerably. In this anthology a variety of interpretations and aspects of 'corporeal practices' is examined and reflected upon. The authors are informed by approaches of cultural anthropologists like Pierre Bourdieu and Michel de Certeau who study everyday practices to trace out the ways in which religious belief is actually appropriated; or by the approaches of critical philosophers such as Michel Foucault and Judith Butler who investigate corporeal practices as 'sites' of repression and resistance; or by the approaches of philosophers like Paul Ricoeur and Luce Irigaray who, each in his or her own way, develop a hermeneutics of bodily and sensory experience.

Although very diverging corporeal practices are scrutinized, and the sources and interpretative stances that are used also vary considerably, in almost all of the contributions everyday practices with clear somatic and sensitive components - like cooking and eating, manual labor and ritual performance, mothering, nursing and educating, suffering illness, pain, and death, as well as creating art - are studied as hermeneutical devices to discover and discuss religious meaning.

In the first part of this book we have gathered articles that look at corporeal practices as forms of religious performance and as particular intersections of daily activities and spiritual interests. Here the hermeneutical advantages of focusing on corporeal practices are explored and spelled out.

In the opening essay titled " 'A Way of Being-in-the-World.' Traces of Divinity in Everyday Life" Maaike de Haardt investigates the religious meaning and theological relevance of everyday practices like preparing food and having a meal together. As a case in point, she turns to the Oscar-winning film *Babette's Feast*, based on a novel by Isak Dinnesen (Karen Blixen). The images, language and narrative of this film show how the leading figure Babette - French, catholic and very vivacious - who, by her 'sense of food', her manifold and refined cooking and feeding practices, gradually unbends and transforms an introverted and fossilized protestant Christian community, giving it 'embodied knowledge' of grace and abundance. Following Michel de Certeau in his analysis of the tactics by which people, day by day, produce meaning in their appropriation of cultural and religious images and attitudes, De Haardt proposes a consideration of everyday practices like cooking and eating as acts of believing, revealing what people believe, and what makes them believe. To reflect on practices like these as processes of appropriation, so De Haardt states, offers methodological and epistemological starting points to detect 'a sense of divine presence' in everyday life, and opens new possibilities to get theological reflection and daily experience more concretely involved with each other.

In "Of Love, Life and Belief: The Story of Mary of Bethany (John 12:1- 8)" Magda Misset-van de Weg continues the anthology's project by offering a contrary reading of Mary of Bethany's gesture of anointing Jesus' feet and wiping them with her hair. Misset-van de Weg points at the many prejudiced interpretations of this 'strange' text, interpretations that are related to an apparent urge to explain this 'uncommon', that is embarrassing, scandalous, and shocking practice. For many interpreters, it seems almost impossible to avoid the traditional connection among women, sexuality, and sin as the model of interpretation. By studying the allusions to the Song of Songs in this text of John, Misset-van de Weg is able to develop a different approach that brings to the fore the various dimensions of the all-embracing love that Mary of Bethany manifests in anointing and wiping Jesus' feet. By interpreting Mary of Bethany's gestures as a 'common' practice of generous hospitality and kind affection, which possibly include a foreshadowing of mourning as well as a sign of prophetic behavior, Misset- van de Weg throws a new light on the meaning of this episode. Furthermore this interpretation adds a specific physical and sensual dimension to the mostly allegorical interpretations of the Johannine love. The limits of language in the case of expressing love not only demand evocative images and imagination, but also the mediation of concrete love-practices in order to understand fully the intersection of the mundane and the spiritual, and to perceive Mary of Bethany's gestures as a woman's way of expressing that she loved God with all her soul, with all her heart, and with all her might.

In her contribution " 'The Pearl Lay Hidden in the Dung' " Mathilde van Dijk explores the same intersection of daily and spiritual life by studying the modeling of female piety in two 'Sisterbooks', collections of biographies originating from communities of Sisters of the Common Life (*Devotio Moderna*) in the Netherlands, and dating from the late fourteenth and early fifteenth centuries. Van Dijk points to the prominent place housework and other forms of manual and strenuous labor have in portraying the religious life recommended for women. She tries to unravel the circumstances and motives that gave rise to this representation and to the intentional effacing of the more intellectual and reflexive aspects of religious life. According to van Dijk, manual labor was seen as a primary device for women to direct the inner self in order to be delivered from the pride and disobedience that had longstanding reputations as 'women's sins'. The authors of the Sisterbooks combined different models to show the sisters how to perform bodily in order to reach perfection. They recurred to the traditional female model of the good housewife, to the examples of the desert fathers, to Augustinian self-direction, and to a gendered form of *imitatio Christi*. The identification of Christ with Divine Wisdom, represented as the good housewife, offered women the possibility to become like Christ by performing domestic tasks, and the physical efforts these tasks required brought them closer to Christ's sufferings. Van Dijk notes that in the Sisterbooks the spiritual meaning of all kinds of mundane activities is emphasized and that demarcations between religious and non-religious activities are not sharply drawn.

In her article "Lebendiges Wasser. Die Geschichte der samaritanischen Frau (Johannes 4) von Rembrandts Perspektive gelesen (Living Water: The Story of the Samaritan Woman read from Rembrandt's point of view)" Anne Marijke Spijkerboer offers an interpretation of the story of the Samaritan woman (John 4) based on a careful exploration of the interrelation between visual and literary interpretation. Building on semiotic text interpretation, she argues that seeing a picture of a story adds new hermeneutical perspectives and different meanings to the textual story. Images, she states, affect the viewer at different and more existential levels than words, affecting people more directly and rapidly. With respect to the general theme of this book, she holds that images remind the viewer of the concrete, material, and embodied character of the imagined. Furthermore, they evoke a heightened awareness of the viewer's own concrete presence and his or her relationship with the imagined. A metaphorical, allegorical, or abstract interpretation of a story is far less likely to emerge from a viewer's perspective than from a reader's.

Spijkerboer demonstrates this position by an interpretative viewing of the two drawings made by Rembrandt of the story of the Samaritan woman at the well. She subsequently relates the insights gained from studying the pictures to a close reading of the text. Central in this process of interpretation is the meaning of the everyday life of the woman, i.e. the drawing of water, in relation to the living water of the eternal life of which Jesus speaks. It becomes clear that the living water and the eternal life can only be understood from the materiality and the activities of everyday life. In this interpretation, the robust materiality of the well, so impressively present in the drawings, points to the multidimensional elements of everyday life as well as to the substantiality of the 'spring of eternal life'.

The contributions in the subsequent part of this book focus upon the corporeal practices and experiences of the failing, limited, or resisting body. This point of departure leads to the articulation of a critical stance towards cultural and religious practices, and to creative interventions in theological and philosophical discourse.

In "Kinship of Soul", Inez van der Spek's musings on Lisa Moren's interactive video book *la_alma* (1999), the reader comes across the central themes of this volume, but from an unexpected angle. The reader becomes part of the interactive process that van der Spek enacts by watching the video of the interactive video book and reflecting on what she sees, hears, and feels. Inevitably, the reader who enters van der Spek's text will have to continue this process of interaction and will be confronted directly with the issue Moren and van der Spek are presenting here: how does physical failing, the shriveling of body, brains and senses, affect and transform our memory, storytelling and conversation? What is communication, in the end, all about? According to van der Spek, *la_alma* is a work of art in which communication, language, and memory are central but have lost their common and logical forms. We meet them in fragmented, incomplete, and fragile forms, embedded in both everyday personal experience and common cultural history, revealing events in some ways more truthfully than conventional history and narrative are able to do.

In her interactive video book, Moren links the personal story and history of her own grandmother Alma, who suffers from Alzheimer's disease, to the history and vicissitudes of Berlin, the city of Alma's ancestors. Moren's installation mediates numerous fragments of stories that reluctantly emerge from the large gaps of memory and history, inviting the spectator to create a unique visual story from a great many narrative possibilities. Van der Spek plays with some of these fragments - family saga, old women, speaking birds, a female Berlin - and shows them to be many layered, touching different moments from the past and the present of both Alma and Berlin, and relating the two in unexpected ways. According to van der Spek, *la_alma* cherishes and evokes a movement, an event of connection based on faith, that she names 'kinship of soul': a nourishing life force that inspires the cautious and creative bridging of gaps of memory, communication, and interpretation among people, times, and continents.

In her article "The Need for 'Another World'. Women's Everyday Life and the Embrace of Pain", Kune Biezeveld urges classical as well as feminist theology to take seriously the injustice and pain that are so often present in the everyday lives of women and men. How can theological discourse stay closer to these experiences and situations? As many other feminist theologians, Biezeveld is convinced that classical theology needs fundamental revision with regard to the validation of everyday life. But a simple change of scene, from heaven to earth, from lofty thoughts to daily pains and needs, will not do. According to Biezeveld, the classical, and by many feminist theologians rejected, image of 'another world' still proves to be a necessary and sustaining image in dealing with pain and injustice. The point of reference here is the emphasis on, or preference for, immanence that has become central to the feminist-theological project of re-writing systematic theology. However important this approach, Biezeveld demonstrates that the notion of transcendence, unmistakably implied in the image of 'another world' as present in biblical texts and developed in dialectical theology, still represents a fundamental and not to be discarded aspect of the Divine. Notably with regard to actual and everyday pain and injustice, and the ongoing need for liberation, this concept preserves a critical potential that in a more immanent approach seems at risk for erasure.

In "A Mixed Blessing. Differently Abled Women and Experiences of Transcendence" Jacqueline Kool questions the central title of this collection, *Common Bodies*, from the perspective of women with differently abled bodies. What are common bodies? Are there any common bodies at all and, if so, what do they look like? Kool criticizes the often-romanticized image of bodies and of embodied knowledge in feminist theology, and points at the far more ambiguous and paradoxical character of bodily existence and the knowledge it produces. Even the 'uncommon' bodies of differently abled persons are more common than common society would expect them to be - although actually dealing with the complexity of a disabled body proves to be a mixed blessing. Discussing the contribution of disabled women to feminist theology, Kool shows that in theological reflection from this perspective, disability, or the disabled body, has become a critical model or metaphor for God, transcendence, or wholeness. But, according to Kool, this prophetic theological approach, however important, does not hold on enough to its critical and spiritual potentials. It is inclined to make abstractions of concrete bodies and risks ignoring concrete physical existence and its actual spiritual meaning. Following theologian Nancy Eiesland, Kool states that this approach needs to be balanced by reflection on the 'unpredictable body' and on experiences of transcendence obtained in and through the body. In the process of the life and death of Treya Killiam Wilber, Kool finds a model of spirituality in which bodily and sensory experiences of everyday life affirm living in a vulnerable body with a 'passionate equanimity'.

Staying close to the body's actual vulnerability is also the starting point of the contribution of Riet Bons-Storm, entitled " 'I Have Only One Body!' The Conflict between 'Love' and Integrity in Everyday Practices of Western Middleclass Women, Reared in a Christian Tradition". The translation of feminist thinking into feminist practices proves to be very difficult, since many women in their day to day lives are exhausted and are often in conflict with themselves and their bodies. Bons-Storm questions and analyses this situation from a practical theological perspective. What causes these continuing conflicts in women's everyday practices? How are these conflicts to overcome? In her contribution, Bons-Storm not only tries to deconstruct the complex patriarchal scripts, including the Christian one, that direct the everyday life of women, but she also critically explores the counter scripts offered by feminist theologians. Bons-Storm doubts the effectiveness of these counter scripts; for example, feminist connection ethics runs the risk of reinforcing the patriarchal scripts instead of transforming them. A better option with which to resist these scripts may be found in strategic concentration on actual bodily existence. Recognizing the particularities and limitations of their own bodies can help women to oppose the confusing and exhaustive scripts that are literally written on their bodies. Bons-Storm stresses the importance of a community of dialogue that supports exploration of our bodies' possibilities and limitations, as well as one that acknowledges the limits of our responsibility and accountability. The acknowledgement of differences is fundamental to these processes, as is a representation of the Divine that supports diversity and dynamics. Only a truly gracious image of the Divine can allow and sustain a 'grace-full' living.

The two closing texts of this book investigate the ethical and theological consequences of reconsidering specific religious practices (moral education and prayer) in light of corporeality, gender, and religion.

According to Grietje Dresen, examining current proverbs can clarify the ethos of cultures and the dialogue between cultures. In her contribution "Reciprocity and Grace in the Golden Rule. Proverbial Wisdom as Source for Intercultural Dialogue and Moral Theology" she attempts to give such clarification in various ways. In the first part of her article she shows why proverbs lost favor as expressions of practical wisdom, and were devaluated to the level of popular conviction. Dresen speaks up for these convictions, both as lead for ethical reflection and as starting point for interreligious discussion, for example, in schools. She concludes this part with a proposal regarding the latter. In order to illustrate the intended hermeneutical consideration of convictions, in the second part of her article Dresen focuses on a single proverb, found in many cultures: the so-called Golden Rule. Using Paul Ricoeur's layered interpretation of the Golden Rule in *Oneself as Another*, Dresen shows the sophistication of a seemingly simple proverb. However, she shares the questions C. Theobald put to Ricoeur's consciously philosophical, secular analysis of the Golden Rule. She does not want to dispute the importance of such autonomous ethical analysis but considers it more appropriate to seek words, *within* philosophical argumentation, for a 'poetry of agape', i.e. for the meaning of the experience of love as a gift, an experience that helps to develop the motivation and ability to step into another's shoes.

What sense does the act of praying make in a (post)modern culture that is dominated by the experience of God's silence or absence? In "Zu dritt, oder: Das Gebet als eine utoptische Erinnerung (Three Together: Prayer as a Utopian Memory)" Susanne Hennecke tries to answer this question by studying the relationship between God and the human being that is installed by the performing of prayers such as the "Our Father". She first turns to the analysis of the structure of prayer offered by the theologian Karl Barth, who emphasizes the asymmetry of the relationship between God and the human being. In the act of praying the huge distance and difference between the two is remembered and installed. But the diminishing of this distance is also foreshadowed when we look at the act of praying as mediating a bilateral involvement. Secondly, Hennecke spells out the thesis of the feminist philosopher Luce Irigaray that believing in God the Father replaces and reformulates the situation of human beings who start their lives inside their mothers' wombs. The original paradisiacal human experience of being in the womb, where mother and child are connected as well as separated by a mediating instance, the placenta and the umbilical cord, is suppressed but not totally forgotten in western culture and religion. According to Hennecke, the acknowledgement of this original triangular structure of connection and dependence in the womb can help to redefine the act of praying as a 'utopian memory'.

At the close of this project we feel tempted to assess how fruitful our 'back to actual bodies' strategy has been. What does the study of corporeal practices of the gendered body in its common, everyday activities and references actually bring about, both theoretically and practically? In fact, as the summaries above already indicate, most authors have pointed out just how *creative* corporeal practices are in inducing, mediating, and contesting religious meaning. Their studies suggest that this creativity itself is religiously meaningful and theologically innovative, but that it is also hard to lay hold of. Perhaps the most interesting and challenging outcome of this anthology lies in the fact that this creativity comes more to the fore when corporeal practices of 'common bodies' are studied and valued not exclusively from a phenomenological or analytical stance. Precisely by considering, reconstructing, and sometimes literally reenacting corporeal practices as articulated and imagined in sacred texts, devotional literature, pictures, films, novels, life-stories, and rituals, their transforming power in the field of gender studies and theology, as well as in daily life, becomes visible. This also holds for the articles in this anthology wherein theological revisions are proposed on a more theoretical level, the incentives of which are mostly generated by 'sensual solidarities', or sensitive engagements with corporeal practices and experiences. In their contributions Anne-Marijke Spijkerboer and Inez van der Spek, each in her own way, elucidates this approach most explicitly. The way they analyze works of art and participate in, as well as reflect on, the artistic performances they engage with, broadens the scope and style of theology and delivers it from its intellectual - or should we say incorporeal? - tightening. So, making the creativity of 'common' corporeal practices palpable and productive in and for theology is what we hope to have started, enabled, and encouraged by the contributions in this anthology.

'A Way of Being-in-the-World'

Traces of Divinity in Everyday Life

Maaike de Haardt

Introduction

In 1943, in the middle of the Second World War, the famous gastronomical writer M.F.K. Fisher wrote, "There is a community of more than our bodies when bread is broken and wine drunk. And that is my answer when people ask me: Why do you write about hunger, and not wars or love?"[1] According to Fisher, the three basic human needs for food, security and love, are so mixed and intertwined that it is impossible to think about them separately. And what is more, she says, "We must eat. If, in the fact of that dread fact we can find other nourishment, and tolerance, and compassion for it, we'll be no less full of human dignity."[2] Eating together, a common meal, seems to be the sacramental expression of this love, tolerance and compassion. Because, as Fisher so obviously states, there is a 'more.'

In this contribution, I want to reflect on this 'more.' This theological or religious interest in food and eating, in the symbolic meaning of food, or in the specific relation between women and food, is nothing new.[3] Religion is traditionally seen as 'nourishment for the soul'; we know the promised land in its images of milk and honey. Many religious practices are food-related. However, it is not my intention to focus on traditional religious food practices. As said, I want to reflect on the 'more' Fisher mentioned, the 'more' experienced in a simple and ordinary meal. As a theologian, I am inclined to speak of 'a trace of transcendence' or 'a sense of presence' in reference to this 'more'. But what is meant by this? As a systematic theologian, I am particularly interested in the theological relevance of such an observation, notably the questions of if and how religious meanings of everyday practices, such

---

[1] M.F.K. Fisher, *The Art of Eating* (New York: Collier Books, 1990), 353. This book is a collection of five earlier volumes, including the 1943 *The Gastronomical Me*, from which the quote is taken.
[2] Ibid.
[3] In particular, from a historical perspective and tightly focused on the symbolic meaning of food, on the handling of food and the gender-specificity of this. There is the renowned work by C. Walker Bynum, *Holy Feast and Holy Fast. The Religious Significance of Food to Medieval Women* (Berkeley/Los Angeles: University of California Press: 1987); Id. *Fragmentation and Redemption, Essays on Gender and the Human Body in Medieval Religion* (New York: Zone Books, 1992). Also: R.M. Bell, *Holy Anorexia* (Chicago: University of Chicago, 1985). In 1995 the *Journal of the American Academy of Religion* dedicated a special theme to 'Religion and Food' (Vol. LXIII, number 3).

as preparing food or having a meal, can prompt systematic reflection on 'God.' I believe that these implications touch systematic theology in content as well as in method. In this contribution, an attempt is made to detect the theological meaning of the 'more' that is said to be found in preparing food or having a meal, by analysing the highly-praised film *Babette's Feast*. It is not only a film about food, but also a film that has given rise to theological interpretations. But before analysing food practices as a method of reflecting on 'traces of transcendence,' the background of this theological turn to everyday life and practices requires some elucidation.

Everyday life as locus and focus of theology
Feminist theology and contemporary cultural studies share a preference for everyday life. This 'anthropological turn' first and foremost criticizes of the dominant academic epistemology and methodology. The French historian and cultural scientist Michel de Certeau used the metaphor of the city to describe the position of scientists and the kind of knowledge they generate.[4] It is like viewing Manhattan from the 110th floor of the World Trade Centre. All one sees is a wave of verticals in which the actual agitation of the city is arrested, for a moment, by vision. De Certeau wonders to what erotics of knowledge the ecstasy of reading such a cosmos belongs. It is probably the pleasure of "seeing the whole." The price, however, is that this panoramic city is a 'theoretical', a visual simulacrum. It is a picture in which the condition of possibility is an oblivion and a misunderstanding of practices. Only by disentangling themselves from the intertwining daily behaviours, by making themselves alien to them, can scientists be the voyeur-gods created by their own fiction. Invisible to the eyes of these scientists are the ordinary practitioners of city life. These city walkers create a manifold story that has neither author nor spectator, and consists of fragments of trajectories and alterations of spaces,in relation to representations. The story remains daily and indefinitely other.

This image contains a strong criticism of 'the ministers of knowledge' who feared any change that would affect their 'city map,' their ideology, and their position. De Certeau did not dispute these ministers on their own terminology, by questioning their 'clear texts.' Just like the Black feminist poet Audre Lorde, he was convinced that "the master's tools cannot dismantle the master's house."[5] Instead, he chose to analyse the microbe-like, singular, and plural practices of everyday life. These unseen practices of space refer to a specific form of *operations* (ways of operating)

---

[4] M. de Certeau, *The Practice of Everyday Life* (Part 1. Arts de Faire) (Berkeley/Los Angeles: University of California Press, 1984), 91-93.
[5] As the title of a famous article by Lorde in A. Lorde, *Sister Outsider. Essays and Speeches* (New York: The Crossing Press, 1984).

to *another spatiality* (an anthropological, poetic, and mythic experience of space), and to an *opaque and blind* mobility characteristic of the bustling city. De Certeau investigated how a migrational, or metaphorical, city slips into the clear text of the planned and readable city, and vice versa. In other words, his research aimed at "the 'disseminated proliferation' of anonymous and 'perishable' creations that *allows people to stay alive* and cannot be capitalised."[6] (italics mine)

In my view, this city metaphor can be helpful in making clear at whom and at what feminist theologians are oriented. Our criticising is aimed at theological distance and abstractions, and therefore their neglect of actual belief and actual believers, in particular women and other marginalised peoples.We dispute the unidimensional concepts and models of the theological canon of knowledge as well as this canon itself, which has its own (mono)-logic, untouched by the movements of 'believers.' Instead, we have a desire to break and transform this patriarchal monotheistic order and highlight and reflect on what, in the early days of feminist theology, was described as the 'experiences of women.' However, growing insight into the dangers of essentialism and false universals in referring to 'women's experiences' has gradually led to a feminist theological interest in far more concrete everyday practices of very different women, their diverse contexts and in their manifold practices of 'belief.'[7]

Influenced by such thinkers as De Certeau and Michel Foucault, feminist theologians are convinced that these practices are expressions of an intelligence and inventiveness of people, regardless of their power or -as is more often the case- lack of formal power. In the words of Foucault, these practices can be regarded as 'subjugated knowledges.' Notably, white feminist theologians often use the works of Michel Foucault to point at the importance of this 'subjugated knowledge.'[8] Using his analytical tools, it is not only possible to make visible that religion indeed can and is be oppressive, but, far more importantly, it is possible to show the religious resistance of the suppressed as well. A central question to this last point,

---

[6] According to L. Giard in her "Introduction to Volume 1: History of a research project" (originally published as: "Introduction de L'Invention du quotidien, I, Arts de faire (Paris, Éditions Gallimard 1990), in M. de Certeau, L. Giard, P. Mayol (eds.), *The Practice of Everyday Life. Vol. 2: Living and Cooking* (Minneapolis, University of Minnesota Press, 1998), xvii.

[7] See, for instance, such different works as: R.S. Chopp, *The Power to Speak. Feminism, Language, God* (New York: Crossroad, 1989); S.D. Welch, *A Feminist Ethic of Risk* (Minneapolis: Fortress Press, 1990); A.M. Isasi-Diaz, *En la Lucha. A Hispanic Women's Liberation Theology* (Minneapolis: Fortress Press, 1993); D.S. Williams, *Sisters in the Wilderness. The Challenge of Womanist Godtalk* (Maryknoll: Orbis Books, 1993); M. McClintock Fulkerson, *Changing the Subject. Women's Discourses and Feminist Theology* (Minneapolis: Fortress Press, 1994); M. de Haardt, "'Kom, eet mijn brood.' Exemplarische onderzoekingen naar het goddelijke in het alledaagse", *Tijdschrift voor Theologie* 40 (2000) 1, 5-22.

[8] See for instance S. Welch, M. McClintock Fulkerson and D. Prosser MacDonald.

is how to trace this resistance in all its different forms and practices. How does one discover these subjugated insights and knowledge of belief? In what ways is this knowledge related to and mediated by a religious tradition? These questions also affect constructive theology: What are the implications of these data for our understanding of a religious tradition, and its contents and forms? What are the implications for academic theological reflection on religion and religious beliefs? What kind of faith is seeking what kind of understanding?

It is with respect to these questions that the works of De Certeau seem to offer further constructive impulses. In privileging the 'others,' the theoretical outsiders, he uses the concept of appropriation as a primary tool in searching for resisting or surviving practices. It is a concept which can also be found in the works of some feminist authors.[9] De Certeau uses it to name an important mechanism or process with which it is possible to describe the act of believing, as well as what makes people believe. According to de Certeau, these are the 'tactics' with which people, day after day, produce a sense of meaning and freedom in their appropriation of cultural, religious, political, and social instruments as well as images, concepts and attitudes.[10]

To reflect on actual (religious) practices as processes of appropriation seems to open up a path to a further theological exploration of a far more differentiated, polyvalent and moreover, ambiguous, religious reality than the uni-dimensional and mono-logic religion and theology that the academy and the churches would like to deal with.[11] It opens up the fundamental and inescapable, although often repudiated, 'intertwinement' of those spheres which in Western culture and sciences are traditionally separated, such as the secular and the sacred, or popular and the 'high' religion/culture. I expect this approach to even offer possibilities for rethinking such often opposite and exclusively conceptual 'spheres' as transcendence and immanence.

---

[9] The most explicit use of a specific 'appropriation' of religious texts, concepts, and symbols in order to 'survive' *and, at the same time,* express their own religious belief and spirituality can be found in the works of D.S. Williams, A.M. Isasi-Diaz and M. McClintock Fulkerson, regardless of their very different methods. Liberation theologians also use the concept of appropriation to describe the empowering use of biblical stories by oppressed people. According to W. Frijhoff, De Certeau is considered as one of the most influential, be it recalcitrant, protagonists of the concept of 'appropriation.' (W. Frijhoff, "Toeëigening: van bezitsdrang naar betekenisgeving", *Trajecta* 6 (1997) 2, 99-118, 113).

[10] De Certeau, *Practices of Everyday*, Ch. III. 29-42.

[11] In 'Kom, eet mijn brood', I elaborated on the meaning of the ambiguous in relation to everyday life.

The wonder of daily life: aesthetics and a sense of presence

The privileging of everyday life is an epistemological and methodological position grounded in an ethical and political conviction that can be translated in a liberation-theological context as 'the option for the poor,' or, in a more post-modern perspective, as the option for 'the other,' or the 'excluded.'[12] However, more can be said on this point. Despite their exclusion, these 'others' 'live' the city, they provide the city with life. And it is this city life we want to highlight in theology, because it shows us not only how people survive (De Certeau), but, as mujerista theologian Asa Maria Isasi-Diaz states, it also reveals people's hopes and expectations.[13] For feminist and liberation theologians, theology has to make clear what 'God' has to do with human life. In other words, theology must not solely examine the adequacy of its language of God, or ponder the question of whether "we can speak of a transcendent God". Likewise, it cannot suffice to answer the challenge of the non-believer by "demonstrating that the belief in God is a sublime form of rationality."[14] I agree with Mary McClintock Fulkerson when she states, "Feminist discourse does not enter the lists over the question of Gods existence."[15] On the contrary, theology should demonstrate *that* and *what* 'speaking of God' signifies in the lives of ordinary women and men.[16] This implies a gradual shift from the 'what of belief' to the 'how of believing' as central to theology or Christian religion. It is, after all, not only for the sake of the 'others', but also for the benefit of the theological city planners, that a change of subject or perspective becomes necessary to create reliable maps, that is, to create a more 'reliable' conceptual language of 'God.'[17]

However, there is another element embedded in this focus on concrete 'practices- of 'God' that refers to perhaps a 'religious attitude' or a spiritual sensibility, rather than explicit political, epistemological and theological convictionsalthough this cannot be separated from these views. This sensibility is related to the 'more' of, for instance, a communal meal. Again, the work and person of Michel De Certeau can be helpful to trace this attitude. Luce Giard, in describing his work, speaks of de

---

[12] This approach from its political and ethical commitment, differs as I see it from, for instance, the actual German practical theological interest in the 'Alltag.' See my " Kom eet mijn brood."
[13] Isasi-Diaz, *En La Lucha*, 34.
[14] As argued by M. Sarot and A. Marcus in "Denken van Wie ons ontsnapt. Rationele Theologie en de transcendentie van God", *Nederlands Theologische Tijdschrift* 54 (2000) 2, 145-157, 146, and by A. Houtepen, *God, een Open Vraag* (Zoetermeer: Meinema, 1997), 18 (note 6).
[15] McClintock Fulkerson, *Changing the Subject*, 372.
[16] See S.D. Welch, *Communities of Resistance and Solidarity. A Feminist Theology of Liberation* (Maryknoll, Orbis Books, 1985), 1. This conviction regarding the task of theology is found in almost every feminist and liberation theology.
[17] In addition to the previously mentioned works (note 3), a defence of this theological reflection on everyday life from a 'city planner's perspective can be found in K. Tanner, *Theories of Culture. A New Agenda for Theology* (Minneapolis: Fortress Press, 1997). It is also overwhelmingly present in the works of almost every theologian from the Third World.

Certeau's optimistic élan, his trust given to others in such a way that no situation appears to him *a priori* to be fixed or hopeless. This attitude, according to Giard, is "fed from an aesthetic sensibility that De Certeau expressed through the maintained capacity for being filled with wonder. If Michel De Certeau sees these wonders everywhere, it is because he is prepared to see them, as Surin in the seventeenth century was ready to encounter "the young uneducated man in the stagecoach" who would speak to him of God with more force and wisdom than all the authorities of Scripture and of the church."[18] This encounter with 'the wonder of daily life' is one of the many forms of the experience of the 'Presence' that reveals itself, according to De Certeau, as "that without which life is impossible."[19]

In recent years, the articulation of this deep sense of wonder, transcendence, or grace, has been given more attention in theology, particularly by those theologians, notably feminists, who criticise the dominant rationalistic and/or exclusive character of academic theological traditions. In my view, this shift in theological attention to 'the sense of presence' in all its different dimensions, has become the bedrock of theological transformation, or, more specifically, of the transformation of reflection on 'God.'[20] Initially this attention was mainly focused upon the arts, and upon artists and writers, at least in a white Western context. Artists seemed to be regarded by theologians as being among the few groups of people in contemporary Western culture who are able to give a voice to a sense of presence that was not only more convincing and vivid, but also more critical, complex and ambiguous, than the univocal and monosemic voices heard in churches or from theologians. Gradually, this interest in the aesthetic sensibility, as the sense of 'presence' is sometimes also called, has been broadened to the day-to-day practices, experiences, and sensibilities of ordinary people. As Diane Prosser MacDonald states, "this dimension goes far beyond the art sitting in protective spaces in museums and performed for selected

---

[18] Giard, "History of a Research Project", xxi-xxii, quotes M. de Certeau from *Culture in the Plural* (Minneapolis: University of Minnesota Press, 1997), and *The Mystique Fable. Vol 1: The Sixteenth and Seventeenth Century* (Chicago: University of Chicago Press, 1992).

[19] See for this 'Presence' M. de Certeau, "Culture and Spiritual Experience", *Concilium* 19 (1966); and also F. C. Bauerschmidt, "Introduction: Michel de Certeau, Theologian", in G. Ward (ed.), *The Certeau Reader* (Oxford: Blackwell Publishers, 2000), 209-213. According to Bauerschmidt, it is not only the postmodernist and historicist perspective, but also the doctrine of Incarnation that shapes de Certeau's thoughts on religious experiences. At this point, it is perhaps good to mention that de Certeau was a member of the Society of Jesus. His theological views, according to Graham Ward, would be considered heterodox. And it is said among the Jesuits that while de Certeau perhaps did not die a Christian, he certainly died a Jesuit. (G. Ward in his introduction to *The Certeau Reader*, 9.)

[20] See, for instance, M.J. Legge, "Inside Communities, outside conventions: What is at stake in doing theology?" *Studies in Religion/Sciences Religieuses* 29 (2000) 1, 3-18.

audiences in symphony halls. In fact, the aesthetic is no work of art at all, but the 'sensate markings' or practices of culture operating in the 'in-between' of everyday life."[21] Additionally, certain Hispanic theologians point out the fundamental rootedness of the aesthetic, the political, and the ethical in a same similar human praxis, just as they have also indicated the interrelatedness of the aesthetic and the ethical in their reflections on Hispanic popular religion. However, it is important to note that the aesthetic does harmonises neither the tragic nor the suffering. Poetry is no luxury, says Isasi-Díaz.[22] To put it more strongly: art express the truth of suffering and hope.[23]

To explore, as theologians, this 'wonder of the daily life, these experiences of a sense of presence' and to articulate its theological implications, requires an attitude that takes seriously these practices of belief that allow people to 'stay alive' or to survive (De Certeau, Williams), and that, as such, also reflect their hopes, visions, desires, relations, love and struggles (Chopp, Isasi-Díaz). It is an attitude in which the 'sense of presence' is not understood through *a priori* theories that work for all times and places, but through the historical, cultural -including gender, ethnic, racial and sexual- specificity which shapes the forms as well as the contents of the articulation of this sense of presence.

One of the important questions that follows from these foundational considerations is *how* to *practice* a theology of everyday life? How does one detect a sense of presence in everyday life, and, subsequently, reflect on it in such a way that contributes to the transformation of theological conceptualisations and, eventually, the transformation of the doctrine of God? After all, recent Western theological transformations, however impressive, seldom start from the concrete practices of everyday life. When theologians indeed depart from practice-analysis and/or anthropological insights, it is often difficult to reach beyond , however necessary and important, a critical deconstruction and reformulation of theological agendas, actors, and fundamental theological outlines.[24] As difficult as it is to reach

---

[21] D.L. Prosser MacDonald, *Transgressive Corporealiy. The Body, Poststructuralism, and the Theological Imagination* (Albany: State University of New York Press,1995), 136.

[22] Isasi-Díaz, *En La Lucha*, 35. The expression is a quote from the title of an essay by Audre Lorde, *Sister Outsider. Essays and Speeches* (New York: The Crossing Press, 1984). For further elaboration on this specific topic see: R.S. Goizueta "US Hispanic Popular Catholicism as Theopoetics" in: A.M. Isasi-Díaz, F.F. Segovia (eds.), *Hispanic/Latino Theology. Challenges and Promise* (Minneapolis: Fortress Press, 1996), 261-288; or more recently, A. Garía-Rivera, *The Community of the Beautiful. A Theological Aesthetics* (Collegeville: The Liturgical Press, 1999).

[23] E. Graham and J. Polling, "Some Expressive Dimensions of a Liberation Practical Theology. Art Forms as Resistance to Evil", *International Journal of Practical Theology* 4 (2000) 4, 163-183.

[24] As, for instance, in the previously mentioned studies by Isasi-Díaz and McClintock Fulkerson. See S. Jones, "Women's Experiences between a Rock and a Hard Place", in R.S. Chopp and S. Greeve Davaney (eds.), *Horizons in Feminist Theology. Identity, Tradition, and Norms* (Minneapolis: Fortress Press, 1997), 33-52, 47-50.

beyond a highly abstract and formal level, that is, to reach beyond the city-view from above.[25]

My interpretation of the film *Babette's Feast*, as presented here, can be regarded as an attempt to overcome these drawbacks. In this sense, my interpretation is an exercise in a style of theology that is still in the making and that can and should take many forms. My interpretation of the film aims at the exploration of the meaning of everyday life practices in relation to theological reflection on divinity. I hope to show that focusing on ordinary everyday life experiences brings to light specific characteristics of 'the sense of presence', so often missing in theological discourse.

Babette's Feast: the narrative

Babette's Feast starts with a voice-over introduction of the central characters and the location of the film. The main characters are Martine and Phillipa, two unmarried daughters of a Danish Lutheran minister who founded a small, sectarian, ascetic community near the coast. Their father is long dead and the sisters have dedicated their lives to serving the people of their little community. The voice-over continues by introducing the third main character, Martine and Phillipa's French housekeeper, which is something very unusual for this small Danish village. After this introduction, we are shown, in flash backs, the story of Martine and Phillipa's past and we discover how Babette, the housekeeper, came into their employ.

The two women, in their youth, were stunning beauties and many men fell in love with them. The film portrays two specific cases. One is of a young army officer, Lorens Loewenhielm, whose aunt lives on a short distance from the little village. Loewenhielm was sent to his aunt in order to rethink and change his style of life because of his 'loose' lifestyle in the army. He falls in love with Martine but does not have the nerve to tell her. Thus he runs from the village, back to the army, determined to make a great career for himself. This he accomplishes. The second love story concerns the relation between a famous French (Papist) opera singer, Achille Papin, and Phillipa. With her father's permission, he gives her voice lessons after hearing her angelic voice in church. Unable to withhold his feeling he kisses her hand after they sing a duet from Don Giovanni. Afterwards, Phillipa asks her father to tell Papin that she no longer wishes to take lessons from him.

Years later, in their middle years, the sisters answer a knock at the door and find a Frenchwoman carrying a letter of introduction from Achille Papin. Fleeing the events in Paris during the 1870s, in which her husband and son were executed, she herself having narrowly escaped, the French woman, Babette, pleads with the sisters to let her stay with them. Reluctantly, they agree. It is the letter of Papin and

---

[25] As in Tanner, *Theories of Culture*. See Jones, "Women's Experiences between a Rock and a Hard Place".

Babette's assurance that she doesnot need any money, but rather only wants to serve the good people of Papin, that induces them to let her stay. In fact, they are a bit afraid, not only of her being a French Papist, but all the more because of French luxury and abundance in eating. Thus they show Babette how to prepare the plain food of the home, including beer and bread soup, and codfish, which are also to be distributed among the poor of het village by Babette. Soon the little community becomes accustomed to the strange French women. They notice the wholesome change Babette has brought to the lives of the sisters and the community, and they include Babette in their prayers.

It is after Babette has lived in the community for twelve years that she wins ten thousand francs in the French lottery. The sisters worriedly expect her to leave them, although they do not voice their concerns to Babette. Then, Babette offers to cook them an anniversary meal memorialising the birth of their father, at her own expense. The sisters reluctantly accept Babette's offer. When Babette goes on two week's leave in order to make all the preparations for the meal, the sisters are haunted by ghosts, anxiety, and guilt for what they have permitted that Babette will cook the anniversary dinner. They confess their guilt to the community, and it is decided that whatever happens, nobody will say a word about the food during the meal. At the last minute, general Loewenhielm arrives in the village and will also be present at the meal. Then, almost near the end of the film, the feast itself is presented in a lengthy (twenty minute) scene. Alternately, we are shown the kitchen and the dining room. In the kitchen, Babette works at the peak of her talents to produce the most wonderful dishes. It is clear that she is enjoying every second of it. There are two other people in the kitchen, the coachman, who receives his share of every dish and drink with an expression of angelic bliss, and the hard-working young boy who assists Babette and serves the guests. In the dining room, amid the most exquisite food and drink, the little community is trying to do its utmost not to speak of their amazing cullinary experience. Instead, they tell one another stories in which they remember their founder and the spiritual wisdom they have learned from him.

During the meal, they, unwillingly, come to enjoy the food, drink, and their own renewed or perhaps previously unknown, cordiality towards each other. They even reconcile old grievances and differences. Throughout the meal, General Loewenhielm is the only one sophisticated enough to recognise and appreciate the fineness of the delicacies served. Fruitlessly, he explains to the community what they are eating and drinking: the finest amontillado, turtle soup, blinis Demidoff, Veuve Cliquot, and a famous main dish, cailles en sarcophage. He can think of but one place in the world where the cuisine was as fine as this, the Café Anglais in Paris with its famous female chef. This chef, Loewenhielm remembers, was said to have the capacity to turn a meal into a love affair, where one was unable to distinguish between physical and spiritual appetites. Inspired by this recollection and the actual experience of the meal of which he is now partaking, in which he recognises this chef, he gives a speech in which he is able to formulate these insights in a spiritual language that opens up both the hearts of the members of the community and his own, long hidden feelings for Martine. At the end of the meal, all the guests leave in a previously unknown, exuberant mood. Only then do the sisters go to the kitchen where Babette is sitting, exhausted but deeply satisfied. There they discover that Babette is not going to leave them, as they had feared. Where would she go without money? The sisters discover, to their horror, that Babette has spent her whole fortune on this one meal. When they speak emphatically of her being poor for the rest of her life, Babette, almost proudly and with a strange smile on her face, assures them that as an artist she could never be poor.

Babette's Feast: theological interpretations[26]

Gabriel Axel's *Babette's Gaestebud* (*Babette's Feast*) is based on a novella by Isac Dinnesen (Karen Blixen).[27] Although Axel's film adaptation follows Dinnesen's text very closely, through adding his own wonderful visual and auditive power, he makes the filma masterpiece in its own right. Some critics and interpreters found the film 'occasionally surpassing its source .... in its succinct visualisation.'[28] The film won the Oscar for best foreign-language film in 1987. The narrative itself seems to be a very simple one, its location seldom changes and there are only a few central characters. Food plays an important role in the story.[29] In the film, this centrality of food is underlined by the highly sensual visual presentation of food, not only during the festive meal, but throughout the film. In the opening shots of the film, in which the little village is presented in images and the characters are introduced in voice-over, we are given a view of the village from under a clothesline on which we see beautiful flatfish drying. The film culminates in the feast. The images of the dishes and the preparation of the dishes are wonderful in their intensity. According to Tim Pulleine, they "unselfconsciously take on a metaphorical resonance in terms of what one of the participants dubs the balance between bodily and spiritual appetite."[30]

---

[26] I will not go into the methodological questions and problems of a theological interpretation of film *as film*, but focus on the elements in the film that theologians grant theological relevance.
[27] I. Dinesen, "*Babette's Feast*", in *Anecdotes of Destiny* (London: Joseph, 1958); G. Axel, *Babette's Gastebrut (Babette's Feast)*, 1987.
[28] C. Marsh cites, in agreement, the review by R. Cobbs in the *Monthly Filmbulletin* 55, 75-74, in his article "Did you say Grace. Eating and Community in *Babette's Feast*" in C. Marsh and G. Ortiz, *Explorations in Theology and Film. Movies and Meaning* (London: Blackwell Publishers, 1997), 207-219, 208. Note the implied supremacy of the text above the film in this statement.
[29] According to J. Thurmans' *Isak Dinesen. The Life of Karen Blixen*, Dinesen was out of money in 1949 and wanted to enter the lucrative American market. An English friend gave her the advise to write about food, because "Americans are obsessed with food." (London: Penguin, 1984), 376.
[30] T.Pulleine, "Review of *Babette's Feast*", *Films and Filming*, February 1988, 28-29.

When I saw *Babette's Feast*, I found it a beautiful, unassuming, sympathetic, moving and meaningful film. I was particularly impressed by Babette's 'sense of food', which so strongly contradicted the religiously motivated dismissal by the religious community of any attention to food. It did not occur to me to call it a 'religious' film. Later on, I discovered that the film has often been interpreted by theologians because of its 'obvious religious' themes. In fact, according to Maria Consuelo Maistro, "*Babette's Feast* has been an important catalyst for some resurgent interest in religion and film over the last decade."[31] Theological interpreters name different elements which point at the 'religious' character of the film, some name the (sectarian) religion and the religious community, others name the figure of Babette. They see Babette as a kind of Christ figure or representative of God. Subsequently, the feast itself is generally interpreted as the highlight of the film. It is seen in the light of the Eucharist and interpreted as a 'redemptive' meal for the community, or as the self-sacrifice of Babette.[32] The opening shots, as well as the hymns, and other 'obvious' Christian elements, such as the many quotes from the Bible and Luther, are considered to reinforce the eucharistic theme and symbols of the film. All of this, according to the interpreters, counts as 'proof' of the theological relevance of the film.

What troubles me in these theological readings is the glibness of the tactics some theological interpreters use to move from the film to the great classic themes of Christian tradition, for example salvation, Eucharist, sacrament, confession, absolution, communion and sacrifice.[33] To give a vivid example, Wendy Wright observes, "In fact, *Babette's Feast* is structured to recapitulate the central dynamic of the foundational Christian myth. It visually presents a movement from death to resurrection. And it does so by introducing a salvific figure who transfigures the main characters' world to a loving act of self-giving."[34] In my view this, and similar enunciations, are not only exaggerated Christian interpretations of the film, but they also miss the sensitive, evocative, and open, indefinite character of the film itself.

---

[31] M.C. Maistro, "Cinematic Communion? *Babette's Feast*, Transcendental Style, and Interdisciplinarity" in D. Jasper, S.Brent Plate (eds.), *Imagining Otherness. Filmic Visions of Living Together* (Atlanta: Scholar Press, 1999), 138.

[32] See, for instance, Marsh, 'Did you say Grace'; G. Hill, *Illuminating Shadows. The Mythic Power of Film* (Boston/London: Shambhala, 1992), 137-158; Maistro, 'Cinematic Communion? *Babette's Feast*, Transcendental Style, and Interdisciplinarity', W. M. Wright, "*Babette's Feast*: A Religious Film", *The Journal of Religion and Film* 2 (1997) 1.
Online; [http://www.unomaha.edu/~wwwjrf/wrightar.thm]; Diana Tolomeo Edwards, "*Babette's Feast*, Sacramental Grace, and the Saga of Redemption, *Christianity and Literature*, 42 (Spring 1993) 3; A M. Greeley, "Images of God in the Movies", *Journal of Religion and Film*, 1 (1997) 1, [http://www.unomaha.edu/~wwwjrf/greeleya.htm].

[33] It could be that a difference in confessional background engenders these different readings. All of the interpretations I read were by Protestant theologians, whereas I was raised and trained in the Catholic tradition.

[34] Wright, "*Babette's Feast*: A Religious Film".

In my opinion, such theological readings of *Babette's Feast* are interpretations 'from above', from a theoretical point of view in which it is clear what counts as religious and what is theologically relevant. From there, one only has to detect these elements in the film or in the recognisable religious practices that are performed in the film, which include prayers, hymns, sermons, and the community meal. However, these interpretations diminish the actual living practices which form the base of the life of the villagers, the practices that 'make people believe.'

It is not to state that these forms of interpretation are impossible, but they do not contribute to a reflection on the religious meaning of everyday practices, since they all focus on the exceptional feast. They show very little of the sensibility of the 'more' Fisher mentioned. On the contrary, they see no trace of a 'more' that is to be detected, because the theological meaning and message of the film is clear and firmly located in the festive meal as a sacrificial, and therefore, redemptive meal.

A sense of food

So, if it is not the explicit Christian themes that indicate the religious relevance of the film, what then makes this film theologically interesting? What kind of religious insights can be discovered in reading/seeing this film? Like the other interpreters, I turn to the food, and to the centrality of food in the film. As was stated before, there is far more food in the film than only Babette's meal. The visual introduction of the sisters in the film - we see them walking in the background while the clotheslines with the fish on them are still in the foreground- is food related. We also see them distributing their simple meals among the poor of the village. We see an old man receive the food and eat it. The little religious community is introduced while singing hymns about heavenly food. In alternate shots, we see and hear the community singing of the Lord who feeds them. We see Babette getting the baking tins from the oven, waiting at the door, holding a tray of tea and freshly baked biscuits. Behind that door we see and hear the community singing hymns in which they express their belief that food shall be given to them. We see the sisters teaching Babette their plain way of cooking and we see Babette's somewhat bewildered expression at that time. We follow Babette as she buys fish, prepares codfish, as well as beer and bread soup, and finally brings it to the old man. We see his grateful face while tasting Babette's meal. We also see his disappointment, later on in the film, when the sisters replace Babette for two weeks. We learn of Babette's gradual acceptance by the village people, effected through her way of communicating with them about food; she discusses the quality of bacon, she negotiates on the price of fish, she saves money on food, she cares for the biscuits during community gatherings. Babette, at first a 'threatening stranger', French, papist, revolutionary, and refugee, becomes a part of the village and is even included in the community prayers.

With this abundance of food images, I find it hard to understand that none of the theological reviewers has commented on these elements, while they *do* recognise the importance of the food, notably in relation to the transformation of the community. But again, as stated before, neither the ubiquity of the food, nor Babette's different 'attitude' towards food, but rather Babette's sacrifice and her redemptive meal, are generally seen as the transforming elements.

In my view, however, the film shows a convincing change in the ordinary lives and practices of the villagers, mainly due to Babette's food practices. Babette's 'sense of food' generates a sensitivity that was not there before. This 'sense of food' involves her attention to food and to the quality of food; it involves her care for the process of cooking, her care for taste, smell, visualisation, and touch. Her sense of food reveals a knowledge at the sensory level, embodied knowledge, and becomes a medium of communication and trust for the sisters, the community and the villagers. This 'strange', hitherto unknown sensitivity is accepted by the little village. They even integrate elements of this sensitive attention into their own lives and come to appreciate it, despite their spirituality and ascetic practices that favour abstinence from this sensitivity and 'worldly' enjoyments. There is no explication or reflection on this process by the community, but then, it is hardly a spectacular transformation. In fact, as I would postulate, because of this greatly invisible, barely noticed, but, nevertheless, actual transformation of everyday life and practices, the community is able to become open to different, hitherto unknown sensations and other, redeeming, ways of relating to each other, all of which can be considered an enrichment of the quality of their lives. To use more explicitly theological terms, it seems adequate to speak in this regard of practices of grace,[35] that is, practices that create space for well-being. These are practices in which people can become more fully human, and are referred to by logians as practices in which people become 'imago dei'.[36] Following this line of thought, Babette's meal can then only be viewed as a culminating point in which these transformations become undeniable and meaningful when seen in the light of, and as a continuation of, the preceding events and changes. Additionally, if one focused solely on the meal, nothing would prevent a more cynical interpretation of the mood of the dinner guests other than as them being 'under the influence,' as they are not used to the consumption of alcoholic drinks.

Creative appropriation
Babette's daily cooking and her attentiveness to food can be interpreted as active ways of resisting the dominant food regimes by her own culinary machinations.

---

[35] McClintock Fulkerson, *Changing the Subject*, 366.
[36] The imago dei motif is an important one in contemporary feminist and/or (inter)cultural theology. It functions as an envisioned, however not fully to be known and thus not fixed, possibility for all, in which the dignity and full humanity of all people are affirmed.

Probably the only way for Babette to 'survive' or 'to stay alive' in her new locus of living is to appropriate the community's food habits in such a way that they, again, become a meaningful way of communication for her. As Loewenhielm remembers, in her former life she could turn a meal into a love affair. So, her current practices - in terminology taken from Michel de Certeau- refer to an 'anthropological, poetical and mythic experience of space,' that is, an experience not determined by the logical structures and discursive practices of the cultural-religious codes of her new domicile. This mode of operating opens up, for Babette as well as for the community, hitherto unknown, unexpected, but nevertheless moving experiences of sensations and communication. They open up, again following De Certeau, an opaque and blind, not clearly planned, mobility and, therefore, 'transform' the little village. As Ronald Grimes has noted, "the film reveals nothing new, only that which has not been truly seen or really tasted before."[37] Babette uses the same familiar ingredients in preparing food, but nevertheless creates different meals and biscuits, which are not tasteless as before, but full of flavour.[38] Her attention to the 'ordinary' strongly contradicts the religious neglect of the ordinary by the community. Her practice of the ordinary, in an extraordinary way, breaks open and transforms conventions. As a result, this generates 'new' or 'other' experiences in the community.

But there is more that can be stated. This transformation can only be integrated when -in a way- it can be conjoined with tradition. As was said, Babette uses familiar ingredients. And like Babette, the general also uses the same familiar religious 'ingredients' (language, prayer and sermon) to name his own and the community's new insights and experiences. In the strange circumstances of *Babette's Feast*, where everything on the table is completely 'other', unknown, and probably suspect as heathen, perhaps only the 'old' language of Scripture and hymns can adequately accompany this disclosing or transforming potential of the meal to become real. In this situation, it is perfectly clear what the relevance of the concept of appropriation can be. For the small community, the appropriation of Scripture in this uncertain situation sustains and makes acceptable a practice of well-being, of becoming more human. It is a use of Scripture in a practice that contradicts their regular practices, a use that stabilises and authorises this new practice through scriptural approbation. The community's sense of the world is nourished by another sensibility.

---

[37] R. L. Grimes, *Deeply into the Bone. Re-inventing Rites of Passage* (Berkeley: University of California Press, 2000), 245.
[38] At this point, my interpretation differs from Grimes who, like others, focuses only on the meal. Grimes however, is interested in the meal as a ritual in which the 'special ordinariness' becomes clear. In this approach, I agree with him. Grimes, *Deeply into the Bone*, 244-346.

Divine presence in the every day world

Why speak of a sense of presence with regard to these practices and the transformations they energise? First of all, there are the 'surviving', 'resisting', and 'self-identifying' qualities these practices have for Babette. The faces of the poor, the silent appreciation of her biscuits, all small signs of the resilience of her talent, her creativity, and the potential meaning of her art. Although her circumstances had changed dramatically, her ordinary cooking practices enable Babette to find her way of being in this new and strange world and to make it her own. She has the courage to live, despite everything. The festive meal, in a way the summit of Babette's way of being in the world as it brings together her old as well as her new world, shows that, even though the power of the attentive sensibility of her art can take different directions, it remains as transformative as it ever was.

In my view, these practices are acts of believing and as such they reveal what people, Babette as well as the community, believeand what makes them believe. For Babette, this belief and what makes her believe is her allegiance to her art and the way she is able to use it to find her way of being in the world. From a theological perspective, this art can be read as a power/practice that is liberating, resisting and life-giving. With respect to the community, its beliefs as well as its religious practices, have gradually become grooved and worn out, lacking their original vividness and dynamism. The old people are a bit moody and even a little vindictive towards each other. The sisters do not know how to handle this situation. Babette's presence and her activities lure them to life again and reinforce their beliefs with unknown, graceful, and saving experiences. These experiences of ordinary, anonymous women and men, show other facets of the life-giving power of presence, of which nourishing and transformation are central elements. Referening Lady Wisdom in Proverbs, it is the simple invitation to eat and drink that seems to be lifegiving, just as the preparation of a meal can be a divine art. This film makes clear that theology, in order to be able to detect this kind of religiosity in everyday practices, perhaps needs a more 'sacramental,' incarnational and, therefore, a more 'ordinary' imagination of the Divine.[39] It is not the 'greatness' of Babette, nor her 'eucharistic meal,' but the greatness, openness and sanity of these ordinary women (including Babette) and men, that make it possible to relate these stories to the stories and narratives of the Christian tradition.

These and other stories manifest that the idea of God is indeed, as Metz once said, a practical idea without which there is no truth in the pure idea of God.[40] In weaving in these stories of women's (and men's) ways of being into the traditionally told

---

[39] L. Sexson, *Ordinarily Sacred* (Charlottesville: University Press of Virginia, 1982/1995).

[40] J. Baptist Metz, "Theology Today. New Crises and New Visions", *Catholic Theological Society of America Procedings* 40 (1987) 7, as cited by E. A. Johnson, *She Who Is. The Mystery of God in Feminist Theological Discourse* (New York: Crossroad, 1995), 244.

stories of the tradition, these stories bubble up to colour the pure idea of God.[41] My reading of *Babette's Feast* makes it clear that on the level of the practices of belief, the God-language of what Metz called the historical order, with its concepts, models, and dogmas, including such distinctions as these between transcendence and immanence or the sacred and the profane, does not make much sense. So far, I have defended the necessity of a preference for radical immanence in feminist theology. However, in practices of everyday life these concepts have a different meaning. In my analysis of *Babette's Feast*, they can function as an indication of both the presence of 'God,' which could be labelled as immanence, as well as the transforming power of this Presence, which could be called transcendence. This 'transcendence,' as I hope my analysis of the film has shown, does not ignore, neglect or diminish the materiality of ordinary existence; on the contrary, it makes the ordinary extraordinary without diminishing its everyday character. The importance of looking at this 'other' meaning of an 'immanent transcendence,' or a 'transcendent immanence', is that it reveals different facets, elements, characteristics of 'God' simultaneously. Reflecting the 'practices-of-God' shows that these facets are not to be converted to a monologic meaning, concept or image. What is more, these manifold, polysemic traces of divinity are theological interpretations not of an unknown distant 'God', but of a sense of divine presence in the everyday world.

---

[41] Johnson, *She Who Is*, 244.

Of Love, Life and Belief: the Story of Mary of Bethany (John 12:1-8)[1]

Magda Misset - van de Weg

Introduction

The story about 'a woman' who anointed Jesus is one of the few narratives that made its way into all four New Testament Gospels, albeit in differing versions. It must have stirred the imagination of many, as it did and does mine. A mass of interpretations can be seen as the sign of the ongoing popularity of the story and reveals that this text can be read so as to yield multiple interpretations, to which I propose to add yet another one. My focus will be the version in the Fourth Gospel (John 12:1-8), in which the evangelist recounts the story of "Mary who anointed the Lord with perfume and wiped his feet with her hair." (John 11: 2)

Love is one of the most vital aspects of human life, yet its concrete presence always seems to evade us. How 'substantially' can we speak about love? Love's intangibility has called upon imagination, evocative images and gestures to express its presence.[2] Examples of such an evocative 'strategy' can be found in the Fourth Gospel where love is a major theme and where pouring out sweet smelling perfume can be read as a poetic way of describing love.

The Fourth Gospel abounds with allusions to what we call the Old Testament and features a number of quotations.[3] In general, allusions are referred to in passing; my interest lies in establishing if and how we can speak in more certain terms about allusions to the Old Testament, in this case a specific allusion in John 12:3c to a specific book: the Song of Songs. Another point of my interest is the impact of such an intertextual element on the interpretation of the narrative in which Mary of Bethany expresses her love for Jesus.

In order to try and appreciate the dimension of love expressed in John 12, an additional interpretative key can be found in the saying in John 3:12: "If I have told you earthly things and you do not believe, how can you believe if I tell you heavenly things?" The contention of this article is that these words, together with the allusions in John 12 to the Song of Songs, bring both the 'earthly', mundane, human level of

---

[1] I would like to express my thanks to Maaike de Haardt and Maarten Menken for their support and their comments on an earlier draft.
[2] Cf. C.E. Walsh, *Exquisite Desire. Religion, the Erotic, and the Song of Songs* (Minneapolis: Fortress Press, 2000), 54.
[3] M.J.J. Menken, *Old Testament Quotations in the Fourth Gospel. Studies in Textual Form* (Contributions to Biblical Exegesis and Theology, 15: Kampen: Kok Pharos, 1996).

meaning and the 'heavenly' dimension into focus. A primary plain-sense reading can make the reader appreciate 'pouring out sweet oil' as a woman's way of expressing that she loved her god/God with all her soul, with all her heart and with all her might, and at the same time lift 'heavenly things' or the spiritual dimension to visibility. In John 12:1-8 love life and belief in God intersect.

The narrative: John 12:1-8

1. Six days before the Passover, Jesus came to Bethany,
   where Lazarus was, whom Jesus had raised from the dead.
2. There they made him a supper;
   Martha served, and Lazarus was one of those at table with him.
3. Mary took a pound of costly ointment of pure nard
   and anointed the feet of Jesus and wiped his feet with her hair;
   and the house was filled with the fragrance of the ointment.
4. But Judas Iscariot, one of his disciples (he who was to betray him), said:
5. "Why was this ointment not sold for three hundred denarii and given to the poor?"
6. This he said, not that he cared for the poor but because he was a thief, and as he had the money box he used to take what was put into it.
7. Jesus said, "Let her alone, let her keep it for the day of my burial.
8. The poor you always have with you, but you do not always have me."[4]

At the end of his public ministry, six days before the Passover, Jesus is on his way to Jerusalem for the third and the last time. He stops at Bethany, the town that had already been identified as "the village of Mary and her sister Martha" (11:1) and "There they made him a supper" (12:1). The location 'there' has been the subject of much discussion and speculation. Was he or was he not in the house of Mary, Martha and Lazarus?[5] It seems to me that the immediate context provides telling

---

[4] All English Translations of the New Testament texts in this article are from the Revised Standard Version.

[5] In efforts to harmonize the four gospels, commentators have located the meal in the house of Simon (the leper/ the Pharisee). Others argue that Jesus was Martha, Mary and Lazarus' guest, or that ἐκεῖ does not refer to the house of Martha, Mary and Lazarus, because if that were the case, why would the evangelist mention that Lazarus was at table with Jesus; some simply leave the matter unsolved. See for example: R.E. Brown, *The Gospel According to John (i-xii). Introduction, Translation, and Notes* (The Anchor Bible, 29: Garden City, NY: Doubleday, 1966), 448; L. Morris, *The Gospel according to John* (New International Commentary on the New Testament: Grand Rapids: Eerdmans, rev.edn., 1995), 509 and 511; H. Ridderbos, *Het evangelie naar Johannes. Proeve van een theologische exegese, deel 2 (Hoofdstuk 11-21)* (Kampen: Kok, 1992), 47; J.N. Sanders, *A Commentary on the Gospel According to St John*

clues to unravel the 'mystery'. From the outset the reader's attention is drawn to the previous, important event - the raising of Lazarus from the dead - and to the other protagonists: Lazarus' sisters Martha and Mary. In John 11 it is also made clear that Jesus loves this family of three (11:5), and that he and his disciples consider Lazarus their friend (11:11). The readers may therefore guess that when Jesus returns to Bethany he has, of course, a meal in their house, a private place, where he is safely among friends who will not follow the order of the chief priests and Pharisees: "that if any one knew where he was, he should let them know, so that they might arrest him." (11:57). Speculations about the reason for Martha serving a meal in somebody else's house or explanations for Mary's presence thus become superfluous.

The remark, "Lazarus was one of those at table with him" (12:2) puts both Lazarus and 'others' on the scene. The others, however, have no role to play, with the exception of Judas. Spotlighted is that Martha serves, that Lazarus is at table with him, and Mary's action. Her gesture was anticipated when she was introduced for the first time as the "Mary who anointed the Lord with ointment and wiped his feet with her hair" (11:2). Remarkable is not the fact of the anticipation, because prolepsis frequently occurs in John.[6] That which is remarkable is the content of the anticipation because it discloses, as it were, what needs to be at the forefront of the reader's or hearer's mind: they/we need to notice that Mary anoints *Jesus* rather than his feet; in 11:2 the wiping of his feet is mentioned as a separate action.

After the anointing, while the scent of the perfume lingers on in the house, Judas fulminates that Mary is wasting money, by which he devalues both Jesus and Mary's gesture. He is, however, immediately denounced. The narrator depicts him as a hypocrite and a thief and Jesus too rebukes Judas, but this reaction is fraught with difficulties. Firstly, Jesus' remark "The poor you always have with you, but you do not always have me", is difficult to digest. It has been suggested that the contrast fits in well with rabbinic theology. Good works were divided into two groups: those that pertain to mercy, e.g. burial and those that pertain to justice, e.g. almsgiving, and the former were superior to the latter.[7] However, the contrast between mercy and almsgiving is not the issue here, whereas the contrasts between the poor and Jesus (accentuated by the emphatic εφμεω) and not always/always, is.

(edited and completed by B.A. Mastin; Black's New Testament Commentaries: London: Black, 1968), 283; J. Gnilka, *Johannesevangelium* (Die neue Echter-Bibel; Neues Testament, 4: Würzburg: Echter-Verlag, 1983), 96; A. Reinhartz, "The Gospel of John", in E. Schüssler Fiorenza (ed.), *Searching the Scriptures. Volume II: A Feminist Commentary* (New York: SCM Press, 1995), 561-600, 582.

[6] E.g. 12:5; 6:64.71; 13:11.38.

[7] See Brown, *Gospel According to John*, 449, who refers to 'J. Jeremias, *ZNW* 35 (1936), 75-82'. C.K. Barrett, *The Gospel According to St John. An Introduction with Commentary and Notes on the Greek Text* (London: SPCK, 1978), 415, refers to *T.Peah* 4.19 and *Sukkah* 49b.

τοὺς πτωχοὺς γὰρ πάντοτε ἔχετε μεθ' ἑαυτῶν
ἐμὲ δὲ οὐ πάντοτε ἔχετε.

Moreover, the context is the refutation of Judas who tries to establish a situation of either/or, while Jesus affirms both Mary's gesture *and* caring for the poor:

> Die Leser begreifen, wovon Jesus redet, ist ihre Zeit doch durch die leibliche Abwesenheit Jesu geprägt. Ihnen bleiben nur die Armen, und der Dienst an ihnen ist der *zukünftige* Jesusdienst.[8]

Commentators have also been grappling with the impression given in John that Mary was to keep the perfume, or some of it, for a future embalming. The problem is that Mary of Bethany has no role in the burial preparation of Jesus' body, so why should she save it? Some find the general sense plain enough after having drawn attention to the problem. Others have suggested different translations, either based on text critical evidence, or on a possible Aramaic original, or on the meaning of τηρέω, or the alternative meaning of ἵνα, but none of these is wholly satisfying.[9] I shall not pretend to have the answer, but the general sense seems to be that Mary must be allowed to do this for she kept the ointment for the day she would have to 'prepare' Jesus for burial and is that not, among other things, precisely what she is doing?

---

[8] Cf. L. Schenke, *Johannes. Kommentar* (Düsseldorf: Patmos, 1998), 240; E. Haenchen, *Das Johannesevangelium. Ein Kommentar* (herausgegeben von U. Busse; Tübingen: Mohr [Siebeck], 1980), 434; X. Léon-Dufour, *Lecture de l'Évangile selon Jean II (chapitres 5-12)* (Paris: Éditions du Seuil, 1990), 449; G.R. O'Day, 'John', in C.A. Newsom and S.H. Ringe (eds.), *The Women's Bible Commentary* (London/Louisville, Kentucky: SPCK; Westminster/John Knox Press, 1992), 293-304, 299.

[9] Examples of suggestions for translations are: 'Lass sie in Frieden! Es soll gelten für den Tag meines Begräbnisses'; 'Laisse-la! Elle se proposait de garder ce [parfum] pour le jour de mon ensevelissement'; 'So Jesus said, Let her be! [She did this] to keep it for the day of my burial'; 'The purpose was that (*hina*) she might keep this for the day of preparation for my burial' - see: G.Voigt, *Licht - Liebe - Leben. Das Evangelium nach Johannes* (Göttingen: Vandenhoeck & Ruprecht, 1991), 187; Léon-Dufour, *Lecture de l'Évangile*, 446; Sanders, *A Commentary*, 285; F.J. Moloney, *Signs and Shadows. Reading John 5-12* (Minneapolis: Fortress Press, 1996), 182 and cf. for example F. Manns, *L'Évangile de Jean à la lumière du Judaïsme* (Studium Biblicum Franciscanum Analecta, 33: Jerusalem: Franciscan Printing Press, 1991), 271, Gnilka, *Johannes Evangelium*, 97, Morris, *Gospel According to John*, 507, Barrett, *St. John*, 414.

Mary's gesture in other interpretations

The reference to Jesus' burial led commentators to connect Mary's gesture with Jesus' death and resurrection, and to regard it as an act of mourning.[10] Some emphasise that Mary, as it were, foresees and foretells Jesus' death so that her gesture is of a prophetic nature or may even have messianic overtones.[11] Others read the event as a proleptic response to the consummate gift Jesus was about to give: his own life.[12] The proximity of the episode of the raising of Lazarus and the reminder of that event in 12:1, has, however, prompted a number of other commentators (or the same) to interpret Mary's gesture as an act of gratitude for bringing her brother back to life. Some add that the extravagance of the ointment,[13] together with Mary's self-effacement and self-humiliation, confirms her devotion born from gratitude.[14] Another suggestion is that it is not coincidental that the anointing is situated shortly before the crowds hail Jesus as the 'King of Israel'; the anointing helps to convey the signifycance of Jesus' kingship. He rides into Jerusalem and dies there, as an anointed king.[15] This view is problematic because it was the custom to anoint the head of a king, not his feet. However, the fact that the evangelist announced (chapter 11) that *Jesus* was anointed, offers food for thought.

As a part of or added to the above-mentioned interpretations, attention is also drawn to the striking parallels between John 12 and 13. In John 13, Jesus washes the *feet* of his disciples and *wipes* them off, during a *meal*, and urges his disciples to do

---

[10] E.g. S. van Tilborg, "The Women in John. On Gender and Gender Bending", in J.W. van Henten and A. Brenner (eds.), *Families and Family Relations as Represented in Early Judaisms and Early Christianities. Texts and Fictions*, (Studies in Theology and Religion, 2: Leiden: Deo Publishing, 2000) 192-212, 200; Ch.H. Giblin, "Mary's Anointing for Jesus' Burial-Resurrection (John 12,1-8)", *Biblica* 73 (1992), 560-564, argues that the coherent and distinctive theological point of wiping off the ointment is that Mary realized the inability of the grave to hold Jesus and that the Evangelist expects the reader to grasp that Jesus' rising as uncorrupt is prophesied.

[11] Among others: Brown, *Gospel According to John*, 452; Haenchen, 439-440; Gnilka, *Johannesevangelium*, 97; E. Schüssler Fiorenza, *In Memory of Her. A Feminist Theological Reconstruction of Christian Origins* (London: SCM Press, 1983), 331; M. de Groot, *Messiaanse Ikonen. Een vrouwenstudie van het evangelie naar Johannes* (Kampen: Kok, 1988), 70-71; C.R. Koester, *Symbolism in the Fourth Gospel. Meaning, Mystery, Community* (Minneapolis: Fortress Press, 1995), 114; Reinhartz "Gospel of John", 583; Moloney, *Signs and Shadows*, 182; M.R. D'Angelo, "(Re)Presentations of Women in the Gospels: John and Mark", in R.S. Kraemer and M.R. D'Angelo (eds.), *Women & Christian Origins* (New York/Oxford: Oxford University Press, 1999), 129-149, 136.

[12] E.g. Koester, *Symbolism*, 114.

[13] 300 denarii = approximately ten month wages of a labourer. The nard may thus be an indication for the social location of the family from Bethany.

[14] Among others: J.F. Coakley, "The Anointing at Bethany and the Priority of John", *Journal of Biblical Literature* 107 (1988) 2, 231-256, 246; Koester, *Symbolism*, 112-13; F.F. Bruce, *The Gospel of John. Introduction, Exposition and Notes* (Grand Rapids, Michigan: Eerdmans, 1983), 255.

[15] Barret, *The Gospel According to St John*, 409; Koester, *Symbolism*, 115.

as he did to them:

> If I then, your Lord and Teacher, have washed your feet, you also ought to wash one another's feet. For I have given you an example, that you also should do as I have done to you. Truly, truly, I say to you, a servant is not greater than his master; nor is he who is sent greater than he who sent him. If you know these things, blessed are you if you do them. (John 13:14-17)

Reading John 12:1-8 with this in mind is seen as lending Mary's gesture added meaning. She fulfils in advance Jesus' request: "The woman Mary is the prototype of the practice of discipleship."[16]

The contrast between the odour of death of Lazarus's rotting corpse (11:39) and the fragrance of nard or "the odor emanating from Mary's extravagant love",[17] and the contrast between Mary's love and Judas's betrayal, are more examples of specific dimensions in the narrative that drew attention. In passing, it is also mentioned that 12:3c may evoke Song of Songs 1:12 or 13, and 4:13-14, casting Mary in the role of the woman lover from Song of Songs 1:12.[18]

Both the theme of love and the allusion introduced here will be discussed in detail. First, however, I shall take a closer look at the manner in which Mary anoints Jesus.

---

[16] T.K. Seim, "Roles of Women in the Gospel of John", in L. Hartman and B. Olsson (eds.), *Aspects on the Johannine Literature. Papers Presented at a Conference of Scandinavian New Testament Exegetes at Uppsala, June 16-19, 1986* (Coniectanea Biblica New Testament Series, 18: Uppsala: Almqvist & Wiksell International, 1987), 56-73, 73. Cf. Schüssler Fiorenza, *In Memory of Her*, 330; C. Vander Stichele, "Een vrouw als apostel", in S. de Jong (red.), *Het testament van de dochters. Een bundel exegeses door vrouwen* (Kampen: Kok, 1992), 116-123; O'Day, 'John', 299; Reinhartz, "Gospel of John", 583.
There are still other readings, for instance those that depart from the viewpoint that John is written in terms of the Lucan story, which involves the conclusion that Mary of Bethany is the sinful woman and that - in agreement with ancient traditions - she and Mary of Magdala are one and the same person. See for example: J.H. Bernard, *A Critical and Exegetical Commentary on the Gospel According to St. John* (edited by A.H. McNeile; Edinburgh: T.&T. Clark, repr., 1963), esp. 412 where Bernard states: "... since the time of Gregory the Great, the Roman Church has been accustomed to identify Mary of Bethany, Mary Magdalene, and the ἁμαρτολό of Lk. 7. The Breviary office for the Feast of St. Mary Magdalene (July 22) draws out this identification, and treats the story of Mary as that of one who, once a great sinner, became a great saint. This identification has been accepted in the present commentary."

[17] O'Dale, "Gospel of John", 229.

[18] See among others: D'Angelo, "(Re)Presentations of Women", 136; Bruce, *Gospel of John*, 256; Léon-Dufour, *Lecture de l'Évangile*, 446, n. 14.

Loose hair and the anointing of feet

The description of the manner in which Mary anoints Jesus gave rise to much speculation, particularly Mary's loose hair and the fact that she anoints Jesus' feet. While referring to a diversity of sources, scholars note, among other things, that loosening hair in public was a mandatory term of divorce and therefore would have scandalised Jesus; that the Jews would have counted it immodest that Mary should unloose her hair at an entertainment where men were present; that it was a mark of loose morals, or that it would have been either, or all at once, extraordinary, shocking, scandalous and embarrassing and out of character for the virtuous Mary of Bethany, even though, curiously, the basis for ranking Mary with the 'virtuous' is never mentioned.[19] Of course, after having established the embarrassing aspects, explanations are sought and found. For instance, that it can best be explained "as a confused transferral of details...during the oral stage of transmission;"[20] or that "Mary did not stop to calculate public reaction. Her heart went out to her Lord, and she gave expression to her feelings in this beautiful and touching act."[21]

Apart from pointing out that it is not dramatised in the narrative that Mary actually loosens her hair and that some commentators mistakenly accentuate the public nature of the event, whereas the scene is precisely of a private nature, I wish to draw attention to data that cast a different light on 'loose hair'.

a. From many cultures it is known that the loosening of hair was a sign of mourning.[22]
b. Loose and unbound hair could be a sign of ecstatic endowment with Spirit-Sophia and a mark of prophetic behaviour (cf. 1 Cor.).
c. Molly Myerowitz Levine, in her essay on the gendered grammar of ancient Mediterranean hair, describes how in Greek epic for women, rich free flowing hair is initially a positive attribute, retaining a primary association with generative vitality. The same quality of luxurious hair may, however, assume a negative valence in contexts where female fertility and/or sexuality is seen as a potential threat. Levine concludes:

---

[19] E.g. Bernard, *Critical and Exegetical Commentary*, 417-8; Bruce, *Gospel of John*, 256; Brown, *Gospel According to John*, 450; Morris, *Gospel according to John*, 512.

[20] Brown, *Gospel According to John*, 450.

[21] Morris, *Gospel according to John*, 512.

[22] See M. Myerowitz Levine, "The Gendered Grammar of Ancient Mediterranean Hair", in H. Eilberg-Schwartz and W. Doniger (eds.), *Off with Her Head. The Denial of Women's Identity in Myth, Religion, and Culture* (Berkeley/Los Angeles/London: University of California Press, 1995), 76-130, 117, n. 66. See also, for example, the martyrdom of the saints Perpetua and Felicitas 20: "... Next she asked for a pin to fasten her untidy hair: for it was not right that a martyr should die with her hair in disorder, lest she might seem to be mourning in her hour of triumph."

with a glance at some actual customs of virgins, brides, and wives in which practice counterpoints myth to enunciate the cultural grammar of hair [...] almost universally the hair of young girls is 'untamed' left flowing and free like that of Ovid's virginal Daphne - *pace* Paul, Tertullian, and many others.[23]

For the time being, these data allow me to imagine Mary as a young or free unmarried woman, which, all things considered, would not exclude that her loose hair can be seen as a sign of mourning and/or as a sign of her prophetic behaviour.[24]

As regards footwashing, it is well known that footwashing was a routine matter of cleanliness and hospitality. Upon the arrival of guests the host provided water, sometimes oil, for the guests to wash and/or soothe their feet, especially before sharing a meal.[25] It was considered a menial task usually performed by slaves. A few sources reveal that children or students wash and/or anoint their parents' or their teacher's feet, a voluntary act through which they show themselves devoted enough to act as a slave.[26] More interesting still, that is with a view to the Johannine narrative, are the examples of footwashing as an expression of love. In Catullus 64.158-63, a woman is said to prefer to be a slave washing the feet of her beloved rather than endure separation from him. In the 1st Century story *Joseph and Aseneth*, we find two examples of footwashing as a voluntary act in which different kinds of emotion find expression: repentance and devotion but primarily love.

> But, my Lord, I entrust him to you, for I love him more than my own soul. Guard him within the wisdom of your graciousness and deliver me to him as a servant, that I may wash his feet and serve him and be a slave to him for all the rest of my life. (*Joseph and Aseneth* 13,11-12)

> And Joseph stretched out his hands and took Aseneth in his arms, and she him, and they embraced for a long time, and their spirits were rekindled. And Aseneth said to him, "Come here, lord, come into my house." And she took his right hand and led him into her house. And Joseph sat down upon the

---

[23] Levine, "Gendered Grammar", 95-96.
[24] The option that Mary was a young girl might provide an answer to many questions and speculations concerning the relation between her and her sister Martha, such as, for example: Martha is more important because she is repeatedly mentioned first; Mary is the silent type in the background because she stays at home when Jesus arrives in Bethany after Lazarus died.
[25] Cf. Gen. 18; 19:2; 24:32; 43:24; Judg. 19:21; 2 Sam. 11:8; b.Menah. 85b; Sifre Deut. 355.
[26] Mekilta, "Nezikin" 1.56-63 (Lauterbach ed., Vol. 3, 5-6) and Aristophanes, Wasps 608. See also 1 Sam. 25:41-42, where Abigail declares that she is prepared to be a servant to wash the feet of her master's servant, and cf. *Life of Aesop* 61-64 [trans. available in L.W. Daly (ed.), *Aesop without Morals* (New York: Thomas Yseloff, 1961)].

throne of Pentephres, her father, and she brought water to wash his feet. And Joseph said to her, "Let one of the virgins come and wash my feet." And Aseneth said to him, "No, lord, for my hands are your hands, and your feet are my feet, and no other may wash your feet." And she constrained him and washed his feet. (*Joseph and Aseneth* 19,2-20,4)[27]

Furthermore, it is known that anointings were performed by wives for their husbands before and after sexual intercourse; the alabastron is often portrayed in private scenes with women.[28]

While I do not wish to contest that Mary's gesture may have prophetic overtones, or is born out of gratitude, I do suggest - in light of the above mentioned examples - that Mary's gesture can be placed within a framework of love rather than in one of humility, of a lower place or the lowliest place.[29] At this point, I would like to add that the history of interpretations in general shows that there has been little or no place for the potential of the Sacred in physicality. Instead, biblical scholarship has shunned placing a positive value on the physicality of the anointing, and too often has resorted to the age-old linkage of between women with sexuality, sin and shame. As Teresa Hornsby states: "The interpreters of Christianity seem to be more comfortable explaining and propagating the violent passion of Jesus rather than acknowledging any other passion concerning Jesus' body."[30]

I shall now work out how the allusion to the Song of Songs in John 12 provides the incentive to place Mary's gesture within the framework of love in all its multifaceted splendour.

Allusions to the Song of Songs

An allusion is a directional signal with evocative potential that refers the readers to another text outside the alluding text and is therefore a relational device. The relational quality lies in the potential to guide the reader to the additional referent and to build up semantically significant links between the alluding text and the alluded-to text. As the allusion is never obvious, the process of actualisation of an

---

[27] Translations from R.S. Kraemer (ed.), *Maenads Martyrs Matrons Monastics. A Sourcebook on Women's Religions in the Greco-Roman World* (Philadelphia: Fortress Press, 1988), 273, 277-8.

[28] K.E. Corley, *Private Women Public Meals. Social Conflict in the Synoptic Tradition* (Peabody, Massachusetts: Hendrickson, 1993), 104 and see there for more examples and literature on the subject.

[29] For the latter interpretations see for example: B. Witherington, *Women in the Ministry of Jesus* (Cambridge: Cambridge University Press, 1984), 112; Morris, *Gospel according to John*, 512.

[30] T.J. Hornsby, "Why Is She Crying? A Feminist Interpretation of Luke 7.36-50", in H.C. Washington, S. Lochrie Graham and P. Thimmes (eds.) *Escaping Eden. New Feminist Perspectives on the Bible* (The Biblical Seminar, 65: Sheffield: Sheffield Academic Press, 1998), 100.

allusion begins with the recognition of the marker or the 'stumbling block' that draws the reader's attention to a text's intertextual relationship(s) and entails recollection of the original form of the marker, which may lead to identification of the evoked original text and context, which, finally, is mandatory for intertextual patterning beyond the modified interpretation of the marker itself.[31]

What then is the marker in John that might cause the readers to pause and ponder? On the one hand, I thus postulate the ideal readers as the reconstruction of all the appropriate responses to a text.[32] To them could be accredited such widely propagated characteristics as: Christians were or had been instructed in assiduous reading of Jewish Scriptures, which includes that they might, or are expected to, recognise allusions to the Scriptures.[33] On the other hand, I, as one of the present-day assiduous readers enter into the reading process and seem to have an advantage over the first readers and hearers for I have additional sources, in this case the versions of the anointing narrative in the synoptic Gospels. Moreover, a few other exegetes have - albeit tentatively - drawn attention to the possibility of an allusion to the Song of Songs in John 12.[34] In any case, the text

ἡ δὲ οἰκία ἐπληρώθη ἐκ τῆς ὀσμῆς τοῦ μύρου (and the house was filled with the fragrance of the ointment), the aspect not mentioned in the Synoptic Gospels but only in the Fourth Gospel, together with the combined occurrence of a woman and a man/king who is reclining at table, plus the fragrance of the ointment made of nard, are the markers that guided me to the Song of Songs 1:12 (LXX) as the alluded-to-text:

"Ἕως οὗ ὁ βασιλεὺς ἐν ἀνακλίσει αὐτοῦ νάρδος μου ἔδωκεν ὀσμὴν αὐτοῦ.
While the king reclined (at table), my nard gave forth its fragrance.

---

[31] My definition is based upon: U.J. Hebel, "Towards a Descriptive Poetics of *Allusion*", in H.F. Plett (ed.), *Intertextuality. Research in Text Theory/Untersuchungen zur Texttheorie* (Berlin/New York: Walter de Gruyter, 1991), 135-164; Z. Ben-Porat, "The Poetics of Literary Allusion", in *PTL. A Journal for Descriptive Poetics and Theory of Literature* 1, 105-128, esp. 109-10; M. Riffaterre, *Semiotics of Poetry* (Bloomington: Indiana University Press, 1978).

[32] I shall not go into the question of the ideal reader as the reconstruction of all the appropriate responses suggested or implied by the text matter here. The matter has been lucidly presented by others, most recently by G. van Oyen, *De lezers van het Marcusevangelie* (Utrechtse Theologische Reeks, 43: Utrecht 2001).

[33] J.A. Sanders, "A New Testament Hermeneutic Fabric: Psalm 118 in the Entrance Narrative", in C.A. Evans and W.F. Stinespring (eds.), *Early Jewish and Christian Exegesis. Studies in Memory of William Hugh Brownlee* (Atlanta: Scholars Press, 1987), 177-90, 178; Menken, *Old Testament Quotations*, 11.

[34] Manns, *L'Évangile de Jean*, 287. D'Angelo, "(Re)presentations of Women", 136.

Because an allusion is like a piece broken off from the context of a more complete and prior utterance and incorporated into a new one,[35] other indicators in the contexts both of the alluded-to and the alluding text can be of major importance for asserting that we are indeed dealing with an allusion. They can, moreover, be of help in establishing that the author of the alluding text was familiar with the alluded-to-text. Even the quickest glance at the wider contexts of both John 12:3 and Song of Songs 1:12 reveals that these contexts certainly have one thing in common, that is the preponderance of the theme of love, but there are other connections as well.

To begin with, the amount of sensory language in John 12,1-8 (and 9) is remarkable.[36] There are references to *taste* ("they made him a meal" vs. 2); *touch* ("Mary...anointed Jesus' feet and wiped his feet with her hair" - vs. 3); *scent* ("the house was filled with the fragrance" - vs. 3); *hearing and seeing* (the crowd *learned* where Jesus was and came to *see* him and Lazarus - vs. 9). In the Song of Songs too the senses go on full alert; the Song celebrates human, sensual life.[37] Or as Jonneke Bekkenkamp has observed in the first four verses of the Song, four senses are immediately stirred: the *hearing* in the 'Song of Songs', *touch* in the loving, *scent* in the scent of the ointment, and *taste* in the kisses.[38]

Points of contact between John and the Song of Songs can also be found in the use of the images of wine and vine.[39] In biblical traditions the images of vineyards and gardens represent, in a sense, the best that creation has to offer,[40] and are appropriated to convey important values, such as the relationship of God with his people.[41] Besides, the vine's delightful product, wine, became the symbol of *eros*, especially in the Song and occupies a choice place in it.[42] Even though the image of the vineyard is not overt in John, Jesus appears as the giver of the best of wines, thus manifesting that the best of God's vineyard can now be shared (John 2). The combination of the wedding and the wine in this Cana narrative is rich in meaning, activating both the image of God's relation with his people and passion.

An important aspect of these images is that mutuality is entailed. The farmer, his workers, and the grapes, as it were, have to be willing to put in the time for successful cultivation. I see reflections thereof in the meal-scenes in John 12 and 13

---

[35] J. Hollander, *The Figure of Echo. A Mode of Allusion in Milton and After* (Berkeley/Los Angeles/London: University of California Press, 1981), 62-63.

[36] Cf. Manns, *L'Évangile de Jean,* 284 and 286.

[37] Walsh, *Exquisite Desire*, 216.

[38] J. Bekkenkamp, *Canon & Keuze. Het bijbelse Hooglied en de Twenty-One Love Poems als bronnen van theologie* (Kampen: Kok Agora, 1993), 260.

[39] Song of Songs 1:2.4; 2:4; 4:10; 5:1; 7:10; 8:1 and John 2:3.9.10 (wine); Song of Songs 1:6.14; 2:13.15; 6:11; 7:12; 8:11.12 and John 15:1.5 (vine).

[40] Cf. Walsh, *Exquisite Desire*, 209-10.

[41] E.g. Isa. 5 and 55.

[42] A. LaCocque, *Romance She Wrote. A Hermeneutical Essay on Song of Songs* (Harrisburg, Pennsylvania: Trinity Press International, 1998), 85 and 187.

and in John 15 where Jesus elaborates on the vine-metaphor and says:

> As the branch cannot bear fruit by itself, unless it abides in the vine, neither can you, unless you abide in me. (15:5)

What Jesus has to offer is the best of both, but it will come to nothing without response, it needs, in essence, reciprocal love.

Next, in the Song of Songs, the identity or the image of the male lover is not a constant but has an elusive quality. His identity is left obscured in the sense that he cannot be fully known, or easily and exactly packaged.[43] In the Fourth Gospel, the fierce altercations with 'the Jews' on the subject of Jesus' identity seem to indicate that the question of Jesus' identity is, in a sense, *not* left obscured, but rather a matter of dispute. On the other hand, the abundance of designations also creates a certain kind of elusiveness. Jesus cannot be easily 'packaged' either, or one might conclude that the readers do not have to commit to any one identity. He is presented as the *logos*, the messiah, the king, the son, the bridegroom, the teacher, the shepherd, the well of living water, the manna from heaven, and so on. A number of these designations bring the Song of Song's lover to mind - he too is called, among others, shepherd, king, son - but the identity marker from the Song that attracts special attention in relation to John 12 and 15 is the image of the beloved as "he whom my soul loves."[44]

Exegetes have often noted that the scene of Mary Magdalene seeking the body of Jesus in the garden (John 20:11-18) distinctly echoes the Song of Songs, in particular chapter 3:1-4 (cf. 5: 6-7.17; 6:1). In this passage of the Song the woman searches him whom her soul loves, in the city, during the night, or near the end of the night. She cannot find him, asks the guards whether they have seen him and when she finally does find him, she holds him and does not want to let him go.[45] I cannot here elaborate on the convergence between John 12 and the resurrection narrative, but draw attention to it because of the love that motivates and is expressed by the two Marys for the one whom their soul loves, which I see as the tie that binds the two narratives in John 12 and 20 together.

---

[43] On the elusiveness of the identity of the lover in the Song of Songs, see Walsh, *Exquisite Desire*, 204. She points out that the obscurity of the identity of the male lover is one of the details that hint at the possibility of God's presence in the Song.

[44] Song of Songs 1:7; 3:1.2.3.4; 5:6.

[45] See for example: M. Cambe, "L'influence du Cantique des Cantique sur le Nouveau Testament", *Revue Thomiste* 62 (1962) 1 and 5-25; A.T. Hanson, *The Prophetic Gospel. A Study of John and the Old Testament* (Edinburgh: T.&T. Clark, 1991), 227-9; D'Angelo, "(Re)Presentations of Women", 136.

A final focal point concerns the overall image of the woman in the Song of Songs that gave me the idea of associating - albeit tentatively - her image with Mary of Bethany. In more or less recent treatises on the Song, the woman is portrayed as fully the equal of the man.[46] Her independence and boldness are underlined, and it is pointed out how she reverses the societal customs of giving and receiving. According to these customs the male in charge supported the woman, who was always the one to receive.[47] Judging from Judas's reaction, Mary of Bethany, like the woman in the Song, sheds societal chains too. Boldly and freely she gives her gift of love.

Love and commandments

'Love is a many splendoured thing' and the Fourth Gospel encompasses many manifestations thereof, ranging from God's love for the world to Jesus' love for his friends:

> For God so loved the world that he gave his only Son,
> that whoever believes in him should not perish but have eternal life (John 3:16)

> Greater love has no one than this, that a man lays down his life for his friends (John 15:13)

To be sure, the evangelist gives pride of place to the love between the Father and the Son, which is the precondition for and determines everything else: "[...] the Father loves the Son, and has given all things into his hand" (3:35) and the Son does as the Father has commanded him, so that the world may know that he loves the Father (14:31).[48] Many more examples could be given; instead I shall focus on one other conspicuous aspect of the love-theme: the relation between love and commandment(s). Although we may or even should wonder how 'new' it is, a new commandment calling for reciprocal love that determines and characterises discipleship is introduced in 13:34:

> A new commandment I give to you, that you love one another;
> even as I have loved you, that you also love one another.
> By this all will know that you are my disciples, if you have love for one another. (13:34-35)

The same theme, or the connection between love and commandment(s), is taken up again in the next chapters. Just as the son out of love for the Father keeps his

---

[46] E.g. Bekkenkamp, *Canon en Keuze*, 118-19 and see there for further references.
[47] LaCocque, *Romance She Wrote*, 115.
[48] Remarkably, this is the only instance where the Son's love for the Father is mentioned explicitly.

commandments and his words, so the son's friends (φίλοι) are encouraged, out of love for him, to keep his words and commandments, which are, of course, one and the same as the Father's (15:9.10.14 - cf. 14:15.21.31; 15:12.13.15.17).
In 15:9-10 the aspects just mentioned are, as it were, summarised:

> As the Father has loved me, so have I loved you; abide in my love.
> If you keep my commandments, you will abide in my love,
> just as I have kept my father's commandments and abide in his love.

M.J. Mulder has argued that in the first century CE, the Song of Songs must still have been a popular, cherished and well-known song that was sung in the vineyards and the taverns. The moral or puritanical inhibitions of a later era and the dualism that favours the spirit over the material had not yet taken its toll; graphic scenes and descriptions of the love between a man and a women were not yet found to be scandalous. At the same time the allegorical interpretation had already begun to win acceptance. The discussion about the Song's canonicity had begun and ended, circa 90 CE, with R. Aqiba's teaching that the Song should be included among the Holy Books, which also meant that the allegorical interpretation was accepted and legalised. The love depicted in the Song was thus interpreted as the love between God and Israel, from which followed that Israel's response to the love of God finds expression in living according to the Torah and the study of Torah.[49]

Therefore, if, and I emphasise *if*, the author of the Fourth Gospel was familiar with Jewish exegetical techniques and devices of the early Rabbinic Period, the Song might resonate behind the insistence of loving God and keeping God's commandments and words.[50]

---

[49] M.J. Mulder, *De targum op het Hooglied. Inleiding, vertaling en korte verklaring* (Exegetica: Oud- en Nieuwtestamentische studiën. Nieuwe reeks, 4: Amsterdam: Bolland, 1975); B. Rapp-de Lange, "The Love of Torah: Solomon Projected into the World of R. Aqiba in the Song of Songs Rabba", in A. Brenner and J.W. van Henten, *Recycling Biblical Figures. Papers read at a NOSTER Colloquium in Amsterdam 12-13 May 1997* (Studies in Theology and Religion, 1: Leiden: Deo Publishing, 1999), 272-291, esp. 272-275. According to F. Landy, *Paradoxes of Paradise. Identity and Difference in the Song of Songs* (Sheffield: Almond, 1983), 14-15, Rabbi Aquiba also taught that human love and divine love are united in Torah, with which the world was created and that is why what remains at the end when everything else is lost is the Song of Songs *id est* the theme of love stronger than death!

[50] On the subject, see: Menken, *Old Testament Quotations*, 14: "We may expect that John uses such techniques and devices in his rendering of OT passages." A. Houtman and E. van Staalduin-Sulman, in their paper "Reverence for Scripture: Treatment of the Hebrew Text in Targum Jonathan and the New Testament", read at the EABS conference, Utrecht, August 6-8, 2000, emphasize the importance of recognizing, albeit with caution, techniques and themes used in the early Rabbinic Period and the far-reaching influence of the Targum on contemporary literature like the New Testament.

LaCocque, like Mulder, points out that the Song of Songs has probably never been read at one level of understanding only.[51] He also notes:

> [...] what actually stirs Rabbi Aqiba's enthusiasm is that "for our sages, the starting point of all love is love of God for Israel, love of Israel for God, and from there, their work commences." Note that "the starting point of all love" is a love not exclusive but inclusive of all other manifestations of love. God-Israel mutual love invites us in return to reflect upon the love between the Canticle's human lovers.[52]

In my view, the evangelist precisely evokes this human dimension as well, through the allusion in John 12:3. This brings me to the next step in the interpretive process: detecting the (larger) meaning or effect the allusion can or is meant to produce for those 'who have ears to hear'.[53]

The anointing story 'revived'

Obviously, different levels of interpretation and multivalent messages can be and are detected in a nearly two-thousand year-old story; it calls and has called forth different responses from different readers and one interpretation does not necessarily exclude another. It is noticeable, however, that many interpretations of the Bible are not oriented towards human emotions, fears, dreams and desires, thus leaving the impression that ancient people did not really live ordinary lives. But of course they did. They knew pleasure, pain, and love; in short there was more to their lives than adherence to God. When I allow these dimensions to surface I am jolted out of spiritual complacency. New horizons open up and I can see that "[...] though spirituality courses through much biblical material [...] texts ponder the meaning of life, customs, and belief in God in terms that matter to the human."[54] Besides, it cannot be ignored that the authors wrote from a human perspective, whether or not they meant to produce a theological treatise. A shift back and forth between the horizontal axis 'human-human' and the vertical axis 'divine-human, human-divine', may therefore be seen as an inherent quality of biblical texts. In the Fourth Gospel it is the theme of love that enlightens such a shift, drawing the readers and hearers to the human as well as the spiritual dimensions in the text. It is in John 3:11-12 that we can find encouragement for such a shift:

---

[51] LaCocque, *Romance She Wrote*, 20: "The presence of the Canticle at Qumran, a community of radical ascetics allowing little room for Eros, would prove that much!"
[52] LaCocque, *Romance She Wrote*, 15.
[53] Cf. R.B. Hays, *Echoes of Scripture in the Letters of Paul* (New Haven/London: Yale University Press, 1989).
[54] Walsh, *Exquisite Desire*, 211.

... we speak of what we know, and bear witness to what we have seen; but you do not receive our testimony. If I have told you earthly things and you do not believe, how can you believe if I tell you heavenly things?

It was through the allusion to the Song of Songs that I discovered the validity to read the anointing story in that vein.

The dimension then, which is thus brought to the fore, are that Mary of Bethany, like the woman in the Song of Songs, loves the beloved. Reciprocating his love - the best there is - she boldly pours out her gift of love - the best there is - for the man her soul loves. She anoints him with sweet smelling oil, touching and caressing him, entangling him with her hair. Her gesture is an expression of and motivated by the most fundamental, enduring and existential human emotion: love. Not the theological-laden disincarnate *agapê* that smothers any real emotion, but *eros*, the love between human beings, the given of creation we cannot live without, because to love is to live.[55]

Finally, it is this love/*eros*, which must first be understood before any allegory of love between God and Israel, or Jesus and the church, could even work, because, as is sung in the Song of Songs, human love is God's love incarnate.[56] The same is expressed in the First Letter of John 4:7-8:

> Beloved let us love one another; for love is from God,
> and everyone who loves is born of God and knows God.
> Whoever does not love does not know God,
> for God is love.

---

[55] On the subject of *eros*, see e.g. A. Lorde, "Uses of the Erotic. The Erotic as Power", in A. Lorde, *Sister Outsider. Essays and Speeches/by Audre Lorde* (Freedom, California: Crossing Press, 1984), 53-59, who argues among others that the erotic is more a question of feelings than acting and therefore is a resource for empowerment.
[56] Cf. LaCocque, *Romance She Wrote*, 207 n. 1.

'The Pearl Lay Hidden in the Dung'[1]

Reaching for God in *Devotio Moderna* Sisterbooks

Mathilde van Dijk

Introduction

Sister Heylewich ten Velthave (d. 1418) lived in 'Master Geert's house', a community of the Sisters of the Common Life in Deventer created by Geert Grote (1340-1384), the founder of *Devotio Moderna*. The sisters lived without vows in common possession of goods. Heylewich was in charge of the convent's livestock, a job that involved a lot of hard and dirty work. She was also frequently sent on various errands, much to her chagrin, as she hated to leave the convent's compound. Such tasks constantly interfered with her work in the stables. However, when a fellow sister advised her to stand up for herself and complain about her workload, she answered: "Good Lord, why should I? The pigs and the cows don't complain, do they?" It was as though she were saying: "I would indeed be entitled to complain, if the animals were not properly cared for. However, I can return to the stables when I get back, so I think that our sweet Lord would be angry with me if I were to complain and grumble." She was always obedient and, whatever order was given to her, she would say: "I'd love to do it." It made no difference to her whether she heard Mass or mucked out the stables. Her obedience was exemplary. The same held for her humility; her behavior, the way in which she dressed herself, her books, and everything else about her bore witness to this. She never desired anything for herself. The pearl lay hidden in the dung, as it were. Worldly people looked down on her because of her appearance, but in the eyes of God, she was beautiful on the inside. Thus, like the bride from the Song of Songs, she could say: "I am black, but I am beautiful." She was beautiful in the eyes of Him who cares only about the state of the heart.[2]

The life of Heylewich is included in the sisterbook of 'Master Geert's house.' It is a typical example of the life of a female adherent of *Devotio Moderna*. She is portrayed as a diligent, obedient, and humble woman whose activities in the convent consist mainly of manual labor. Her inner self is what matters. The perfect state of

---

[1] *Hier beginnen sommige stichtige punten van onsen oelden zusteren naar het te Arnhem berustende handschrift*, D. de Man (ed.), (The Hague: Nijhoff, 1919), 11r: "Die margaerite lach verborgen in den meste." I thank Riet Bons-Storm for her comments.

[2] *Hier beginnen sommige stichtige punten*, 10v-11v.

her heart makes her a proper bride for the sisters' Groom.

A sisterbook is a collection of biographies of sisters of a particular house, usually written by a fellow sister. Its purpose is educational: the author intends to present her subjects as models of piety for her fellow sisters and for future sisters. From *Devotio Moderna*, only two sisterbooks survive, though it is obvious that more existed at the time.[3] The other example is from a convent of Regular Canonesses at Diepenveen, that of Saint-Agnes and Saint Mary. This community was a member of the Chapter of Windesheim.[4] These sisterbooks belong to the very few surviving works from *Devotio Moderna* written by women.[5] They therefore provide rare insight into the ideas and practices of female members of this religious movement.[6] The practice of writing educational biographies was by no means restricted to the female adherents of *Devotio Moderna*. Male authors felt the same about saving the memories of exemplary brothers of the past and educating their fellow brothers by their examples. The contents of male and female biographies are different. This is striking because the ideal of piety, to which the sisters and brothers had to conform, was the same for both sexes, as we shall see presently. However, the means of reaching this goal were different.

---

[3] I.e. in their original form. Another sisterbook from the convent of Saint Agnes at Emmerik was destroyed in the Second World War. Rev. W. Richter made a copy in the years 1921/1922. The City Archives of Emmerik acquired this copy in 1969. See: G. Hövelmann, "Das Emmmericher Süsternbuch. Eine verlorengeglaubte Hauptquelle zur Geschichte der Devotio Moderna", in *Thomas von Kempen. Beiträge zum 500. Todesjahr 1471-1971*, (Kempen: Stadt Kempen, 1971), 43-62, esp. 43-44 and W.F. Scheepsma, "Zusterboeken. Bijzondere bronnen voor de Moderne Devotie", in *Het zaad der Middeleeuwen. Jaarboek voor vrouwengeschiedenis* 16 (1996), 153-170, esp. 156-157. The Emmerik sisterbook has been edited by Anne Bollman and Nikolaus Staubach in Anne Bollmann and Nikolaus Staubach (eds.), *Schwesternbuch und Statuten des St. Agnes-Konvents in Emmerich* (Emmerich: Emmericher Geschichtsverein, 1998), esp.31-308.

[4] D. de Man edited the Deventer sisterbook in *Hier beginnen sommige stichtige punten*. The sisterbook of Diepenveen exists in two versions. The shorter version was entitled *Van den doechden der vuriger ende stichtiger susteren van Diepen Veen (Handschrift D)*, D.A. Brinkerink (ed.), (Leiden: Sijthoff, 1904). I am grateful to W.F. Scheepsma for allowing me to work with his transcription of the longer version, as described in manuscript DV (= Deventer, Stads- en Atheneumbibliotheek, hs. 101 E 26). Both versions have been used for this paper. For an outline of the differences between the two versions, see W.F. Scheepsma, *Deemoed en devotie. De koorvrouwen van Diepenveen en hun geschriften* (Amsterdam: Prometheus, 1997), 135-141.

[5] For a study of writings by women in the Windesheim chapter, see the aforementioned study by Scheepsma, *Deemoed en Devotie*.

[6] Furthermore, they belong to a rare genre. The only other surviving sisterbooks come from the convents of Dominican sisters in the south of present-day Germany and the Elzas. These predate our material by over a century. For a study of these sisterbooks, see G. J. Lewis, *By Women, for Women, about Women. The Sisterbooks of Fourteenth-Century Germany* (Toronto: Pontifical Institute of Mediaeval Studies, 1996).

For the purpose of this essay, I shall concentrate on one issue: the proportion of manual work and study. Both were traditional features of religious life for both men and women. However, manual labor is much more prominent and is different in character, as compared to the situation for brothers, in the lives of *Devotio Moderna* sisters.[7] In the sisterbooks, manual labor appears to be the prime duty. Furthermore, the sisters engage in all kinds of heavy and dirty work. If manual labor is referred to in men's biographies, the authors usually mean the writing of books, both as copier and as author.[8] In general, study is not mentioned in the sisterbook texts as a favored occupation. This is in keeping with the prescriptions for both Deventer and Diepenveen. The statutes of 'Master Geert's house' do not address study, and the Windesheim statutes for women make little room for study in a sister's day. In this respect, the sisters at Diepenveen deviated from the Augustinian tradition, in which the reading and writing of texts had always been an important feature of religious life for both male and female canons.[9] At the same time, it is obvious that some sisters were educated women. Moreover, the sisterbooks praise some sisters for their abilities in this respect. How is manual labor described in the sisterbooks? Why is it such an appropriate pursuit for women? How do the sisterbooks deal with those sisters who excel in study? How could this activity be presented as an example for the readers or hearers?

This essay consists of five parts. In the first place, I shall look into the nature of *Devotio Moderna* and its views of the religious life. Secondly, I shall deal with the place of women in *Devotio Moderna*. As we shall see presently, women were a constant concern, at least for the male adherents, and probably for themselves as well. Part three will investigate the ways in which manual labor is presented in the sisterbooks as an appropriate pursuit for women. In the fourth part we shall look into two examples of two studious sisters; the ways in which they are presented give clear insight into what true piety was all about, at least for women. The fifth part will give a conclusion. It will be followed by a postscript.

The religious life according to *Devotio Moderna*

Devotio Moderna had its origins in the lowlands around the IJssel in the 1370s. From there it spread through the whole of the Low Countries and parts of the Holy Roman Empire. By the eve of the Reformation, it was the predominant influence on

---

[7] R.T.M. van Dijk, *De constituties der Windesheimse vrouwenkloosters voor 1559* (Nijmegen: Katholieke Universiteit Nijmegen, Centrum voor Middeleeuwse studies, 1986), 437-439; J. de Hullu, "Statuten van het Meester-Geertshuis te Deventer", *Archief voor Nederlandsche kerkgeschiedenis* 6 (1897), 70.

[8] See M. van Dijk, "En zuster Jutte lachte ... Vroom en vrouwelijk in het zusterboek", in *Het ootmoedig fundament van Diepenveen. Zeshonderd jaar Maria en Sint-Agnesklooster 1400-2000*, in W. F. Scheepsma en T. Hendrikman (eds.), (Deventer: Ysselacademie, 2002), 95-112, 143-145, 167-169

[9] Scheepsma, *Deemoed en devotie*, 76-77.

religious life.[10]

It was a typical medieval reform movement, along the lines of the better-known Poverty Movement of the Thirteenth Century. Its purpose was to return to the piety of the early church, to the examples set by Christ and the apostles. According to the adherents, the best way to do so was to follow the example of the desert fathers. These were the holy men and women who had invented religious life. After religious persecution ended in the fourth century, they were the first to withdraw into the deserts of Egypt and Syria as hermits or monks and nuns in religious communities. Their lives and aphorisms, as described in the *Vitae patrum* and the *Collationes patrum*, had been a traditional part of monastic libraries throughout the centuries. The adherents of *Devotio Moderna* were also influenced by other early church saints: the martyrs and the church fathers, particularly Saint Augustine.[11]

The most important influence on adherents of *Devotio Moderna* was, however, the desert fathers. Johannes Busch, the fifteenth century historian from Windesheim, boldly announced that if these first monks and nuns could be regarded as the 'old devotion' (the *Devotio Antiqua*), he himself and his fellow brothers and sisters represented the 'modern devotion' (the *Devotio Moderna*).[12] They took over many of the ideals and practices of their illustrious religious forebears, including the writing of educational biographies of exemplary brothers and sisters.

At the most fundamental level they were in agreement with the desert fathers' views of the purpose of religious life and the ways in which such a life should be lead. In their eyes, religious women and men ought to aspire to "purity of the heart."[13] They strove to become the complete opposites of people in the world – in carnal bondage – and this entailed a total reversal of the self. It was commonly held that humankind's perfection was lost at the Fall. Adam originally had been created perfect, in the image and likeness of God. The Fall was the result of Adam diverting his will from that of God's. In reaching for the apple, he had contracted a desire for carnal pleasure that would be shared by all his sons and daughters. The challenge for religious people was to recover humankind's state at creation, to clean their hearts of all carnal desire in order to recreate these hearts as pure. Along with the

---

[10] E. Persoons, "De verspreiding der Moderne Devotie", in A. G. Weiler, E. Persoons and C. C. de Bruin, *Geert Grote en de Moderne Devotie* (Zutphen: Walburg Pers, 1984), 57-101.

[11] See for this: K. Stooker and T. Verbeij, *Collecties op orde. Middelnederlandse handschriften uit kloosters en semi-religieuze gemeenschappen in de Nederlanden* 1 (Leuven: Peeters, 1997), 231-234.

[12] J. Busch, "Liber de viris illustribus", in K. Grube (ed.), *Des Augustinerprobstes Johannes Busch Chronicon Windeshemense und Liber de reformatione monasteriorum* (Halle: Hendel, 1886), c. 3.

[13] See for this: Johannes Cassianus, *Conférences*, E. Pichery (ed.), (Parijs: Ed. du Cerf, 1954, 1958, 1959), coll. 1.

desert fathers, the adherents of *Devotio Moderna* felt that this could be achieved only if a woman or man devoted her or himself entirely to this lofty goal. Everyday life was seen as the daily battleground for sisters or brothers striving for perfection. All their practices, thoughts, and feelings were to serve their goal of self-reformation. As such, mucking out a stable could be as useful as hearing Mass, if done with the right intention.[14]

Both men and women had to conform to the same ideal, as the original model of perfection was perceived as being sexless. Their biographies show that their means of reaching this goal, however, were *gendered*. This was inevitable in view of the differences between the sexes as the adherents of *Devotio Moderna* perceived them.

Women in *Devotio Moderna*

From the start, the pastoral care of religious women was a major focus of *Devotio Moderna*. Female adherents outnumbered males throughout the movement's history.[15] This is why it has become customary to address *Devotio Moderna* as the 'second wave' of the religious women's movement. The 'first wave' was in the thirteenth century, as a part of the Poverty Movement. Its effects were mainly felt in the southern part of the Low Countries. In this movement too, the women had outnumbered the men by far. Most of these women lived as Beguines.

Much of *Devotio Moderna* can be regarded as a reply to the Poverty Movement. While this movement's ideas were generally considered sound, in the eyes of Grote and his followers, they had become corrupted. Furthermore, and particularly with regard to women, their way of life was seen as being seriously flawed. The Beguines were thus subjected to considerable *Devotio Moderna* criticism. When Geert Grote offered his home to the sisters of the future 'Master Geert's house', he intended them to do better than the Beguines.[16]

Grote's greatest concern was the lack of spiritual guidance in communities of Beguines. Compared to nuns, they were very much on their own. They did not follow a monastic rule. They had their own parishes, separate from the rest of the town, and for which they chose their own rectors. In Grote's eyes this was a recipe for trouble. A true man of his times, he was convinced that women were physically and morally weaker than men.[17] This was obvious from the fact that many Beguines

---

[14] A.G. Weiler, "Over de geestelijke praktijk van de Moderne Devotie", in P. Bange, C. Graafland, A.J. Jelsma and A.G. Weiler, *De doorwerking van de Moderne Devotie. Windesheim 1387-1987* (Hilversum: Verloren, 1988), 29-45, esp. 32-33.
[15] Scheepsma, "Zusterboeken", 155.
[16] The best-known treatise against the Beguines is that by Geert Grote, *De simonia at Beguttas*, W. De Vreese (ed.), (The Hague: Nijhoff, 1940). In this work, he attacked the practice of paying an entrance fee for admission into a community of Beguines. He regarded this as simony. Furthermore, he felt that poverty should not be a barrier to the religious life.
[17] This was due to their physical natures. For an analysis of the nature of male and female bodies and consequences for the state of the soul, see J. Cadden, *Meanings of Sex Difference in the*

had drifted into heresy, particularly the Free Spirit heresy. In view of their natural inclination for sin, it was much more difficult for women to reach perfection than for men. They had to be kept in much stronger bonds than men if they were to have any success in their struggle. The statutes of 'Master Geert's House' placed the sisters under the jurisdiction of the local parish priest. Contact with the outside world was to be avoided. Begging was forbidden. The sisters had to provide for their own livelihood by working with their own hands, preferably inside the convent. Leaving the house was supposed to distract them from their focus on God, and was the reason that the statutes prohibited the sisters working as dry nurses. Manual labor also served another purpose. Idleness could encourage the sisters to engage in musings about theology, the pitfall of the Beguines. The statutes of 'Master Geert's house' explicitly forbade them to engage in theological speculation.[18]

Nevertheless, those who were further removed from *Devotio Moderna* found little difference between the Beguines and Sisters of the Common Life.[19] This is why many of the houses of the Sisters of the Common Life later became convents of regular canonesses. Diepenveen was founded with the assistance of sisters of 'Master Geert's house.'[20] Unlike the Sisters of the Common Life, regular canonesses, such as the sisters of Diepenveen, had a clear religious status. They were therefore less open to charges that they were in fact Beguines. The brothers of the Chapter of Windesheim provided for their spiritual guidance. The sisters were subjected to a very strict regime of claustration.[21] In practice, this left little room for female theological initiative. Daring mystics of Hadewych's ilk had no place in *Devotio Moderna*, as is shown by the fate of Alijt Bake (1405–1455), the prioress of a Windesheim convent in Gent. She wrote several works on mystical theology and was subsequently deposed as a prioress.[22] Her actions resulted in a decision by

---

Middle Ages. Medicine, Science, Culture (Cambridge: Cambridge Univeristy Press, 1993).

[18] De Hullu, "Statuten van het Meester-Geertshuis te Deventer", 63-76, esp. 69-70. The author of the statutes was particularly concerned that the sisters might be drawn into the heresy of the Free Spirit, regarded as being a common one among the Beguines. G. Dresen, "God in het hart sluiten. Ingekeerde vrouwen aan de vooravond van de Nieuwe Tijd", *Amsterdams sociologisch tijdschrift* 15 (1988), 310-336, esp. 315 and 317-318.

[19] F.W.J. Koorn, "Ongebonden vrouwen. Overeenkomsten en verschillen tussen begijnen en zusters des gemenen levens", in *Geert Grote en de Moderne Devotie*, J. Andriessen, P. Bange and A.G. Weiler (eds.), (Nijmegen: Katholieke Universiteit Nijmegen, Centrum voor Middeleeuwse Studies, 1985), 393.

[20] Scheepsma, *Deemoed en Devotie*, 18.

[21] Van Dijk, *De constituties der Windesheimse vrouwenkloosters voor 1559*, 444-445, 458-459.

[22] G. Dresen, "God in het hart sluiten", 318-324; Id., *Onschuldfantasieën. Offerzin en heilsverlangen in feminisme en mystiek* (Nijmegen,: SUN, 1990), 53-93 and Id., "Het vuil vlees versterven, een nieuw vlees verwerven. De tweeslachtige waardering van het lichaam in de

the general chapter to forbid all women in the Chapter of Windesheim to write about mystical theology.[23]

The sisterbooks came into being in this context. They had to provide women with examples that could show them how to reach spiritual perfection. This was a tough challenge, as women were perceived to be so meagerly equipped to reach this goal. Moreover, even if their own brothers and sisters were convinced of their value, they had to convince those further removed that they were not Beguines, and thus could be trusted to have orthodox views. The authors solved the problem by providing impeccable models of piety that were especially appropriate for women.

The sweat of thy face

The sisters of 'Master Geert's house' needed manual labor to survive as a community. This was not the only reason that their work was given such a prominent place in their sisterbook. It was also seen as a means of inducing obedience and humility, especially if the work was dirty and unpleasant. That the sisterbook describes exemplary sisters as unkempt in appearance indicates their success. Their humility was visible in the state of their clothes.

Though Geert Grote had intended his house to be occupied primarily by poor women, many of the Deventer sisters clearly came from well-to-do burgher families, even though their social status is not mentioned.[24] Heylewich was no exception. Since she could apparently read, she was obviously not of low birth. Had she stayed in the world, or for that matter, had she entered a different convent, she would never have touched a dung fork in her life. In most religious communities, the menial work would have been done by lay sisters of humble origins or servants. Heylewich's humility and obedience, as shown by her diligence and good cheer, were models for aspiring sisters. The crucial thing was that Heylewich was so thoroughly focused on God that she did not mind doing menial work or being laughed at for her grubby appearance.

The Deventer sisterbook was not only directed at sisters like Heylewich, for whom conforming to Master Geert's house regulations was apparently not difficult. It was also directed at sisters who were less compliant. Another sister, Stijne Zuetelinckx (d. 1445), found it hard to suppress her resentment at having to perform menial work. She was the daughter of a rich burgher family and a niece of Florens

---

vrouwenmystiek", in *Is dit mijn lichaam? Visioenen van het volmaakte lichaam in katholieke moraal en mystiek* (Nijmegen: Valkhof Pers, 1998), 83-105, esp. 93-94. See for a list of Bake's works and their reception Scheepsma, *Deemoed en Devotie*, 251-264.

[23] S. v.d. Woude (ed.), *Acta Capituli Windeshemensis. Acta van de kapittelvergaderingen der Congregatie van Windesheim* (The Hague: Nijhoff, 1953), 53.

[24] Compare the Brandesshouse, another Deventer convent of the Sisters of the Common Life. When these sisters had a quarrel with their rector, they asked family members to mediate with the Council of Deventer. Their families obviously had some clout. G. Dumbar, *Het kerkelyk en wereltlyk Deventer* 1 (Deventer: by Henrik Willem van Welbergen, 1732), 599-600.

Radewijnsz, one of the founding fathers of *Devotio Moderna*. The rector of Master Geert's house, Father Johannes Brinckerinck, advised her to say "I'd love to do that", whatever the task was. This medieval version of pep talk psychology actually worked; in the end she came to mean it and became as patient and humble as Heylewich.[25]

Manual labor was also used as a meditative tool to help the sisters identify with the Lord. Sister Lubbe of Zwolle encouraged her fellow sisters to spin while reflecting on the wounds of Christ.[26] While doing this, they would come to associate their own toil with His suffering.

The prominent place given to manual labor is even more striking in the Diepenveen biographies. For the sisters at Saint Agnes and Saint Mary, manual labor was not a necessary part of life: land and rents provided for their livelihood. Moreover, in real life, it can hardly have taken up their lives to the extent that the stories in the sisterbooks suggest. After all, choir took up a large part of the day. In practice, this cannot have left much room for other activities. However, the descriptions in the sisterbook suggest that cheerful diligence in manual labor was what set the exemplary sister apart from others.

This is even more obvious if we look at the ways in which the work and the sisters themselves are described. Compared to Deventer, the accounts of the various tasks in Diepenveen are much more detailed. Furthermore, much more is made of the unpleasantness, the dirtiness, and the constant humiliation of having to work with one's own hands. Unlike the Deventer book, the Diepenveen author always mentions the status of the sisters in the world. Without exception, those mentioned in her book were of noble descent or, at the very least, daughters of wealthy burgher families. With them too, their humility was visible in their clothes, though compared to Deventer, there was a much greater difference between the sisters prior to entering the convent and after entering it. In some stories, the sisterbook elaborates at length on the sisters' love of expensive clothes when still living in the world, describing in detail the lavish clothes they were wearing when they entered. These sisters were to come to prefer the dowdiest and most threadbare clothes.

Pampered upper class ladies accustomed to luxury (such as the Diepenveen sisters were) found it hard to overcome their longings for carnal pleasures and comforts. Many of the sisters are depicted as having to battle fiercely against their own natures; this is why they elect to do the dirtiest and heaviest tasks. Moreover, even if they were willing enough, some of the Diepenveen sisters were hampered by their lack of experience, and thus they had to endure not only the humility of manual labor itself, but also the ridicule of others. The Diepenveen sisterbook proudly

---

[25] *Hier beginnen sommige stichtige punten*, 91r-92v.
[26] *Hier beginnen sommige stichtige punten*, 23v.

recalls the shocked reactions of outsiders, thus showing how extraordinary the behavior of the sisters was. A visiting lady is appalled when she recognizes in a shabby figure her former acquaintance, Sister Jutte of Ahaus, once the abbess of a convent of aristocratic secular canonesses. Jutte and the other sisters cooked meals for the men who were constructing the convent's buildings. The men's amazement that such noble ladies were serving people of a lower class like themselves is described at length by the author of the sisterbooks.[27]

As for the nature of the work, it consisted of all kinds of housework: cleaning, laundry, cooking, tending the livestock, spinning, weaving, and so on. At Diepenveen, some of the sisters literally helped with the building of the convent. They not only cooked for the builders, but also carried heavy loads of bricks. The copying and writing of books is conspicuously absent, as are reading and choir activities.

However, if a sister did indeed read and write, how was her life described? The biographies of two studious sisters, Salome Sticken and Katharina of Naaldwijk, illustrate this.[28]

Studious sisters

Salome Sticken and Katharina of Naaldwijk were obviously educated women. Salome wrote at least one original work, the treatise *Super modo vivendi*.[29] She started her religious life at Deventer, later transferring to Diepenveen. She occupied an executive position in both convents, as a mother in Deventer and as a prioress in Diepenveen. Katharina was the librarian and Diepenveen's subprioress. She was responsible for the supply of books, as it was customary for a convent's librarian to copy relevant works for the library.[30] Though no original works by her survive, we may assume that she wrote at least one text. Both Salome's and Katharina's lives are described slightly differently than are other accounts in the sisterbooks. Both sisters appear to have been subjected to special acts of grace, something that is rather unusual in *Devotio Moderna* sisterbooks.

---

[27] *Van den doechden*, 42v and 37v and DV, 145v and 137v.
[28] Biographies of Salome Sticken are included both in the Deventer and the Diepenveen sisterbooks: *Hier beginnen sommige stichtige punten*, 119r-120v, *Van den doechden*, 1r-21r and DV, 190r-225v. The biography of Katharina of Naaldwijk is included in *Van den doechden*, 45v-70r and DV, 226r-266v.
[29] Salome Sticken, "Super modo vivendi", in W. J. Kühler, *Johannes Brinckerinck en zijn klooster te Diepenveen* (Leiden: Van Leeuwen, 1914), 362-380. J. van Engen translated Salome's text into English in his *Devotio Moderna. Basic Writings* (New York: Paulist Press, 1988), 176-186.
[30] Compare J. Deschamps, "Handschriften uit het Sint-Agnesklooster te Maaseik", in *Album M. Bussels* (Hasselt: Federatie der Geschied- en Oudheidkundige Kringen van Limburg, 1967), 167-194, esp. 170.

Salome is described in the sisterbooks of both Deventer and Diepenveen. The accounts exhibit both remarkable similarities and remarkable differences. The Diepenveen biographer describes various instances of paramystical phenomena experienced by Salome: she faints, radiates light, flames appear at her mouth, and so on. We are not told what Salome's visions are of. This sister is claimed to have had a close relationship to supernatural forces, and the author of the life also gives several accounts of appearances of the devil. These visions and diabolical apparitions are not referred to by the Deventer writer.

Neither sisterbook addresses Salome's activities as a writer. Instead, she is praised for her diligence and aptitude in manual labor, her humility, and her qualities as a leader. According to the sisterbooks, she was very strict. She insisted that the sisters always keep their minds on the Lord; manual labor, obedience, humble clothing and so on were the means for achieving this.[31] She was admired both at Diepenveen and Deventer because she worked alongside the sisters despite being a mother and a prioress. At the end of the Deventer life, her move to Diepenveen is described in the following words:

> She was such an outstanding example of virtue and she built her foundation on the Lord to such an extent that great things could be built on her. Consequently she was sent to Diepenveen, and she went in all obedience: a convent had been started there, and her job was to help found it on the proper virtues, a job that she did faithfully.[32]

Salome was the Saint Peter of Diepenveen, as it were.

The sisterbook of Diepenveen gives a different version of Salome's move. She initially appears as an unlikely candidate to serve as an example for the sisters. She is portrayed as being a difficult and perhaps somewhat unbalanced young woman, prone to diabolical delusions and even rebellion to some extent. The latter is evidenced in the account of her move to Diepenveen. As mentioned before, she had been chosen to be a mother at Deventer. She was not at all pleased and tried all she could to get out of doing the job. This was not because she had no sense of responsibility; she simply felt unworthy of the job. As a final resort, she ran away, thus forfeiting her place.[33] In a surprise move, Johannes Brinckerinck invited her to

---

[31] The same subjects are treated in Salome Sticken's treatise *Super modo vivendi*.

[32] *Hier beginnen sommige stichtige punten*, 120v: "Ende hieromme, want si aldusdanigen geheelen exempel der doechden was ende oer fondament soe vaste in onsen lieven Heren gelecht hadde soe datmen daer grote dijnge op stichten mochte soe wart si overmids gehorsomheit, doe dat cloester ten Diepen-vene begonnen waert, daer gesat, opdat si dat solde helpen stichten ende fondieren inden rechten doechden, als si oeck trouweliken gedaen heeft."

[33] As ordered in De Hullu, "Statuten", 68.

Diepenveen. She accepted on the condition that she be a humble lay sister. This would make her ineligible for the administrative functions in the community. However, she was installed as a choir sister on the day of her initiation. According to the sisterbook, she had been tricked; the sisters had made her believe that the clothes that she was given were the habit of the lay sisters. Three years later, she was again appointed a prioress, which would not have been possible if she had become a lay sister. She served as prioress until she was finally excused because of old age and ill health. The sisterbook makes it quite clear that she did not like her job any better than she had in her earlier term at Deventer. Upon retirement, she humbly devoted herself to manual labor as though she had never been called to a higher position.

As for Katharina, she was probably among the highest ranking sisters at Diepenveen as far as her social status was concerned. She was descended from an aristocratic family that had its seat in the county of Holland. She had been raised by the Benedictine nuns of the Abbey of Rijnsburg, a convent that only took in girls from the upper levels of society.

At the end of the account of Katharina's life, the author gives a lengthy account of a prayer by Katharina that she had received in a special act of grace. The prayer contains an elaborate allegory on the sisters' wedding with Christ. It seems strange that there was no written version of it, either one written by Katharina or one that she dictated to another sister or to her confessor. The author of the sisterbook does not reveal how she came by the information about Katharina's vision.

Katharina was the librarian and later the subprioress of Diepenveen. She is praised for her learning, especially her knowledge of Latin. Her favorite saint was Saint Augustine, himself a learned doctor. Katharina is also portrayed as a lover of books. The sisterbook fondly remembers how she used to carry a little basket with books that she read while she was doing manual labor, during choir, and at other times. Nothing is said about her actual work in the library. As a librarian, copying was her job, but we are not told anything about this. We learn nothing about her maintenance of the books, about the books she acquired, or how she got them. As a librarian, she must have exercised a decisive influence on the spiritual development of her fellow sisters. The statutes prescribed that the sisters were to ask the librarian for a book after prime. She decided which book would be useful for each sister.[34] However, we are told nothing about what Katharina thought the sisters should read and how she decided which book to give to each sister.

The sisterbook praises Katharina primarily for her community values. She has many *spreekzusters* ("sisters to have discussions with") assigned to her; her job is to further their spiritual growth. Furthermore, her diligence in doing the more menial kinds of manual labor such as spinning is clearly seen as a model for others, even

---

[34] Van Dijk, *Constituties*, 366, 773.

if this is not dwelt on at length. She is also praised for her lack of snobbishness. This highly aristocratic lady consorted with all sisters, even if they were far below her as far as social class was concerned.

Models above suspicion

The writers of sisterbooks had a tricky task to perform. They had to educate women in the religious life using examples set by other women. They had to prove that their subjects were indeed a rare kind (or at least that they had advanced considerably on their path to becoming such): new 'non-carnal' people after the model of Jesus Christ or of Adam before the Fall. Women in particular were deemed unlikely to ever reach that status (though the possibility was not excluded). It is equally important that the authors of the sisterbooks distance themselves from the Beguines. They had to do their utmost to avoid the smear of heresy that clung to their forbears in the first wave of the religious women's movement.

Their solution was to return to tradition, notably the tradition of the desert fathers. In all of the Deventer and Diepenveen lives, the focus is on the inner self. The sisters had to re-model themselves as religious personalities in the image of Jesus Christ or of humankind before the Fall. For women, manual labor (and especially housework) was the primary tool to accomplish this. Their shabby appearance was a sign of their perfection. In all these aspects, their lives corresponded to the lives of those women who are numbered among those collectively called the desert fathers.

With ordinary sisters like Heylewich, manual labor is presented as though it is almost their only activity. This had been a traditional feature of women's lives from the time of the desert fathers onward, as has been shown by the American historian, Lynda Coon, in her study *Sacred Fictions*.[35] Manual labor was traditionally seen as a training device for the inner self, to gain in humility and obedience. While this applied to both men and women, it was even more relevant for the latter. Traditionally, pride and disobedience were seen as being the most important sins. Pride had caused the downfall of Lucifer, disobedience the Fall of Adam. As women were seen as more inclined to sin than men, they would thus also suffer more from pride and disobedience. They would thus have to train harder than men to eradicate these sins. In *Super modo vivendi*, Salome Sticken describes manual labor as a plaster on the wounds of sin.[36]

---

[35] L. Coon, *Sacred Fictions. Holy Women and Hagiography in Late Antiquity* (Philadelphia: University of Pennsylvania Press, 1997), 41-44.
[36] Salome Sticken, *Super modo vivendi*, 374.

The most humiliating and least attractive work had the best effect. Neither at Deventer nor at Diepenveen were the majority of the women from the lower classes. For such women, excelling at prayer, study, or at copying books was nothing exceptional. In these areas, they could excel to the same extent in the world or in a different convent. However, cleaning the floor (as though they were women from the lower classes) and meekly obeying orders (as though they were not born to rule) would have been huge feats of humility and obedience for such women. This would have been proof that they really had rejected their former lives. From the *Vitae Patrum* to later writings, the contrast of high birth with a predilection for menial work is a frequent element in women's lives.[37]

Manual labor had a profound theological meaning for the sisters of *Devotio Moderna*. Traditionally, housework was particularly seen as a way for women (as opposed to men) to imitate Christ. He was traditionally identified with Divine Wisdom, who was represented as a good housewife.[38] Being a good housewife made a woman take on the quality of Wisdom, and thus become like Christ. Manual labor was also perceived as entailing suffering, and thus it acquired yet another function: it turned a sister into an imitator of the suffering Christ.

As much as the adherents of *Devotio Moderna* claimed that they were the new desert fathers, it is equally clear that they were not. Contrary to the biographies in the sisterbooks, the lives of the desert fathers contain many accounts of visions and appearances of demons or the devil. Except for a few exceptions, these are absent in most sisterbooks' lives. If visions are referred to at all, their contents are rarely mentioned. This should be seen in the context of the fear of heresy. Some Beguines had participated in theological debates and had acted as spiritual leaders. They had claimed authority on the basis of their visions. Some of these women had fallen into heresy, which was seen as only natural because of women's carnal nature. They could not be expected to distinguish the messages of God from those of the devil. Moreover, when they started to interpret their visions, they could easily be lead astray. In short, they could not be trusted to think for themselves.[39] The sisterbooks therefore had to avoid all remarks that might lead the audience to think that the sisters had ideas of their own, or that they desired and strove to attain them.

Another difference between the sisterbooks and the *Vitae Patrum* is that the former is not a hagiography. As a rule, they portray ordinary women who, like the readers themselves, had a constant daily struggle to avoid deviating from the path to perfection. While saints ideally resemble each other, there was room for difference in the sisters' lives, even if all the sisters ultimately had to conform to the

---

[37] Compare Coon, *Sacred Fictions*, 128. See, for instance, the life of Euphraxia in J.P. Migne, *Vitae patrum* (1894) 1, 623-643.
[38] *Proverbs*, 9.
[39] Compare R. Voaden, *God's Words, Women's Voices. The Discernment of Spirits in the writing of Late-Medieval Women Visionaries* (Woodbridge: York Medieval Press, 1999), 66-71.

same sexless ideal, which was to become like Jesus Christ and the saints. The stories about Heylewich, Salome, and Katharina provided the sisters with models that were applicable to sisters of different statuses within the convents: the ordinary sister, the mother or prioress, and the librarian. The virtues that were ascribed to them and the paths that they followed were especially fitting for sisters in such roles.

Ordinary sisters like Heylewich had to work with their hands and be humble and obedient. As for Salome, she was the ideal leader according to the definition of *Devotio Moderna*. Following the traditional Augustinian ideal, she taught *verbo et exemplo*, by word and deed. This is why she continued to work with her hands, despite her status as mother or as prioress: it was to set an example for other good housewives. The same was said of many a holy abbess.[40] Salome's key virtue appears to be her humility; this is the reason why she did not want an executive position. Her revulsion at the idea of holding such a position and her exemplary behavior as far as ordinary manual labor is concerned appear to have been shared by other Deventer and Diepenveen leaders.[41] Furthermore, like some other sisters, she was an example of a woman who, despite many falls by the wayside, successfully overcame her nature and reached perfection. She thus provided hope for sisters who despaired of ever reaching this goal. As a warrior, she conformed to the example set by the founder of the Diepenveen rule, the church father Saint Augustine, another early church saint. According to his spiritual autobiography, the *Confessions*, he had to wage a lengthy war on himself before he was able to devote himself entirely to God. His works were among the most important read in *Devotio Moderna*.[42]

Katharina was the librarian and the subprioress. It would thus have been unlikely if the sisterbook had shown her life as being devoid of books. The story constantly stresses that she uses her books in the right way; that is, to focus her attention on God. Her life shows that learning was not *per se* an obstacle to accomplishing perfection; it merely needed to be put to a proper purpose. In this, she mirrored her favorite saint, Augustine, whose learning assisted his conversion. She is particularly praised for her community values – using her education to help other sisters on their spiritual paths – and it is stressed that this sister, one elevated in social standing, did her share of manual tasks such as spinning. The anecdote about her basket of books shows that her love of study did not compromise her diligence in the more humble kinds of work. Her copying is not mentioned, since unlike the more menial tasks, this would have been expected of her.

---

[40] For instance, Saint Clare of Assisi. F. Pennachi, *Legenda sanctae Clarae virginis tratta dal mss. 338 della biblioteca communale di Assisi* (Assisi: Tip. Metastasio, 1910), c. 28.
[41] See for instance *Hier beginnen sommige stichtige punten*, 60r-61v and DV, 56v.
[42] See note 11.

Heylewich, Salome, and Katharina represent different types of sisters: the ones who did not have administrative duties, the leaders, and the librarians. Each in her own way, they show the way for sisters doing these jobs to reach perfection. The authors of the sisterbooks combine different models to achieve this: the traditional female model of the good housewife, and of male saints like Augustine, in his roles as a struggler for perfection and as a scholar applying learning in the proper way. As they combine housework, battles against the natural self, and teaching and learning abilities, they provide examples for sisters of all types to imitate. Furthermore, they give an orthodox alternative to the Beguine model.

Postcript: historia magistra theologia feministica?

The Middle Ages are different. Historians repeat this cliché over and over again in studies, if not always in as many words. Nevertheless, in feminist theology, medieval religious women have traditionally been seen as examples for the theologians or even the Christians of today. Incidentally, the same applies for feminist historiography, at least in the earlier stages of it. As a historian, I have always been uneasy about this. It is hard to use historical figures as points of reference for people today. To a twenty-first century audience, their messages are, at best, ambiguous. Our Salome Sticken is a good case in point. On the one hand she is portrayed as an independent woman. On the other hand, what is a feminist to do with her outdated virtues, her abject humility and her eventual submission to the Diepenveen rules?

As a historian, I am inclined to duck the question of what medieval women mean to us today. This paper lays claims to nothing more than an analysis of the spirituality of two medieval communities of religious women in their contexts, especially as far as housework and other manual labor were concerned. I do believe, however, that if historical research shows that in the past, categories such as male and female, sacred and profane, divine and earthly, were defined differently, this can have some relevance for present day theological disputes. However, also as an historian, I feel that it is not my place to participate in this particular arena. I supply tales, which may have some relevance for twenty-first century theological discussions. In view of the theme of this volume – everyday life as a source of knowledge of God or as a means of piety – it is striking that in the sisterbooks there was no division between religious and non-religious activities: every activity could be used to reach for God.

Lebendiges Wasser

Die Geschichte der samaritanischen Frau (Johannes 4)
aus Rembrandts Perspektive gelesen

Anne Marijke Spijkerboer

Einleitung

Im Rahmen meiner Tätigkeit als Rektorin des Predigerseminars der *Nederlandse Hervormde Kerk* (das mittlerweile eine gemeinsame Einrichtung der drei *Samen op Weg*-Kirchen ist) führe ich seit 1995 Biblische Studien mit Studierenden und Pfarrern durch. Ich verbinde dabei die Betrachtung einer Darstellung aus dem Bereich der Bildenden Kunst mit der Lektüre des entsprechenden biblischen Textes.

In der - vor allem deutschsprachigen - religionspädagogischen Tradition bin ich der von mir praktizierten Methode so noch nicht begegnet. Es wird zwar vielfach mit Bildmaterial gearbeitet, auch im Zusammenhang mit biblischen Erzählungen, aber nirgendwo stieß ich auf eine Methode, bei der das Bild nicht lediglich als Illustration dient,[1] sondern sowohl die hermeneutische Position der Betrachtersin bzw. Leserin klären hilft als auch eine andere Sicht des Textes ermöglicht. Ein Ansatzpunkt für eine solche Methode findet sich - von der Semiotik her - bei Mieke Bal. Sie nennt vor allem den Unterschied zwischen Bild und Text, arbeitet dies jedoch nicht systematisch aus und konzentriert sich auf das Bild.[2] Jacques Maas und Nico Tromp kommen ebenfalls von der Semiotik her; sie unterziehen das Verhältnis von Bild und Text aber ebenso wenig einer systematischen Betrachtung. Außerdem stellen sie den Text dem Bild voran.[3] Auch Bernadette Neipp[4] arbeitet in ähnlicher Weise, auch sie stellt den Text voran und reflektiert ihre Methode kaum.

Es wird immer wieder deutlich, dass die Betrachtung eines Bildes zu einer anderen Sicht des Textes führt als ein Arbeiten mit dem Text allein. Außerdem spricht das Betrachten eines Bildes in anderer Weise existenzielle Schichten an als

---

[1] Vgl. M. Künne, *Bildbetrachtung im Wandel. Kunstwerke und Photos unter bilddidaktischen Aspekten in Konzeptionen westdeutscher evangelischer Religionspädagogik 1945-1996. Ästhetik-Theologie-Liturgik*, hrsg. H. Schwebel, Bd.8 (Münster/Hamburg/London: LIT Verlag, 1999).

[2] Vgl. M. Bal, *Verf en Verderf* (Amsterdam: Prometheus, 1990), 97f.

[3] Vgl. N. Tromp/J. Maas, *Voorlezen uit Rembrandt. Visies op bijbelse verbeeldingen* (Tielt: Lannoo, 1999).

[4] B. Neipp, *Le Christ du Rembrandt. L'evangile lu en Dialogue avec l'Image* Diss.theol. (Lausanne, 1997).

ein Text und dies obendrein schneller.⁵

In dem hier vorgestellten Ansatz steht das Betrachten der Abbildung deshalb auch immer vor dem Lesen des Textes. So entsteht eine Bewegung vom Betrachter zum Bild hin, die dann über den Text wieder den Betrachter - und mittlerweile Leser - erreicht.

Wenn man so vorbereitet den Text liest, erscheint er in einem anderen Licht als bei der umgekehrten Vorgehensweise, die ebenfalls möglich wäre: erst der Text und dann das Bild.

Das Bild hilft der Betrachterin zum einen bei der Klärung des hermeneutischen Standortes. Zum anderen löst die Betrachtung des Bildes Fragen an den Text aus, die sonst unzureichend berücksichtigt würden. Das Verhältnis zwischen Betrachterin und Bild gestaltet sich dann so, dass der hermeneutische Standort der Betrachterin mitbestimmend ist für die Interpretation des Bildes ist. Gleichwohl geht die Bedeutung des Bildes nicht in der subjektiven Interpretation auf. So mag man vielleicht in einer Wolke auf einer Rembrandtzeichnung das Antlitz Gottes sehen, aber Rembrandt zeichnete nie das Antlitz Gottes, und schon gar nicht in einer Wolke.

Außerdem handelt es sich bei den Fragen, die nach dem Betrachten schließlich an den Text gestellt werden, um Fragen, die bis dahin unterbelichtete Möglichkeiten des Textes selbst ans Licht bringen. Sowohl das Bild als auch der Text wahren dabei eine gewisse Selbständigkeit gegenüber der Betrachterin/Leserin. Bei der sich daran anschließenden Methode wird jede Interpretation anhand des Bildes ständig am Text überprüft.

Bei der Arbeit mit Bild und Text zu einer Bibelstelle ist es in diesem Zusammenhang besonders interessant, auf die unterschiedliche Wirkung von Bild und Text hinzuweisen. Abgesehen davon, dass ein Bild manchmal schnelleren Zugang zu verschiedenen Ebenen des Menschseins zugleich ermöglicht, kann es auch mehrere Facetten einer Geschichte gleichzeitig beleuchten, während ein Text zumindest die Zeit für das Lesen der Wörter und damit die Abfolge der Szenen erfordert. Überdies

---

⁵ Vgl. z.B. S. Berg, *Kreative Bibelarbeit in Gruppen. 16 Vorschläge* (München: Kösel-Calwer, 1991), 28: "Der biblische Text soll ja nicht nur mit dem Verstand aufgenommen werden, sondern dem Menschen ganzheitlich begegnen"; sowie dies., *Biblische Bilder und Symbole erfahren* (München: Kösel-Calwer, 1996), 12: "Dabei machen wir die Erfahrung, dass Bilder mehr beinhalten als das vordergründig Sichtbare. Wir sehen heute nicht nur etwas aus ihnen heraus, sondern sehen in sie hinein, sehen uns in sie hinein und erschließen uns neue Dimensionen. Franz Marc hat einmal gesagt: 'Bilder sind das Auftauchen an einem anderen Ort'". Vgl. auch: R. Bartlema, "De kruisweg in viering", in G.D.J. Dingemans u.a. (Hgg.), *Kaïn of Abel* (Zoetermeer: Boekencentrum, 1999), 13 sowie N. Jongsma-Tieleman, "Overwegingen van een godsdienstpsycholoog", ebd., 151f.

- und darum geht es hier - vermag ein Bild das Abgebildete konkreter, materieller, körperlicher in das Bewusstsein der Betrachterin zu bringen als ein Text. Ein gezeichneter Brunnen wird weniger leicht zu einer Metapher, einer Allegorie oder einer Abstraktion als ein beschriebener oder genannter Brunnen.[6]

Wenn ich den Text von den Fragen her lese, die durch das Bild ausgelöst werden, gehe ich in exegetischer Hinsicht eklektisch vor, abhängig von den gestellten Fragen. Im Folgenden wird deutlich werden, dass die erste Frage lexikologischer Art ist (nämlich was die allgemeinere Bedeutung der zwei Wörter für 'Brunnen' und 'Quelle' ist). Außerdem werde ich bei der Bearbeitung der ersten und der zweiten Frage durch die 'Fokalisierungsmethode' geleitet.[7]

In dem vorliegenden Aufsatz wird es um die Lektüre der Erzählung von der samaritanischen Frau in Joh. 4 gehen, wie sie sich von einer Zeichnung Rembrandts her ergibt. Das Ziel der Betrachtung einer Rembrandtzeichnung der samaritanischen Frau ist es also, zu überprüfen, welche Bedeutungsebenen des Textes für mich als Betrachterin bzw. Leserin aufgrund der Betrachtung zum Vorschein kommen.[8]

Bei der Suche nach den Bedeutungsebenen des Textes, die durch die Betrachtung des Bildes ausgelöst werden, leitet mich die Frage, was das 'Alltägliche' in der Erzählung von der samaritanischen Frau sein könnte. Beim 'Alltäglichen' geht es dann um die Verbindung mit dem 'Nichtalltäglichen', also um das, was im Alltäglichen nach etwas oder jemandem außerhalb der sichtbaren Wirklichkeit verweist. In dieser Erzählung handelt es sich um den Frauenaspekt: das Schöpfen von Wasser ist nicht nur in Joh. 4 Frauensache.[9] Das Materielle und Alltägliche des Wasserschöpfens aus dem ebenfalls sehr materiellen Brunnen wird bei der Metapher vom 'Wasser des ewigen Lebens' eine Rolle spielen. Beim Betrachten wird außerdem deutlich, dass das Bild die Materialität und das Alltägliche des Brunnens in dem Maße verstärkt, in dem sich aus dem Text andere als die bislang gebräuchlichen Motive abheben.

---

[6] Vgl. Künne, *Bildbetrachtung im Wandel*, 219; Neipp, *Le Christ du Rembrandt*, 5.

[7] M. Bal, *De theorie van vertellen en verhalen. Inleiding in de narratologie* (Muiderberg: Coutinho, 1978), 104-117.
Mit der Methode der Fokalisierung werden folgende Fragen an den Text gestellt: Wer ist Subjekt, wer handelt, wer ist Objekt dieses handelns? Wer handelt nicht? Wer spricht und wer nicht? Mit wem zusammen schaut der Leser? Das Ziel der Methode ist, an der Oberfläche zu bringen, wie sich der Leser durch den Aufbau des Textes in bestimmte Personen hineinversetzt und in andere nicht. Mit anderen Worten: Wie kommt es zu einem Urteil über die beteiligten Personen?

[8] Der Rahmen dieser Darstellung erlaubt es nicht, auf das Verhältnis der reader-response-Methode bei der Lektüre des Textes (was sehe ich im Text?) zur strukturalistischen Methode (was hat der Text zu sagen?) näher einzugehen. Sowohl Paul Ricoeur als auch Umberto Eco bewegen sich zwischen diesen beiden Polen, ohne dass sie einen davon aufgeben wollten. Vgl. P. Ricoeur, *Tekst en betekenis. Opstellen over de interpretatie van literatuur* (Baarn: Ambo, 1991) und U. Eco, *De grenzen van de Interpretatie* (Amsterdam: Bakker, 1993).

[9] Vgl. Anmerkung 35.

Bei der Suche nach der Bedeutung des Frauenalltags in Joh. 4 stellt sich die Frage nach dem Verhältnis des konkreten Wasserholens und des konkreten Brunnens einerseits und der Metapher 'Quelle des ewigen Lebens' andererseits. Im Folgenden verbinde ich das Sichtbare und Konkrete mit dem Alltäglichen und die metaphorische Bedeutung mit dem, worauf das Alltägliche verweist. Das eine ist ohne das andere nicht vorstellbar. Im Text bleibt 'ewiges Leben' unverständlich, wenn die Betrachterin und die Leserin sich nicht gründlich das Bild des Brunnens beschäftigt haben. Mehr noch: Die bereits vorhandene Vorstellung von 'ewigem Leben' selbst verändert sich möglicherweise durch den Anblick von Rembrandts Brunnen. So bekommt die Metapher quasi die Materialität ihres ursprünglichen Bildes zurück. Wenn auf diese Weise das Alltägliche mit Materialität und konkreter Sichtbarkeit eng verbunden ist, erfährt das, worauf das Alltägliche und Materielle verweisen, eine greifbare und konkrete Füllung. Das Alltägliche wird etwas weniger eindimensional, und das, worauf es verweist, wird vom Leben der Frau her mit Bedeutung gefüllt.

Was ich in diesem Zusammenhang vorhabe, ist Folgendes: Nach einer kurzen Einleitung (1.) zu Rembrandts Zeichnungen zur Bibel, seinem Verhältnis zur Geschichte der samaritanischen Frau und der Bildtradition in der Kunstgeschichte vor Rembrandt werde ich die Leserin und die Betrachterin auf eine Sehübung (2.) mitnehmen. Dazu lege ich eine Zeichnung Rembrandts zur Samaritanischen Frau vor. Im Hintergrund stehen zwei Radierungen Rembrandts über dasselbe Thema, die hin und wieder zum Vergleich herangezogen werden. Aus der Sehübung leiten sich (3.) Fragen ab, die dann an den Text herangetragen werden. Im Schlussteil (4.) wird diesen Fragen im Text selbst nachgegangen.

Rembrandts Zeichnungen zur Bibel
Biblische Erzählungen haben Rembrandt - auch im Vergleich mit seinen Zeitgenossen - oft zu Radierungen, Zeichnungen oder Gemälden angeregt. Einige Erzählungen hat er sogar mehrfach bildlich umgesetzt. Man hatte bei Rembrandt ein besonderes Interesse für die Erzählung von der Frau aus Samaria vermutet, weil dazu unter seinem Namen eine große Zahl von Gemälden, Radierungen und Zeichnungen verzeichnet war.[10] Bei der strengen Auswahl, die in den letzten dreißig Jahren unter den Rembrandt ursprünglich zugeschriebenen Werken stattgefunden hat, ist davon allerdings vieles auf der Strecke geblieben, u.a. die Gemälde.[11] Die übriggebliebenen Arbeiten rechtfertigen es nicht, bei Rembrandt von einem

---

[10] Vgl. H.M. Rotermund, *Rembrandts Handzeichnungen und Radierungen zur Bibel* (Lahr/Stuttgart: Verlag Ernst Kaufmann, 1963), 186, sowie H. Hoekstra, *Rembrandt and the Bible* (Weert: Magna Books, 1990), 300f.
[11] Vgl. C. Tümpel, *Rembrandt* (Amsterdam: H.J.W.Becht, 1986), 288; 357.

Interesse zu sprechen, das über das für andere biblische Stoffe hinausgeht. Er hat vielmehr ein Motiv aus der Bildtradition aufgegriffen und auf seine Weise gestaltet. Die samaritanische Frau wurde bereits in den Anfängen der christlichen Kunst dargestellt. Wir finden sie in den Katakomben, und sogar auf den ältesten erhaltenen Abbildungen in der aus dem dritten Jahrhundert stammenden Kirche von Dura Europos[12] in Syrien steht sie am Rand des Brunnens.[13] Das lebendige Wasser aus Joh. 4 wurde von Anfang an mit dem Wasser der Taufe in Verbindung gebracht. In Dura Europos ist die Erzählung folgerichtig in der Taufkapelle dargestellt. Inwieweit dieser Zusammenhang bei Rembrandt noch eine Rolle spielt, lässt sich nicht mit Sicherheit sagen. Fest steht dagegen, dass er sich trotz der ihm (vor allem durch die Romantik) zugeschriebenen Originalität in großem Umfang der Bildtradition bediente. Auch in seiner eigenen Zeit war er nicht der einzige, der diese Erzählung darstellte, sie war im 16. und 17. Jahrhundert sogar ziemlich populär.

Die Zeichnung

Das Betrachten und Beschreiben einer Abbildung ist weniger einfach als es scheint. Beim wiederholten Betrachten eines Bildes leuchten immer wieder neue Elemente auf, die zuvor im Dunkeln lagen. Auch die Deutung und 'Exegese' der Zeichnung bekommt dadurch ständig andere Akzente, obwohl die Zeichnung dieselbe bleibt. Im Folgenden lege ich eine Beschreibung der Zeichnung vor, die deutlich meine Handschrift trägt, d.h. anderen Betrachterinnen werden sicherlich andere Dinge auffallen. Jede Leserin, jede Betrachterin ist aufgefordert, selbst mit zu betrachten und eigene Akzente zu setzen. Bei der Betrachtung der Zeichnung werde ich diese hin und wieder mit zwei Radierungen von Rembrandt[14] vergleichen, die hier allerdings nicht abgedruckt sind. Die Unterschiede zwischen der Zeichnung und den Radierungen können einzelne Akzente noch verstärken.

Beschreibung der Zeichnung

Auf der Zeichnung sind sowohl Jesus als auch die Frau deutlich erkennbar.[15] Er sitzt auf der rechten Seite, die Frau steht auf der linken Seite.[16] Der Brunnen ist sehr groß gezeichnet. Man kann erkennen, dass Rembrandt den Brunnen sogar noch größer

---

[12] Vgl. O. Eißfeldt, "Dura-Europos", *Religion in Geschichte und Gegenwart*, 1986³, Bd. II, 287f.
[13] Vgl. *Lexikon der christlichen Ikonographie*, hg. von E. Kirschbaum, Bd. IV, (Rom-Freiburg-Basel-Wien: Herder, 1994), 27f. sowie G. Wellen, *De verbeelding van het woord* (Baarn: Gooi en Sticht, 1999), 94 und E. van den Brink, *Van Romeins tot Romaans. Kunstgeschiedenis van Europa van 200 tot 1200* (Zoetermeer: Meinema, 2000).
[14] Vgl. E. Ornstein-van Slooten u.a., *Het Rembrandthuis. De prenten, tekeningen en schilderijen* (Zwolle: Waanders, 1999), 60.
[15] Vgl. Hoekstra, *Rembrandt and the Bible*, 303.
[16] Auch diese Positionen sind früh bezeugt. Bereits in der Alten Kirche saß Jesus, während die Frau stand. Vgl. Van den Brink, *Van Romeins tot Romaans*, 36.

gemacht hat: Er geht über die vertikale Mittellinie hinaus und ist auf diese Weise sehr präsent. Möglicherweise wollte Rembrandt den Brunnen verkleinern - in jedem Fall hat er Spuren seines Zögerns in den Strichen am rechten Brunnenrand hinterlassen, was die Aufmerksamkeit auf dieses Bildelement lenkt.

Jesus, die Frau, der Brunnen und die kleine Mauer links sind mit deutlichen Linien gezeichnet. Der Hintergrund ist weniger deutlich: In der Mitte sind zwei Gestalten zu erkennen, bei denen unklar bleibt, ob sie uns zugewandt oder von uns abgewandt sind. Etwas weiter hinter ihnen laufen eine Figur und ein Reittier, das jemanden auf seinem Rücken trägt. Noch weiter hinten lassen sich zwei Personen ausmachen, die sowohl auf uns zu als von uns weg laufen könnten. Hoch über und hinter ihnen sind die Umrisse einer Stadt oder Burg sowie Bäume. Darüber ist die Andeutung eines Rahmens oder eines Torbogens, in dem bzw. unter dem sich die Frau und Jesus befinden. Nahe am linken Rand der Zeichnung verläuft eine vertikale und parallel zur Unterkante eine horizontale Linie, die eine Abgrenzung anzudeuten scheinen.

Die Frau ist an der Jesus zugewandten Seite dunkler gezeichnet als an ihrer rechten Seite, so als sei ihre linke Seite im Schatten. Von ihrem Kopf bis zum Handgelenk verläuft eine seltsame Linie.

Ihr Blick ist nach unten gerichtet, aber offensichtlich nicht auf einen bestimmten Punkt. Ihre Augen sind zwei winzige, sich deutlich abzeichnende kleine Kreise. Die Linie über ihren Augen ist, genau wie ihr Mund, eine gerader Strich. An der leichten Beugung ihres Ellbogens kann man erkennen, dass sie sich ein wenig auf den Brunnen aufstützt.

Jesus sitzt neben einer Mauer auf einer nicht näher definierbaren Sitzgelegenheit und stützt sich nach hinten auf seinen linken Ellbogen. Seine rechte Hand streckt er in Richtung der Frau aus. Er blickt auf den Arm der Frau oder auf ihren Eimer.

Bildaufbau[17]

In der Bildmitte ist zunächst wenig zu sehen. Beim näheren Hinsehen wird für mich deutlich, dass sich die Mitte genau auf der Verbindungslinie zwischen den Köpfen von Jesus und der Frau befindet. Dann sehe ich dort die zwei Köpfe der Männer, die

---

[17] Es geht hier um technische Fragen wie z.B.: Welcher horizontale, vertikale oder diagonale Aufbau ist erkennbar? Wie ist das Verhältnis zwischen Licht und Dunkel oder zwischen kräftiger und dünner Linienführung? Was steht im Zentrum? Was befindet sich im Vorder- bzw. Hintergrund? Vgl. A. de Visser, *Hardop kijken. Een inleiding in de kunstbeschouwing* (Nijmegen: SUN, 1990[4]); H. Mante, *Kompositie. Vormgeving in de fotografie* (De Bilt: Cantecleer, 1970); John Berger, *About looking* (New York: Vintage International, 1991[2]); A.J. Gelderbom, "Ceci n'est pas une pipe. Kunstgeschiedenis en semiotiek", in M. Halbertsma/K. Zijlmans (Hgg.), *Gezichtspunten. Een inleiding in de methoden van de kunstgeschiedenis* (Nijmegen: SUN, 1993), 271-311.

- so nehme ich an - auf mich zukommen. Bildmitte und Vordergrund fallen nicht zusammen. Was machen die beiden Männer da? Worüber unterhalten sie sich? Horizontale und vertikale Linien halten sich in etwa die Waage. Der Brunnen ist ein massiver horizontaler Akzent.

Jesus sitzt gegen die vertikale Fläche des Torbogens gelehnt. Obwohl das bei Rembrandt nie ganz sicher ist, vermute ich, dass mein eigener Standort niedriger gelegen ist. Ich kann gerade eben über den Rand des Brunnens sehen. Wasser sehe ich keines. Ich vermute, dass sich der Eimer auf unserer Augenhöhe befindet. Die Frau ist mir zugewandt. Jesus sehe ich von der Seite. Ich könnte auf meiner Seite des Brunnens meinen Platz einnehmen. Ich bin Zeuge von etwas, das die gezeichneten Personen nicht sehen können, nämlich der Reaktion der Frau auf Jesus. Rembrandt hat seine Zeichnung so komponiert, dass ich als Betrachterin Zeuge dessen bin, was zwischen diesen beiden geschieht. Ich habe sogar den Eindruck, dass ich mich in Hörweite befinde. Nicht mehr lange, und die zwei näher kommenden Männer sind es auch.

Eindrücke

Viele Menschen, die die Zeichnung zum ersten Mal sehen, sind von der Frau fasziniert und gerührt. Wie ist sie zu deuten? Schämt sie sich? Fühlt sie sich schuldig, wie manche beim Betrachten vermuten? Wenn ja, weswegen? Im Text ist 'Schuld' kein Thema.[18] Oder blickt sie zornig? Oder einsam? Oder konzentriert sie sich? Manche tun sich mit dem hier gezeigten Jesus schwer, weil er zurückgelehnt dasitzt und ziemlich unbeteiligt scheint. Fast jeden faszinieren die beiden undeutlich gezeichneten Männer im Mittelgrund. Manche vermuten, dass die Männer sich nicht auf uns zu, sondern von uns weg bewegen.[19]

Möglichkeiten

Der Brunnen nimmt mitten in der Zeichnung enorm viel Raum ein. Auf der ältesten Radierung ist er wesentlich kleiner. Auf der Zeichnung kann ich als Betrachterin nicht ausweichen, höchstens dorthin zurückweichen, von wo ich herkomme.

Der Brunnen steht hier nicht zwischen Jesus und der Frau, wie es bei der genannten Radierung der Fall war, obwohl beide auf den Eimer bzw. den Brunnen blicken (und nicht einander ansehen). Es verbindet sie meinem Eindruck nach mehr als der Brunnen und der Eimer. Jesus streckt seine Hand zu ihr hin. Ist das

---

[18] Der Gedanke, dass die Frau schuldig ist, weil sie fünf Männer hatte (V. 18) findet großen Widerhall, wie ich in meinen biblischen Studien mit Theologinnen und Theologen gemerkt habe.
[19] Zu der Frage, ob es einen spezifisch weiblichen Blick gibt, kann ich hier nur Vermutungen anstellen. Meine - nicht durch Statistiken belegte - Erfahrung geht dahin, dass Frauen sich beim Betrachten schneller mit dieser Frau identifizieren als Männer und sie dann auch weniger schnell für schuldig erklären.

abwehrend gemeint oder handelt es sich um eine Geste der Annäherung?[20]

Dass die beiden einander nicht anblicken, aber gleichwohl auf verschiedene Weise miteinander verbunden sind, löst die Frage aus, was dann zwischen ihnen das 'Thema' sein könnte. Rembrandt hat die zwei miteinander sprechenden Männer buchstäblich zwischen sie hineingezeichnet. Das ist umso auffallender, als die Männer auf den beiden Radierungen rechts neben Jesus und die Frau gezeichnet sind. Auch das verbindet sie miteinander: zusammen sind sie jedenfalls der Gesprächsgegenstand der beiden Männer. Aber es gibt auch etwas zwischen ihnen, was mit den Männern zu tun haben könnte. Das unterstreicht die Tatsache, dass sie etwas Gemeinsames haben, neben ihrer Verbundenheit untereinander durch Jesu Hand, den Eimer und den Brunnen.

Allerdings besteht noch eine ganz andere Möglichkeit: Jesu ausgestreckte Hand gilt demnach nicht der Frau, sondern dem Eimer, so wie auch sein Blick in Richtung Eimer geht. Die Frau blickt vor sich hin, und ich gehe davon aus, dass sie nachdenkt, konzentriert ist (vgl. den Strich über ihren Augen). Sie macht keine Anstalten, etwas mit dem Eimer zu tun. Das würde bedeuten, dass sie in den Augen der Männer hinter ihnen tatsächlich etwas Gemeinsames haben, aber ihrerseits in Gedanken versunken sind, die sich nicht oder kaum berühren. Jesus möchte Wasser und die Frau möchte etwas begreifen. Das Gemeinsame zwischen ihnen ist etwas, das Rembrandt andeutet, das sie selbst aber (noch) nicht erkennen.

Der Effekt eines Bildes liegt darin, dass gleichzeitig verschiedene Akzente und Möglichkeiten geboten werden, die aber nicht notwendigerweise ein kohärentes Ganzes bilden. Ich lasse die verschiedenen Deutungsmöglichkeiten nebeneinander stehen, konzentriere mich aber im Folgenden auf einige Akzente.

- Zunächst ist da die massive Präsenz des Brunnens. Der Brunnen ist nicht nur groß, sondern ich stehe als Betrachterin auch nahe beim Brunnen, bei dem Mann und der Frau. Sowohl die Größe des Brunnens als auch mein Standort als Betrachterin scheinen etwas bei mir auslösen zu wollen. Aber was? Woran kann ich nicht vorbei? Der Brunnen trennt und verbindet Jesus und die Frau und er verweist auf das Wasser. Aber der Brunnen ist so massiv, dass er sich nicht in einem Verweis oder einer Metapher erschöpft. Ich soll mir als Betrachterin anscheinend Gedanken darüber machen, was Jesus und die Frau verbindet, wie auch über die materielle Präsenz des Brunnens selbst.

---

[20] Zum Zusammenhang zwischen Sprache und Gebärde in der Malerei des 17. Jahrhunderts vgl. S. Alpers, *De kunst van het kijken. Nederlandse schilderkunst in de zeventiende eeuw* (Amsterdam: Bert Bakker, 1989), 248-264 (= *The Art of Describing. Dutch Art in the Seventeenth Century* (Chicago:The University of Chicago, 1983).

- Dann gibt es die Blickrichtungen. Sie spielen eine Rolle, weil sie die Sichtweise der Betrachterin beeinflussen.[21] Jesus und die Frau erregen die Aufmerksamkeit der Männer im Hintergrund (zumindest, wenn man davon ausgeht, dass die Männer in ihre Richtung blicken). Auf der Radierung ist das noch nicht der Fall. Das verleiht ihrer Blickrichtung auf der Zeichnung Gewicht, wo sie den Platz zwischen den Köpfen Jesu und der Frau einnehmen. Bei mir löst das die Frage aus, was die zwei Männer eigentlich sehen und worüber sie denn sprechen. Und weil sie sich nahezu in der Mitte der Zeichnung befinden, habe ich den Eindruck, dass sie mich ansehen. Das löst die nächste Frage aus, nämlich was ich selbst eigentlich sehe und was für ein Bild von ihnen beiden ich von meinem Standort aus bekomme. Mir ist bewusst, dass ich mehr sehe als die beiden Männer. Ich sehe die Gesichter der Frau und Jesu, während sie lediglich den Rücken der Frau sehen. Außerdem bin ich wesentlich näher am Geschehen.
Die Männer verstärken so das Unausweichliche meiner Situation: Ich muss meine Position mit Blick auf Brunnen, Mann und Frau bestimmen. Die Männer nötigen mich dazu. Weil sie mich auf meinen Standpunkt festlegen, will ich auch umgekehrt wissen, was sie beschäftigt. Der Umstand, dass Rembrandt ihnen keine Gesichtszüge gegeben hat, vergrößert meine Neugier noch.
- Es gibt allerdings auch noch die Blickrichtungen Jesu und der Frau. Wir hatten sie als uneindeutig bezeichnet. Deutlich ist nur, dass sie sich nicht anblicken. Aber blickt Jesus nun auf den Eimer und den Brunnen oder blickt er vor sich hin? Blickt die Frau in den Brunnen oder 'in sich hinein'? Ich werde ausgesprochen neugierig, worüber die beiden reden. Denn an Jesu Hand lässt sich erkennen, dass er spricht. Was sagt er, und was hat die Frau soeben gesagt? Oder was will sie gleich sagen?

Fragen an den Text[22] und erneut an die Zeichnung

Aufgrund des Vorangegangenen möchte ich folgende Fragen an den Text stellen:
- Welche Rolle spielt der Brunnen in Joh. 4, und zwar sowohl für Jesus wie für die Frau?
- Was ist das Thema der beiden Männer zu dem Zeitpunkt, als sie näherkommen?

Der Brunnen und die Quelle

Hinsichtlich des Brunnens in Joh. 4 fällt auf, dass zwei Wörter gebraucht werden: φρεαρ, das ich mit 'Brunnen' (V.11 und 12) und πηγη, das ich mit 'Quelle' übersetzen werde (V.6 [zweimal] und 14).[23] Auf den ersten Blick werden sie ohne

---

[21] Vgl. Bal, *Verf en Verderf*, 21-53.
[22] Die deutsche Übersetzung folgt, soweit nicht anders angegeben, dem Text der Luther-Bibel in der revidierten Fassung von 1984.
[23] In der deutschen Textfassung unterscheiden die Lutherbibel und die Zürcher Bibel nicht immer zwischen den beiden griechischen Begriffen; sie übersetzen überwiegend mit 'Brunnen'.

wesentlichen Bedeutungsunterschied durcheinander gebraucht.[24] Gleichwohl besteht ein Unterschied in der Bedeutung: Während bei πηγη fließendes Wasser unterstellt wird, handelt es sich bei φρεαρ um unbewegtes Wasser.[25] Außerdem wird bei genauer Lektüre deutlich, dass das Wort πηγη durch den Erzähler (V.6 [zweimal]) und durch Jesus (V.14) gebraucht wird, φρεαρ dagegen nur durch die Frau (V.11b und 12). Beide Wörter kommen bei Johannes sonst nirgends vor.

πηγη ist in V. 6 offenkundig mit der Tradition verbunden: es geht um die Jakobsquelle. Die Frau nennt eben diese Quelle wenig später (V.12). Abgesehen davon, dass das Zufall sein kann und der Erzähler gerne die Wörter variieren wollte, besteht noch eine andere Möglichkeit, die sich der heutige Leser zu Nutze machen kann. Es ist möglich, dass Jesus und die Frau nicht zufällig verschiedene Wörter für dasselbe gebrauchen, sondern dass sie beide bei dem selben Gegenstand an etwas anderes denken: Jesus an fließendes Wasser, die Frau dagegen an unbewegtes Wasser. Der Erzähler seinerseits hat dann bereits einen Akzent gesetzt, indem er in V.6 erwähnt, dass sich Jesus an die 'Quelle' Jakobs gesetzt hat. Die Quelle der Tradition, der Geschichte Israels ist offenkundig eine mit fließendem, lebendigem Wasser. Auch Jesus selbst verwendet das Wort πηγη und bringt es auf eine metaphorische Ebene. Er unterscheidet zwischen 'diesem Wasser' (V.13) und 'dem Wasser, das ich ihm geben werde' (V.14 [zweimal]). Das letztgenannte ist ein anderes Wasser, das sich nicht in dem an Ort und Stelle vorhandenen Brunnen findet. Doch soll es zu einer πηγη des Wassers werden, das in das ewige Leben quillt'. So ergibt sich zwar nicht für die Frau, wohl aber für den Leser eine Verbindungslinie von der Quelle Jakobs zur Quelle des ewigen Lebens. Zwar sagt Jesus, dass 'sein' Wasser hier nicht zu finden ist, aber die Übereinstimmung im Wortgebrauch (Quelle Jakobs und Quelle des ewigen Lebens) ist bedeutungsvoll. Aspekte und Assoziationen aus der Geschichte Jakobs und der Tradition Israels fließen zwangsläufig in die Vorstellung vom ewigen Leben mit ein.

Lediglich in V. 14 ist von 'Quelle' die Rede. In der niederländischen NBG-Übersetzung u.a. wird dagegen 'φρεαρ' mit 'put' (Brunnen) und 'πηγη' mit 'bron' (Quelle) oder 'fontein'([Spring-]Brunnen [V.14]) wiedergegeben (Anmerkung des Übersetzers).
[24] So jedenfalls die Sicht von C.K. Barret in ders., *The Gospel according to St. John. An Introduction with Commentary and Notes on the Greek Text* (London: S.P.C.K., 1987²), 234: 'φρεαρ' may be distinguished from πηγη as an artificially constructed well over against a natural spring, perhaps supplying it; but it is probable that John intended no difference between the words. The use of synonyms is characteristic of his style.
[25] Zu 'πηγη' vgl. Liddel/Scott, *Greek-English Lexicon*, New Edition (Oxford: Clarendon Press, 1977), 1399. Zu 'φρεαρ' vgl. ebd., 1954. Michaelis (*Theologisches Wörterbuch zum Neuen Testament*, Bd. VI, (Stuttgart-Berlin-Köln-Main: Kohlhammer, 1959), 122) unterscheidet zwischen 'πηγη' - Laufbrunnen und 'φρεαρ' - Schöpfbrunnen.

Inzwischen spricht die Frau jedoch von einem 'Brunnen'. Was bedeutet das? Als Figur weiß sie nichts von der Gleichzeitigkeit von Verbindung und Bruch zwischen Jakobsquelle und Quelle des ewigen Lebens. Für sie befindet sich fließendes (nämlich 'lebendiges') Wasser im Brunnen (V.11), wenn sie Jesus fragt, wie er ohne Schöpfgefäß an lebendiges Wasser kommen wolle. Aber sie gebraucht als einzige das Wort φρεαρ 'Brunnen'. Offenkundig steht ihr etwas anderes vor Augen als Jesus: das alltägliche, konkrete Wasser, für das sie sich jeden Tag auf den Weg macht. Selbst wenn hier kein großer Bedeutungsunterschied zwischen φρεαρ und πηγη bestehen muss - sowohl Jesus als auch der Frau geht es ja um 'lebendiges Wasser' -, so lohnt es doch, den möglichen Ertrag dieser Unterscheidung zu würdigen. In Jesu Worten und den Worten des Erzählers besteht eine Verbindung und ein Bruch zwischen Jakobsquelle und Quelle des ewigen Lebens. In den Worten der Frau liegt die Assoziation mit dem ganz Konkreten und Momentanen. Und trotz der Tatsache, dass auch sie vom lebendigen Wasser spricht, verbindet sich mit φρεαρ die Assoziation des unbewegten Wassers, das in erster Linie dazu da ist, geschöpft zu werden, Durst zu löschen und zum Kochen verwendet zu werden. Die Bilder, die sich sowohl Jesus als auch die Frau vom Gegenstand ihres Gesprächs machen, unterscheiden sich voneinander. Der Wortgebrauch des Erzählers macht diesen Unterschied deutlich. Es geht um das fließende Wasser der Tradition unterwegs zum lebendigen Wasser des ewigen Lebens und daneben um das konkrete, alltägliche Wasser, das mühevoll geschöpft werden muss und zum Essen und Trinken bestimmt ist. Beide Bedeutungen können m.E. nicht nebeneinander gebraucht werden ohne sich wechselseitig zu beeinflussen. So beeinflusst das Lesen der Wörter für 'Brunnen' und 'Quelle' das Denken und Wahrnehmen des Wassers.

Rembrandts Brunnen
Was geschieht nun, wenn wir von dem Brunnen bzw. der Quelle in Joh. 4 zum Brunnen auf Rembrandts Zeichnung zurückkehren? Der Brunnen ist in seiner ganzen materiellen Präsenz groß und nicht zu umgehen. Rembrandt selbst war sich offenbar über die Größe unschlüssig. Während im Text das 'Wasser' über die Verbindung mit 'Quelle' ein stark metaphorisches - und bei Johannes oft vergeistigtes - Verständnis[26] nahelegt, rückt Rembrandts Brunnen das dinglich Konkrete und Alltägliche des Wassers wieder ins Blickfeld. Nicht nur von der Jakobsquelle sondern auch vom Brunnen aus der Darstellung der Frau, verläuft eine Linie zur "Quelle des Wassers, das in das ewige Leben quillt". Auch die Assoziationen rund um das stehende Wasser des Brunnens fließen in das Bild des ewigen Lebens mit ein. Auch da geht es offenkundig um einen Durst, der - nach Trockenheit und Staub - gelöscht wird, um Essen und Trinken. Die Frau gelangt

---

[26] Der Text selbst gibt zu einer solchen Deutung Anlass. Vgl. dazu auch: C. M. Carmichael, "Marriage and the Samaritan Woman," *New Testament Studies* 26 (1980), 335, der das Evangelium als "a work so much given to producing higher meanings" bezeichnet.

schließlich mit Hilfe ihres eigenen Bildes vom Brunnen und ihrer damit verbundenen Assoziationen zu dem Wasser, über das Jesus verfügt. Wenn wir die Episode aus ihrer Perspektive betrachten, dann entfalten die alltäglichen Bedeutungen des Brunnens ihre Wirkung. Die materielle Präsenz des Brunnens macht auch das Bild vom ewigen Leben konkreter und materieller. So besteht also von der Jakobsquelle her sowohl eine durchgängige Verbindung als auch ein Bruch mit der Quelle des ewigen Lebens. Dieselbe durchgängige Verbindung und derselbe Bruch existieren zwischen dem Brunnen im Sprachgebrauch und in der Vorstellung der Frau einerseits und der Quelle des ewigen Lebens andererseits. Der Bruch wird ohne die Kontinuität unverständlich. Die Quelle des ewigen Lebens lässt sich ohne das Bild des Brunnens nicht verstehen.

Was geschieht nun, wenn das Materielle und Alltägliche des Brunnens den Inhalt der Quelle des ewigen Lebens mitbestimmt? Offensichtlich ist in der bisherigen Exegese die Materialität des Brunnens und die Vorstellung der Frau nicht in das Verständnis von 'Quelle des ewigen Lebens' mit eingeflossen. Das dort dominierende Bild ist das einer Frau, die etwas nicht begreift und die von ihrem Missverstehen befreit werden muss.[27] Was die 'Quelle des ewigen Lebens' ist, steht dann quer zu dem, was sie als konkretes Wasser aus dem Brunnen vor Augen hat. Diese Exegese hat vieles für sich, weil Jesus selbst einen Gegensatz herstellt: 'Wer von diesem Wasser trinkt, den wird wieder dürsten; wer aber von dem Wasser trinken wird, das ich ihm gebe, den wird in Ewigkeit nicht dürsten' (V. 13b; 14a).

Dennoch scheint mir von der Betrachtung der Zeichnung her eine Lesart möglich, bei der - wie oben ausgeführt - nicht nur ein Bruch, sondern auch eine Kontinuität zwischen 'diesem Wasser' und 'dem Wasser, das ich ihm geben werde' besteht. Die Veränderung in der Perspektive der Frau ('Herr, gib mir solches Wasser' [V.15]) und die Tatsache, dass sie ihren Krug stehen läßt und als Apostelin in der Stadt von 'dem Christus' erzählt, werden nicht nur durch etwas vollkommen Neues zuwege gebracht. Das völlig Neue kann sie nur dann begreifen, wenn das Neue noch etwas mit dem Alten gemeinsam hat. Ist das nicht der Fall, dann berührt das Alte das Neue nicht, auch nicht als etwas Neues. Das Neue kann nur neu sein, weil es mit dem Alten kontrastiert und dennoch mit dem Alten verbunden ist. Kontrast und Verbindung, Bruch und Kontinuität, das Andere und das Selbe - alles braucht es, damit für die Frau Verstehen möglich ist.

Bei der Frau und Jesus am wassergefüllten Brunnen liegt in dem Kontrast von 'Quelle' und 'Brunnen' doch zugleich Verbundenheit und Kontinuität. Die Kontinuität liegt in dem von Rembrandt gezeichneten Brunnen und dem Wort 'Wasser', das in beiden Fällen dasselbe ist. Bei der Betrachtung von Rembrandts Zeichnung wird deutlich, dass es sich bei 'Quelle' und 'Brunnen' um ein und

---

[27] So etwa C.K. Barret, *The Gospel According to St John*, 234.

dasselbe steinerne Ungetüm handelt. In der Zeichnung kann von Kontrast keine Rede sein. Metaphorische Brunnen lassen sich nun einmal schlecht zeichnen. Der Unterschied im Wortgebrauch (des griechischen Urtextes) zwischen Jesus und der Frau spiegelt sich in der Zeichnung nicht wieder. Hier ist selbstverständlich das Konkrete und Alltägliche des Brunnens zu sehen, vor allem das Alltägliche im Leben einer Frau, das sich mit Wasserholen, Trinken und Kochen verbindet. Für die Betrachterin gibt es beim Nachdenken über die Quelle kein Vorbeikommen mehr an diesem Brunnen (für die Zeichnung gilt das wortwörtlich). Das bringt die Betrachterin durch Rembrandts Verarbeitung der Erzählung zuallererst zum Wasser im Brunnen, zum Eimer, den man hinablassen muss, zum Rasseln der Kette oder zum Knarren des Seils am Flaschenzug, zum klatschenden Aufprall auf dem Wasser und schließlich, wenn der Eimer wieder oben ist, zu dem Becher, aus dem getrunken, und zum Essen, das zubereitet wird. Alles, was dazu gehört, das Geräusch des Eimers, das Seil oder die Kette, der Flaschenzug, das Strömen und Spritzen des Wassers, das mühevolle Hochziehen, die Schlepperei mit dem Wasser und schließlich das Trinken und Kochen spielen nach der Begegnung mit der Zeichnung eine Rolle in dem Bild der 'Quelle des Wassers, die in das ewige Leben quillt'. Was geschieht dann mit der Quelle bzw. dem Brunnen im Text? Das Verhältnis zwischen dem Materiellen und Alltäglichen des Brunnens und der Metapher 'Quelle' kehrt sich um. Nicht der Brunnen wird von Anfang an zur Metapher 'Quelle', sondern die Quelle als Metapher wird in der Vorstellung der Frau vom Brunnen her inhaltlich gefüllt. Das Bild des ewigen Lebens wird mit Bildern des Frauenalltags gefüllt.

Die Jünger
Von der Betrachtung der Rembrandtzeichnung her ergibt sich als Frage an den Text, was die Männer beschäftigt, die knapp außer Hörweite auf Jesus und die Frau blicken. In dem langen Gespräch der beiden kommen die Männer nicht vor. Nach Jesu einleitendem Satz: 'Gib mir zu trinken' erwähnt der Erzähler, dass sie in die Stadt gegangen waren, um Essen zu kaufen (V.8). Nach Jesu abschließenden Worten 'Ich bin's, der mit Dir redet' (V.26) kehrten sie zurück. Der Erzähler nimmt daraufhin die Perspektive der Männer ein: Sie kamen mit Essen aus der Stadt zurück und 'wunderten sich, dass er mit einer Frau redete'. Dass sie in Gedanken auch mit dem mitgebrachten Essen beschäftigt waren, wird erst später deutlich. Aber das Erstaunen über Jesu Gespräch mit der Frau wird nicht ausgesprochen. Mehr noch: Der Erzähler bringt aus seinem Blickwinkel diese Möglichkeit selbst ins Spiel: 'Doch sagte niemand: Was fragst Du? oder: Was redest Du mit ihr?'.

Vor allem die vom Erzähler gewählte Formulierung 'Was suchst Du?'[28] wirft Fragen auf. An keiner Stelle ist in dem Kapitel die Rede davon, dass Jesus etwas sucht. Im Gegenteil: In Joh.1,38 hat Jesus die Frage seinerseits an die Jünger

---

[28] Anstatt 'Was fragst Du?' (Lutherübersetzung) übersetze ich mit 'Was suchst Du?'.

gestellt, als sie ihm nachfolgen. Und in 4,23 ist die Rede davon, dass 'der Vater solche Anbeter (nämlich Anbeter, die im Geist und in der Wahrheit anbeten) sucht.[29] Jesus sucht vor allem eines nicht: den eigenen Willen[30] oder die eigene Ehre.[31] Im erstgenannten Fall fügt er hinzu, dass er allerdings den Willen des Vaters sucht, und das ist abgesehen von Joh. 4 das einzige Mal, dass Jesus im Johannesevangelium etwas sucht. In diesem Sinne reagiert er dann auch, als ihm die Jünger zu essen geben wollen: 'Meine Speise ist die, dass ich tue den Willen dessen, der mich gesandt hat, und vollende sein Werk.' So erweist sich die vom Erzähler suggerierte Frage 'Was suchst Du?' bereits als verborgener Hinweis auf ein 'Essen', das anders sein wird als das, was die Jünger aus der Stadt mitgebracht haben. Der Erzähler lässt uns als Leserinnen mehr wissen als die Jünger.[32]

Die andere vom Erzähler suggerierte Frage – "Was redest Du mit ihr?" – nimmt die Perspektive der Jünger auf: "und sie wunderten sich, dass er mit einer Frau redete". Für den Erzähler liegen beide Themen in der Luft, sowohl das Essen als auch das Gespräch mit einer Frau. Für die näherkommenden Männer geht es vor allem um letzteres.

In V. 31 bitten die Jünger Jesus: "Rabbi, iss!" Darauf antwortet er: "Ich habe eine Speise zu essen, von der ihr nicht wisst", und eröffnet damit ein Gespräch mit den Jüngern, das die selben Züge aufweist wie das Gespräch mit der Frau.[33] Bei ihr geht es um Wasser, hier um Nahrung.[34] Und auch hier verwenden die Jünger ein anderes Wort als Jesus. Die Jünger reagieren dann, indem sie sich untereinander fragen: "Hat ihm jemand zu essen gebracht?" Auch sie halten an ihrer konkreten Vorstellung von Essen fest. Sie sind in erster Linie von dem erfüllt, was Jesus vorgesetzt bekommen soll.

---

[29] Luther: 'haben will'.
[30] Joh. 5,30.
[31] Joh. 8,50.
[32] S. Schneiders, *The Revelatory Text. Interpreting the New Testament as Sacred Scripture* (San Francisco: Harper, 1991), 192 sagt über 'ζητειν': "In the forth gospel 'ζητεω' (to seek) is often used as a quasi-technical theological term for the deep desire that finalizes religiously significant attitudes and actions." Der geübte Leser des Johannesevangeliums wird daher bei diesem Wort besonders hellhörig sein. Für B. Ollson, *Structure and Meaning in the Fourth Gospel. A Text Lingistic Analysis of John 2:1-11 and 4:1-42* (Gleerup Lund: CWK,1974), 157 ist das 'ζητειν' ebenfalls etwas positives: "So the fact that in the Samaria narrative they ask no questions must in an Johannine context be regarded as something negative". Auch er erwähnt, dass das 'ti dzèteis' auf V.34 voraus weist.
[33] G. R. Beasley-Murray (*World Biblical Commentary*, 36, Word Books, (Waco: Publisher, 1987), 63) weist, nachdem er die Übereinstimmungen konstatiert hat, vor allem auf die Unterschiede hin.
[34] Der Erzähler gebraucht in V.8:'τροφαι', Essen (Liddel/Scott, 1827: nourishment, food); die Jünger sprechen in V.33 von 'φαγειν', essen; Jesus gebraucht in V.32 'βρωσις', Speise (ebd., 332: meat eating) und in V.34: 'βρωμα', Speise (ebd.: that which is eaten, food, meat).

Mit anderen Worten: Eine erste Antwort auf die Frage, was im Text das Thema der Männer in dem Moment ist, als sie näherkommen, lautet: das Unübliche eines Gesprächs zwischen einem Mann und einer Frau. Ein zweite Antwort ist, dass ihre Gedanken vom Essen erfüllt sind. Der Blickwinkel des Erzählers verstärkt das letztere und lässt uns dadurch vermuten, dass es noch um eine andere Art Nahrung gehen wird.

Rembrandt und die Jünger

Wenn ich die Zeichnung erneut betrachte, dann sehe ich, dass die Gesichter der beiden Männer, die zwischen Jesus und der Frau stehen, 'offen' gelassen sind, d.h sie sind nicht ausgefüllt. Man kann lediglich aus ihrer Haltung etwas schließen. Der linke neigt sich etwas zum rechten, vielleicht um etwas zu sagen. Auf den Radierungen sind die Gesichter ausgefüllt: Auf der älteren sehen sie noch nichts (außer einer kleinen rembrandtartigen Gestalt zur Rechten, die mit den Jüngern mitzulaufen scheint) und sind miteinander beschäftigt. Auf der jüngeren Radierung scheint es, als wären sie stehengeblieben. Wiederum sagt die Gestalt zur Linken etwas zu dem rechts Stehenden. Die auf der Zeichnung dargestellte Situation bleibt der Deutung der Betrachterin überlassen.

Wenn ich als Leserin bereits weiß, dass es gleich um Nahrung in einem 'höheren' Sinn gehen wird, aber die Jünger mit ihren Gedanken noch bei der Frau und dem Essen sind - was bewirkt das, wenn ich erneut auf die Zeichnung blicke? Anders als auf den Radierungen füllen die Männer den Raum zwischen Jesus und der Frau aus. Wenn ich mir klar mache, dass mit den Männern ein neues und doch vergleichbares Missverständnis auftaucht wie mit der Frau und dem Wasser, nämlich der Zusammenhang von konkreter Nahrung und der metaphorischen Speise, dann verstärkt für mich das Missverständnis mit dem Essen das Merkwürdige an dem Gespräch über das Wasser.

Ging es im ersten Abschnitt von Joh. 4 über das Wasser in zweierlei Bedeutung, dann kommt jetzt das Essen, im konkreten und im übertragenen Sinn. Die beiden Männer erhöhen so die Spannung. Aber mich fasziniert auch die Situation mit der Frau und dem Mann am Brunnen. Nicht nur, weil sie bei den Jüngern unausgesprochene Fragen auslöst, sondern auch, weil ich, wenn ich 'zurückblättere' und zurückblicke, bereits verschiedene implizite und explizite Anspielungen auf dieses Thema gehört und gesehen habe:

- Ein Mann und eine Frau an einem Brunnen, das lässt an die Geschichte von Isaak und Rebekka, Jakob und Rachel, Moses und Zippora, an Saul, seinen Knecht und die Mädchen aus der Stadt denken.[35] In drei von vier Fällen lief die Begegnung

---

[35] Gen. 24,10-27; 29,9-14 (L. Eslinger, "The wooing of the woman at the well: Jesus the Reader and Reader-Response Criticism", *Journal of Literature and Theology* 1 (September 1987) 2, 175, gibt zu bedenken, dass es hier um den Jakobsbrunnen geht, was zwar geographisch nicht zutrifft, aber ein literarischer Anknüpfungspunkt sein könnte); Ex. 2,15-22 (auch Moses läßt sich nach

auf eine Verbindung[36] hinaus. Was wird hier geschehen? Außerdem hat eine Quelle bzw. ein Brunnen nicht nur etwas mit Wasser und Leben zu tun, sondern ist auch Metapher für die geliebte Frau.[37] So ergeben sich nicht nur durch das Lesen assoziative Verbindungen zur Liebesmetaphorik, sondern auch durch die Traditionen der Wahrnehmung und Deutung.[38] Bei letzterem wäre vor allem an die Assoziation der Frau an der Quelle mit Maria als Mutter Gottes zu denken, was zugleich das Thema der Frau am Brunnen als 'gefallener Frau' beziehungsreich variiert. Im Zohar, in der jüdischen Mystik, ist die Quelle bzw. der Brunnen das Sinnbild für die Verbindung von Mann und Frau.[39]

- Die allererste Frage der Frau an Jesus („Wie, du bittest mich um etwas zu trinken, der du ein Jude bist und ich eine samaritanische Frau?") suggeriert ja nicht nur, dass die Juden nicht mit den Samaritanern sprechen, sondern auch Männer nicht ohne weiteres mit Frauen.

- Als Jesus die Frau auffordert "Geh hin, ruf deinen Mann", kommt das Thema Mann-Frau erneut zur Sprache. Es ist auffällig, dass viele Exegeten, die den vorangegangenen Abschnitt in erster Linie metaphorisch interpretierten - die Quelle bzw. der Brunnen ist für sie von Anfang an Sinnbild des ewigen Lebens - , in dieser Szene die Metaphorik verlassen und gerne so buchstäblich wie möglich lesen wollen.[40] Große Aufmerksamkeit erfährt dann die Frage, wie das Leben mit den fünf Männern zu verstehen ist und ob (im günstigsten Fall) das Nacheinander von fünf Männern von den Bestimmungen der Thora nicht doch

---

einer langen Wegstrecke an einem Brunnen nieder); 1.Sam. 9,10-14. In den Augen von A. Fehribach, *The Women in the Life of the Bridegroom. A Feminist Historical-Literary Analysis of the Female Characters in the Fourth Gospel*, (Collegeville/Minnesota: The Liturgical Press, 1998), 47, ist das Faktum, dass die Frau "as a fictive betrothed and bride of the messianic bridegroom" präsentiert wird, der Schlüssel zur Episode mit der samaritanischen Frau.

[36] Dieser Zusammenhang verweisen auch Eslinger, "The wooing of the woman at the well",170f., Schneiders, *The Revelatory Text*, 187 und Carmichael, "Marriage and the Samaritan Woman," 336.

[37] Vgl. Hoheslied 4,15 und Sprüche 5,15-18.

[38] So konnte in der Kunstgeschichte das Bild von Maria als Brunnen entstehen. Vgl. A. Thomas, "Brunnen", in *Lexikon der christlichen Ikonographie*, hg. von E. Kirschbaum, Bd.1, (Rom-Freiburg-Basel-Wien: Herder, 1994^2), 335.

[39] Vgl. J. Chevalier/A. Gheerbrant, *A Dictionary of Symbols* (London: Penguin, 1996^2), 1095.

[40] Vgl. z.B. Ollson, *Structure and Meaning in the Fourth Gospel*, 249, der stellvertretend für viele andere genannt sei; vgl. andererseits Carmichael, "Marriage and the Samaritan Woman,", 335, sowie S.D. Moore, "Are there Impurities in the Living Water that the Johannine Jesus dispenses? Deconstruction, Feminism and the Samaritan Woman", *Biblical Interpretation* I (1993) 2, 215, die in Anknüpfung an Schneiders und an A. Link, "Kritische Bestandsaufnahme neuer methodischer Ansätze in der Exegese des Johannesevangeliums anhand von Joh 4", *Theologie und Glaube* 81 (1991), 267, auf diesen Mechanismus hinweisen.

gestattet war.[41] Wenn wir die Blickrichtung der Jünger und die Präsenz des Brunnens bei Rembrandt berücksichtigen, dann verstärkt diese Episode im Text jedenfalls die Spannung zwischen dieser Frau und diesem Mann am Brunnen.

Aber auf der Zeichnung geschieht noch mehr. Der Standort der Männer nötigt mich zu der Frage, was ich selbst bei diesem tête-à-tête zu suchen habe, denn ich stehe als Betrachterin sehr nahe dabei. Was sind meine Gedanken? Was für eine Verbindung entsteht dabei? Diese Frage wird durch das Betrachten ausgelöst und sie findet im Text nicht so schnell eine Antwort.

Mindestens zwei Themen sind es, die mich nach dem Anblick der beiden Männer und dem Nachvollziehen ihrer Perspektiven im Text weiterhin beschäftigen:
- Wie ergeht es mir, wenn ich über die zweierlei Nahrung nachdenke? Bekommt das Konkrete und Alltägliche bei der 'anderen Speise' ebenso Raum wie das Gewöhnliche des Brunnens Raum bekommt im ewigen Leben? Zum Materiellen des Essens aus der Sicht der Jünger lässt sich sagen, dass es sie Energie und Zeit kostet und dass sie das Essenholen für Jesus stark beschäftigt. All das kann mit hinein spielen in das Bild der 'anderen Speise'. Inwiefern erfordert diese Zeit und Energie und ist jeden Tag lebensnotwendig? Für Jesus ist das 'Tun des Willens des Vaters' jedenfalls kein philosophischer Gedanke, sondern etwas, das seinen Alltag konkret füllt.
- Wie können sich Liebe, Anziehungskraft und das Zusammensein von Männern und Frauen auswirken bei der Suche nach dem 'anderen Wasser' und dem 'anderen Essen', wenn diese bei Jesus zu finden sind?

Das Alltägliche

Meines Erachtens sind im oben Ausgeführten verschiedene Dinge geschehen:
- Durch die Betrachtung einer Zeichnung von Rembrandt wird für die Betrachterin die Situation, in der sich die Erzählung vollzieht, so plastisch, dass sie dem Text mit anderen Augen begegnet, als sie es ohne die Abbildung täte.
- Infolgedessen ist das, was man auf der Abbildung sehen kann, materiell stark präsent, stärker als beim Lesen des Textes allein. Rembrandts Zeichnung sorgt dafür, dass die Metapher vom Materiellen durchtränkt wird.
- Was den Brunnen, das Wasser und das Essen betrifft, so folgt daraus, dass Alltägliches - das Wasserschöpfen der Frau, ihre Existenz als Wasserträgerin, das Herbeischaffen des Essens durch die Jünger - in das Nicht-Alltägliche mit hinein spielt, in die Quelle des ewigen Lebens, in die "Speise, dass ich tue den Willen dessen, der mich gesandt hat". Beides ist offenkundig tägliches Brot und

---

[41] Eine symbolische Deutung - allerdings in einem für die Frau ungünstigen Sinn - ist durchaus möglich, indem man die Frau als Symbol für Samaria und die fünf Männer als symbolisch für die fünf fremden Stämme mit jeweils einer eigenen Gottheit versteht; vgl. Barret, *The Gospel According to St John*, 235.

Wasser, notwendig für das alltägliche Leben. An beidem kann Mangel herrschen, und bei beiden wird das rasch deutlich. Beide sind durch die Situation und durch die Spannung, die zwischen dem Mann und der Frau besteht, auch mit Liebe, Sehnsucht und Anziehungskraft verbunden. Wasser und Essen sind keine Dinge, die man, wenn man sie einmal geschöpft oder geholt hat, wegräumt, um sie bis zur nächsten Mahlzeit zu vergessen. Sie vermitteln Freude, Energie und Kraft. Diese Bedeutung fließt in vollem Umfang mit ein in die 'Quelle des ewigen Lebens' und die 'Speise, dass ich tue den Willen dessen, der mich gesandt hat'.

Rückblick

Bei unserem Durchgang spielten verschiedene Dinge eine Rolle. Zunächst (1) war da das Dreieck Leserin - Zeichnung - Text - Leserin. Der Text kommt der Leserin nicht unvermittelt unter die Augen, sondern vermittelt durch die Zeichnung. Ich gehe bei meiner Methode davon aus, dass die Betrachterin, noch bevor sie den Text gelesen hat, eine Erinnerung an die Erzählung hatte. Was den Blick der Betrachterin mitprägte, war die - noch nicht präzisierte - Frage nach dem Alltäglichen in Bild und Text. Als Eigenart des Arbeitens mit Bildender Kunst erwies es sich, dass sie die Aufmerksamkeit auf die materielle Seite des Alltäglichen, hier: auf die Größe des steinernen Brunnens lenkt. Außerdem (2) kam meine Position als Betrachterin explizit vor. Der Umstand dass der Betrachterin die Personen auf dem Bild fast greifbar nahe sind, unterstreicht die eigene materielle Präsenz in der Erzählung. Schneller und noch unausweichlicher als im Text als solchem wird man herausgefordert, die eigene Position zu klären. Diese beiden Einsichten brachten andere Bedeutungsebenen des Textes ans Licht als bislang üblich. Sowohl die Frage nach dem Alltäglichen als auch die Betrachtung der Abbildung hat der Leserin einen größere Bandbreite an Bedeutungen erschlossen, als das ohne diese beiden Gesichtspunkte möglich gewesen wäre.

Kinship of Soul

Lisa Moren's *la_alma* Interactive Video Book[1]

Inez van der Spek

Introduction

People trying to communicate: What could be more common than people talking and gesturing to each other about their feelings, wishes, thoughts, memories, and histories? On the other hand, sometimes nothing seems more tiresome and confusing than the processes of communication. All the misunderstandings and barriers existent inside and between people limiting the expression of their views and emotions! And what if brain functions suddenly or gradually are damaged due to an accident or disease. To what extent can we still talk about communication? In what ways cerebral transformation affected language, memory, and sense of history? And furthermore, does the distortion of the brain faculty inhibit people from story-making, or do they make different stories?

Such are the questions raised in *la_alma*, an interactive video book released by the American artist Lisa Moren in 1999. The gallery or museum offer an out of the ordinary setting for exploring them. Alma was the name of Moren's grandmother of German descent. She was suffering from Alzheimer's disease, which at an advanced stage resulted in a virtually complete loss of language. Moren uses the form of communication she had with Alma during that period as a model for her installation. Her conversations with a woman whose language had become void of chronology or logical links are reflected in the viewer's fragmentary 'conversation' with historical images projected on the video book. 'Speaking with Alma was like jumping through a word search for remember'.[2] Her mind let her down but her physical instinct of talking was still intact. While *la_alma* deals with the discontinuity and the fragility of memory, it also seeks to find access to the crumbled and scattered memories so as to create a different narrative of history.

---

[1] The research for this essay was supported by the Dutch Organization for the Advancement of Research (NWO). An embryonic version was published as "De kwestbaarheid van de herinnering. Loopbruggetjes in L. Morens *la_alma*" *Lover. Tijdschrift voor feminisme, wetenschap en cultuur* 27 (2000) 4, 48-52. I wish to thank A. Simons and A.-M. Korte for their suggestions.

[2] Quotations without references are from *la_alma* itself, various artist's statements of Moren's or personal information provided by e-mail or otherwise. Translations from Dutch or German sources are mine, unless stated otherwise.

Moren's *la_alma*, in my view, is an intriguing and multi-layered work. It does not treat the questions of memory and communication in an abstract manner but shows that they are embedded in both everyday personal experience and common cultural history. Although I had the opportunity to have a look at some of the preparations, I was not actually at Moren's installation. Therefore I use the nine-minute video taken from it as my point of departure. In addition, Moren provided me generously with artist's statements and other background information. In writing about *la_alma*, I intend to contribute to its interactive commitment from a reflective angle. I will relate the matter of memory and language/communication to several other topics implied in the installation. An important issue is the meaning of Berlin, from where Alma's ancestors originated, as a site of cultural memory. Special attention will be given to the link between Berlin and images of the feminine. Furthermore, I will explore the limits and preconditions of writing history as they are set out in *la_alma* - that include Alma's history, the history of Germany in the twentieth century, and any history.

Ultimately, Moren's interactive installation offers a refreshing revision of the notion of the soul. To make a case for this, I make use of a fortunate coincidence. In Spanish, (el) *alma* means soul or spirit of life, while the Latin *almus/alma* means nourishing, fertile.[3] I want to connect these connotations to the meaning of Alma/*la_alma*. Moren's piece was not intended as a tribute to her grandmother Alma, nor as her portrait. It has been inspired by both Moren's conversations with Alma and, as we will see, scraps of information on their ancestry, aiming at an alternative narrative about history. However, her interactive experiment which presents more faithful ways of writing history on the basis of her arduous word search with Alma, is not only intellectually stimulating but also emotionally moving. It creates what I will name 'kinship of soul'. Naturally, the notion of soul figures in an enormous range of discourses, from western classical philosophy to New Age spirituality, from the classical texts of Persia and India to the Oprah Winfrey show, from neo-Platonism to the celebration of the soul in African-American cultural expressions. However, I have neither surveying nor polemical aspirations here. Instead, I hope to depict and value the sense of (the) soul that is emerging from *la_alma*.

The installation: images and sounds

la_alma is an intricate piece of technological art which takes several days to be properly installed. It consists of a video projector, an audiotape, and a computer-directed book. The book is a hand-made hard-cover clothbound accordion book, opening to 17" x 22" with heavy vellum pages. On touching the book, the viewer sets digital video images in motion which are projected on the blank pages. 'Inside the

---

[3] For phonetic reasons the Spanish *alma* has the masculine article *el*, even though it is a feminine word.

accordion pages are keys from a Macintosh keyboard modified into flat sensors.' The keys trigger new images and montage of those images. 'The tabs used to turn pages offer major program changes to the piece's functions, just as turning to a new chapter would offer a new set of thoughts.'

'The databased movies range from 10 seconds to one and a half minute loops. Therefore, besides triggering movies randomly, the viewer may also compose a second movie onto the first, creating a montage. Finally, a third layer will juxtapose a live video of the viewer's own hand interacting, or conversing with *la_alma*.' 'Each viewer who interacts with the book will create a unique visual story from the thousands of narrative possibilities.' In other words, the video derived from *la_alma* is just one of these possibilities.[4] The more than sixty Quicktime movies the viewer is invited to edit include imagery of microfiche, obsolete German handwriting, hands playing the piano, spots in Berlin, a church's stained glass windows, and the Brooklyn Bridge.

Parallel to the visual component is an audiotape of about twenty minutes looping throughout the installation. There are linear and non-linear tracks of the same audio files. In the video we hear just the linear track, containing sounds of a variety of ticking machines, piano music, a scribbling pen, and a woman's voice relating reminiscences of a grandmother. She tells the somewhat sad but at times funny story about Alma Herson, and 'I figured Herson came from the fact that her son was my father, Art'. The story pivots on the likeness between Alma and the talking parakeet Peter in their inclination to fill moments of silence with a lot of noise. What's more, the woman and the bird mimick each other's sounds. Peter has a predilection for talking during quiet moments, for example when the narrator's grandparents renew their marriage vows. When everybody is silent in prayer, Peter all of the sudden shrieks 'Whatcha doin'?' The family of the couple appreciated the humour of the incident more than the minister did.

After the golden wedding-anniversary, Alma started being struck by bouts of Alzheimer's. She carried two peculiarities with her disease, the narrator explains. First was her ability to remember in detail events of more than forty years ago, and second was the remarkable way Alma retained her habits. In her home, space was always filled with jokes, stories, music and Brooklyn colloquialisms and phrases. No one was allowed to feel alone. Apparently, she did her best to keep the house filled with these happier sensations. The narrator compares her to the women in Virginia Woolf's novels, where the mother fills the space with a loud and happy family. When the mother is gone everyone becomes lost in their own disjointed thoughts, too absorbed in self-pity to hear anyone else.

---

[4] *la_alma* primarily uses the experimental video software Image/ine developed by Tom Demeyer at STEIM in Amsterdam. The voice-over is Aliyah Baruchin's.

At a certain stage Alma could no longer remember words. Her thoughts seemed 'clear enough in those long lost days' but the present was 'a blur', just as her family still living was a blur. But she seemed to always remain conscious of empty space and struggled to fill the silent moments. When the narrator's parents celebrated their thirtieth anniversary, history repeated itself in a grotesque manner. Because of her unpredictability, Alma was seated in the back of the room where she would cause the least disturbance. During the solemn silence of the renewal of the vows, Alma seemed to believe everyone was caught up in the horror of their own lonely thoughts and had to be glued back into community.'Alma began entertaining the room with the loudest gibberish that made Peter the parakeet sound poignant. Alma's long loud syllables had no sense but much sensation.'

Her relatives all knew Alma to be in her eighties when she died. On the night of her death, however, they found inconsistent birthdates on various driver's licenses, certificates and other documents. Additionally nobody knew the maiden name of Alma's mother which was required for the death paperwork. 'No one can name what Alma did during her life and no one can say how long she did it'. Alma never really did anything, the narrator says, so they decided she was 'a hostess, you know, for all the parties that would naturally gather around my grandfather's piano'.

Compared to the actual interactive installation, watching the video is likely to produce a shortcoming because one tends to take the images as illustrations with the story. Evidently looking for the plot remains an imperative need; I even inserted my own plot into the story, moved by other memories relating to old women and speaking birds. When I had outgrown my children's books in my early teens, my mother introduced me to the Dutch translation of the *Jalna* series by the Canadian writer Mazo de la Roche. Throughout the at-least twelve volumes of this family saga, covering more than a century, the everlasting figures of Adeline and her pet parrot form the vital link. They keep each other company, terrorizing the rest of the family, until they are old and weary of life, which is not until they are over onehundred years old! I loved reading the novels, which, as I believed, gave me an important insight into the world of grown-ups. At times I was a bit puzzled by the protagonists' ever-varying life-style and physical appearance on the cover because my mother had forgotten to explain to me the meaning of chronology. More important, though, was - and still is - the cherished experience of shared reading.

Even though I think *la_alma* leaves room for this kind of personal association - (so I cheerfully wrote it down), emphasizing the anecdotal, however, would mean a disregard of the installation's historical and philosophical outlook. *la_alma*'s anecdotal import, moreover, is strongly toned down by the fact that the story about Alma ends in confusion and indeterminacy instead of the witty and pithy characterization of anecdotes. This concerns both the visual and the narrative dimensions. While the latter concludes with the absence of a distinct identity for Alma, the visual side of the video also develops into indeterminacy. Its images literally turn into patches and scraps, then into cloudy spots, blurring eventually into a haze, only still vaguely showing the profile of a film-strip. The old woman's history vanishes through the gaps in her memory.

The Berlin story

We see a remarkable parallel of this fading of history on the cultural level. The city of Berlin, especially in its architectural appearance, seems to vanish into a gap as well. Besides fragmentary images of Berlin's postwar reconstruction, the video shows a book called *The Berlin Story*, with a hole in it that is becoming bigger and bigger. The Berlin story is both the city's and, in a derived sense, Alma Herson's. Both are stories of bits and pieces, of amnesia and reconstruction, of historical and present times. The actual link between Alma, who lived in Brooklyn, and Berlin was concealed in a box she carried with her all her life. This box contained over eighty letters, documents, and photographic portraits from the period between 1860 and 1890, mostly from Berlin and Brooklyn.

In some way or another all of these papers related to Alma's grandparents, Amalie and Ferdinand Friederici, who had lived in Friedrichstrasse in Berlin and, after a stop in London, moved to the United States in 1869. We see the image of a large ship in the video; an ocean-going ship, apparently, yet also under sail, as if the mechanical power of the engines could not be trusted sufficiently. It turns out to be a photograph of an otherwise unknown painting of the Steamer Minnesota which Moren had discovered in some American nautical archives. Prior to that, she had found out in the National Archives in Washington DC that Alma's grandparents crossed the Atlantic on this ship. Although Alma's grandparents died in 1888, and Alma herself was born circa 1902 thus never having known them, she nevertheless safeguarded the paper witnesses to their lives.

After her grandmother's death, Moren traced this box in the attic of her parents' house. In the 1970's, the television series *Roots* had inspired her mother to sort out at least for a while the papers, 'until she got bored with it because so many of the letters were about money'. This time Moren herself decided to go deeper into her grandmother's family background. In the video, we see recurring samples of the handwritten family documents, accompanied by the almost incessant scratching sounds of an old-fashioned ink pen. To be able to decipher the documents from the box, Moren first had to become familiar with Kurrent, or Alte Deutsche Schrift, the obsolete German handwriting in which they were set. The vicissitudes of this script can be hardly more illustrative of the intertwinement of language and politics, in particular in the German context.[5]

---

[5] See O. Weiss, http://www.germanscript.com, from whom I derived all information on this topic.

Evolved from Gothic cursive handwriting, the 'modern' form of Kurrent script was established by the end of the 18th century. However, it was difficult to write because of its sharp angles, straight lines and abrupt changes in direction. To give schoolchildren an easier start, the Viennese graphic artist Ludwig Sütterlin devised a form of Kurrent that consisted of wide curves and very few sharp angles as a basic script. This Sütterlin Kurrent was accepted as the primary script in all Prussian schools in 1915, and by 1934 it was firmly established in virtually all German Schools. Nevertheless after the turn of the century, both Kurrent and its printed counterpart, Fraktur, declined in popularity, especially with more cosmopolitan Germans who favoured Antiqua over the national style of writing. With the rise of the Third Reich, however, Antiqua and Latin script were declared 'non-German' and 'non-Aryan'. Only the Fraktur and Gothic typefaces were to be considered German. In 1941, however, Hitler issued an order, effectively terminating the use of Fraktur and Kurrent. The motive for this change was the realization that they created a serious communications barrier with the people of the occupied countries in Europe. After a short time Kurrent was no longer taught in schools, although in the 1950's some German schools still taught Kurrent script in optional afternoon classes, using locally printed primers.[6]

In tracing Alma's ancestral whereabouts and decoding the papers, Moren surely resembles the protagonist of a detective story. However, her project hardly fits the modernist code of the detective genre. While the dominant drive of modernist fiction is, as Brian McHale advances, epistemological, the detective story is the epistemological genre par excellence. It foregrounds questions such as: How can I interpret this world of which I am a part? And what am I in it? What is there to be known? What are the limits of knowledge? These themes are investigated by dint of such characteristic devices as 'the multiplication and juxtaposition of perspectives [and] the focalization of all the evidence through a single "center of consciousness"'.[7] Moren, on the other hand, is not weighing evidence and making deductions in order to reveal a solution to the mystery. In a sense, the focusing function of the 'private eye' has been transferred to the editing activities of the viewer. However, unlike the gathering of information in order to deduce what has happened, the process of editing does not offer a conclusive outcome. For the most part, Alma's life and identity ultimately remain a mystery, while we see barely more than flashes and scraps revealing information about her grandparents' lives. In other words, the gap in *The Berlin Story* and the gaps in Alma's memory are not lamented and filled. Instead, they serve as an eye-opener to the fragmentary and inconclusive character of *any* history.

---

[6] About the remarkable post-war fate of Fraktur in Hollywood, see www.germanscript.com and A. Kapr, *Fraktur. Form und Geschichte der Gebrochenen Schriften* (Mainz: Schmidt, 1993).

[7] B. McHale, *Postmodernist Fiction* (London and New York: Routledge, 1987), 9.

Berlin and the feminine

In the previous section Alma and Berlin were associated, not only by the content of the box, but also by connecting Alma to the hometown of her grandparents in a metonymical mode. That is to say, Alma and Berlin were related by means of the imagery of gaps: memory gaps, holes in history and even building pits. What, however, does it mean to posit a parallel between Alma and Berlin? It is a time-honoured tradition in the western history of mythology, religion and art, to relate women and cities. I want to outline some of this relationships' features and developments, with a special focus on Berlin, explaining, finally, how this tradition is abandoned in *la_alma*.

The representation of women and cities, particularly in terms of metaphorical analogy, has enjoyed great popularity from ancient foundation myths to the modern novel. The city has been portrayed as whore and heavenly bride, as mother and maternal womb, forbidden love, (mother)goddess, soldier's sweetheart, or conquered virgin. Berlin too has been subject to many projections, one of the most well-known being Alfred Döblin's polarization of the angelic prostitute Mieze and the apocalyptic whore Babylon in his novel *Berlin Alexanderplatz*. The most obvious manifestation of the imaginary relation between woman and city are the numerous allegorical statues of female figures in Berlin (and every city in the world, for that matter) To give just one example, for that matter, from the Statue of Liberty in New York to the figure of Justice: the female allegories of philosophy, poetry, and tragedy seated on the plinth of the Schiller memorial in the Schiller-Park. In these petrified representations of abstract ideas and virtues, as Sigrid Weigel notes, 'the rigidity of images of femininity is pushed to extremes, while the represented female figure has been deprived of any concrete meaning'.[8]

Contrasting with the image of the city as a conquered and domesticated woman, there is the complementary image of the boundless female nature. She is the wilderness in the founding myths of antiquity, the dragon, the hydra, or the snake, which must be kept back from the city gates. In the literary representation of the modern metropolis, we see this wild side of femininity return inside the city. To the male writer, Baudelaire being a well-known example, the 'rampant' metropolis becomes a site of subjectivity and reminiscence, of self-reflection as well as loss of self. In this process the city is disclosed as a site for encountering otherness/the other, which is, as often as not, female identified. The city becomes a semiotic space, a signifying body, associated with the dark and sensual sides of femininity.

---

[8] S. Weigel, "'Die Städte sind weiblich und nur dem Sieger hold'. Zur Funktion des Weiblichen in Gründungsmythen und Städtedarstellungen", in S. Anselm, B. Beck (Hg.), *Triumph und Scheitern in der Metropole. Zur Rolle der Weiblichkeit in der Geschichte Berlins* (Berlin: Dietrich Reimer Verlach, 1987), 207-227, 215. See also S. Wenk, "Die steinernen Frauen. Weibliche Allegorien in der öffentlichen Skulptur Berlins im 19. Jahrhundert", in Anselm & Beck, *Triumph und Scheitern*, 91-114.

However, this modern metaphorization of the feminine still has in common with the allegorical petrification petrifaction of woman that women are not portrayed as subjects. In neither case is the feminine credited with history and individuality.

In light of *la_alma*, the different perspective on the relation between city and women Weigel finds in Walter Benjamin's autobiographical *Berliner Kindheit um Neunzehnhundert* is rather interesting. In what he describes as 'ominous-tender miniatures', Benjamin follows the traces of his memory through Berlin, re-creating the city as a written panorama of images.[9] The representation of places with a female character forms a part of this;statues in parks and caryatids in porches, the safety of his grandmother's house, his bird-like Aunt Lehmann, market women who are like 'priestesses of Ceres', and labyrinthine streets outside the districts of the well-to-do, promising escape from mother's authority. By pointing out that these signs are informed by desire and fantasy, and by discussing their cultural meaning, Benjamin, in Weigel's view, abandons the analogous identification between woman and city.

> He does not depict the city as feminine but follows the traces along which the feminine turns into an image or a sign. (...) he does not carry on the series of images in which city and woman are made analogous, but exposes their origins in a childhood's story and follows their traces in his memory.[10]

Benjamin's 'miniatures' were written between 1933-1935, but unfortunately the dark shadow of Nazism would most probably have influenced Benjamin's childhood memories.

One of the most drastic outcomes of the historical catastrophe of World War II was the divide of Germany into East and West, made utterly concrete by the Berlin wall. In 1978, a remarkable book was published in the former GDR, *"Guten Morgen, du Schöne"*, which was a volume of interviews with women living in the GDR by the journalist Maxie Wander.[11] With surprising frankness, the seventeen women interviewed, between 16 and 74 years of age (though, curiously, there were no interviews with women in ther fifties and sixties) and who had all kinds of professional and personal situations, talk about their lives and loves, dreams, disillusions and ambitions. The German history of the twentieth century, with the split Berlin at the centre, is not a protagonist in their stories, and yet it is a backdrop which cannot be removed. Here, woman and city link rather differently. Neither turns into allegory nor traces in the male memory, rather the feminine as representation makes

---

[9] W. Benjamin, *Berliner Kindheit um Neunzehnhundert* (Frankfurt a/M: Suhrkamp, 1950).

[10] Ibid., 226.

[11] M. Wander, *"Guten Morgen, du Schöne". Frauen in der DDR. Protokolle* (Darmstadt und Neuwied: Luchterhand, 1978).

way for women speaking up as embodied subjects.

Returning to *la_alma*, then, I suggest that we understand Moren's installation as a postmodern and post-1989 radicalization of both Benjamin's break with the analogous representation of woman and city, and Wander's 'hearing women into speech'. In a way, the medium is the message. Benjamin's childhood memories and the monologues of the women in *"Guten Morgen"* reflect the modern investigation and formation of the self in literature. The multimedia and interactive character of *la_alma*, on the other hand, constantly puts the self at stake. Authorship is uncertain: is it Moren's, the editing viewer's, the critic's? As Moren herself formulates, 'multiple horizons ultimately fuse the artist, the interactive device, and the viewer as well as their "performative gestures" interacting within the entire process'. And where is *la_alma* located: in Berlin, Brooklyn, the art gallery? 'Post-cognitive' questions are implied in this, such as "Which world is this? What is to be done in it? Which of my selves is to do it?"[12] questions which are inextricably bound up not only with the loss of confidence in the rational and controllable self, but also with the collapse of the seemingly neatly arranged world order of the cold war period.

In this perspective, the relations between Berlin and the feminine also become further unsettled. They are not sketched in subtle shades, as in Benjamin's memoirs, nor used as an almost dull backdrop for women's actual lives, as in Wander's interviews. rather, there is indisputably a female presence in *la_alma*; the maker is a woman, and there is a female voice relating memories about grandmother Alma who was herself the inspiration for the work of art. Yet women are absent on the visual level in *la_alma*. While we do see images of Berlin, there are no pictures of women. It is during the very processes of film making, of projecting and editing in the gallery, and of writing about *la_alma* that Berlin and the feminine are being connected. Not as statements about identities, however, but as possible relations that are continuously formed and undone again.

Globes

The Friederici's were completely settled in another part of the world by the time Germany's tragic and horrifying history of the twentieth century broke out. The traces of the family in Berlin even seemed entirely erased. Alma's box, however, offered Moren a code for making these traces visible again. By *la_alma* she relocates her family and herself in German history, while showing, on the other hand, that this history itself has been absorbed into the culture of transnational ICT (Information and Communication Technologies) capitalism at the end of the second millennium. By their voyage on the SS Minnesota, the Friederici-Herson-Moren family became integrated into the irreversible processes of world-wide migration and economic globalization. They were among the millions of Europeans, first from West and North European countries and later mostly from East and Central Europe, who since the

---

[12] McHale, *Postmodernist Fiction*, 10, quoting Dick Higgins, *A Dialectic of Centuries*, 1978.

1860s had set foot ashore at Hoboken to try their luck on this unknown continent.
When Moren went looking for the address in the Friedrichstrasse where Alma's grandmother had lived, it turned out to be now at the heart of the reconstruction activities in former East-Berlin. On the very spot of the ancestral house now stands an ultra-fashionable shopping mall.

> On both sides of the Friedrichstrasse there are office blocks of polished stone. From here to Unter den Linden, a couple of hundred metres, there are two glassy walls. No protusions. A building line drawn by an architect on his drawing-board, which, however, never returns in the reality of buildings and variations. At this place it does.[13]

In the video there is a light-blue ball popping up time and again. According to Moren, the ball is not only a convenient graphic and photographic device for creating some pattern in the non-linearity of the video, but also it refers to the dome-shaped tower of the complex built by Sony Germany on the Potsdamer Platz. All Berliners recognize it as an icon of the reconstruction efforts of their city. I would also add that the logo of Germany's own company Blaupunkt is of course a light-blue ball. Moren adds that her 'favourite part of the blue ball is that it looks like a crystal ball, especially when it accidentally becomes a portion of the image behind it'. However, unlike the fortune-teller's crystal-gazing or the scientific speculations of futurology, the transparency occuring now and again in *la_alma* is retrospective. It does not offer us a look into the future but a vision of history, displaying the blue balls of the national and transnational corporations as the icons of global powers. Perhaps not accidentally, then, the blue ball also conjures up, in my mind at least, the absurd dance with the globe performed by Charlie Chaplin as Hitler in *The Great Dictator*.

Writing history

Paradoxically *la_alma* abandons the book by using (the form of) a book. In her artist's statements, Moren speaks about the 'palimpsestual' nature of the former East Berlin. A palimpsest is a parchment manuscript from which the original writing has been removed in order to create space for new writing. By using ultraviolet rays, it is often possible to reveal the underlying writing. The vellum pages of *la_alma* randomly show architectural highlights from Berlin's modern history: cranes used in the reconstruction of present-day Berlin, photographs of the Friedrichstrasse in the old days, a silent film with images of the Brandenburger Tor. Berlin could be called palimpsestual because new buildings take the place of destroyed buildings, and therefore new history covers the past. But what actually is *la_alma*'s palimpsest? Is

---

[13] D. Niedekker, H. Naayer, *Berlijn/Berlijn* (Rijswijk: Elmar, 1999), 26.

it the vellum pages of the book? These pages, however, do not contain an original text which can be recovered. On the contrary, they are totally blankContinouosly Continuouslycovered with video projections, they are fundamentally blank, compelling the viewer to 'compose' history differently over and over again. Therefore, instead of 'palimpsest'. I suggest the use of the word 'subjectile' for this context. This notion is derived from Derrida's reading of Artaud. In his interpretation of this reading, Heinz Kimmerle writes:

> 'Subjectile' is the French word for the underlying surface (the canvas, paper, wall, board) on which the drawing or painting is being made. Lying beneath the drawing, it does not have meaning itself yet carries all the meanings applied to it. We cannot think of this 'lying underneath' as meaningless, but by sacrificing it or playing his cruel game with it, the artist [Artaud] is able to take it in the direction of the thinkable. He makes visible that which is without meaning. In this manner, the boundaries can be distinguished between the subjectile and the coherence of meaning applied to it. Could we then call language, not a particular language, but language as such, the subjectile par excellence?[14]

Of course, Moren's approach to the subjectile largely differs from Artaud's artistic strategies. The subjectile is not 'sacrificed', that is to say, destroyed or damaged, but manipulated with technological means. Nevertheless, I see striking resemblances in the way both Moren and Artaud, paradoxically enough, make the subjectile visible only to erase its meaning again. In Artaud's case, this is related to the collapse of Nazism and the concomitant collapse of traditional idea-bound values and linguistic and artistic forms of expression. There had come into being a situation of absolute zero that, however, was hardly acknowledged by the post-war generation. Artaud refused to join the restorative political and artistic forces aimed at rebuilding the pre-war world. Both by ruining his drawings and paintings and useing deliberately inferior shapes, Artaud testifies to his belief that the subjectile cannot be carrier of meaning again nor participate in new attempts at establishing an idea.

la_alma's subjectile, that is to say the projection screen of the blank pages, carries the forms and contents which together make a piece of art, whereas its basic blankness refutes meaning or an idea. In *la_alma*, as I see it, the impossibility and undesirability of an underlying sense or coherence of meaning is motivated politically as well as linguistically. Both the history of Berlin and Alma Herson's forgotten history are told

---

[14] H. Kimmerle, "De projectie van het ware lichaam. Derrida over Artaud", in H. Oosterling and A.W. Prins (eds.), *La chair. Het vlees in filosofie en kunst* [Rotterdamse filosofische studies VIII;] (Rotterdam: Erasmus Universiteit, 1988), 69-83, 75. Known mainly as a writer, actor and director, particularly in connection to the 'theatre of cruelty', Antonin Artaud has also made a great number of drawings and paintings. Cf S. Herel, *Antonin Artaud. Figures et portraits vertigineux* (Montreal: XYZ, 1995).

and written down but they are carried by the blank surface underneath the story, a blank surface that points to the renunciation of a foundational meaning or idea, as do the gaps in Alma's memory and *The Berlin Story*. In place of simulating the existence of a meaningful and coherent story by filling in the gaps, Moren's video book acknowledges the gaps as an invitation, or even obligation, not to tell history as if it makes sense. In this perception of reality, *la_alma* is distinctly modeled on Moren's communication with Alma during her bouts of Alzheimer's, when speaking with Alma was like 'jumping through a word search for remember'. It is moving to read about both Moren and her father dealing with what she names the absence of 'reality anchors'.

> When my father and I would visit Alma, she wasn't able to sit quietly with us, it made her too nervous. As in the story, she had to fill space by being social. Because her faculties were unable to do this it was an awful thing to look at her and look at my dad, and see the reality of a person who couldn't follow words. So I would go alone. When I did this I began to learn to talk to her, to jump through topics, making things up that would work and feel polite. Without my dad there, I had no constant reality anchor and could loosen up to enter her world. I never told anyone I was doing this because then I would have to talk about it. Being with her didn't make me depressed. Rather, making bridges for people who didn't understand Alzheimer's, creating reality anchors for me, made me depressed.
>
> After she died I found out my dad secretly visited her and did the same thing.

Moren's story underscores the subjectile-like character of language, laid bare through the agonies of Alzheimer's. Broken language and communication, against all odds, become the realities on which (writing) history is modeled in *la_alma*, as Moren herself explains:

> It is this physical instinct of talking I wanted to capture in the piece and in the end it seemed these scraps of information in the box were like scraps of words. The scraps are true but everything we fill in means we're making up links to feel logical. My essay talks a bit about when the historian does this, because I feel *la_alma* could be considered an alternative view of communicating historical events. Perhaps not very logical, but in some ways more truthful than the conventional narrative.

Kinship of soul

The way in which *la_alma* is written also reveals the unmendable gaps of Alma's memory and the Berlin story: there is a gap between the mirror image of the two sides of 'la' and 'al(ma)'. Nevertheless the title also contains a kind of foot-bridge, promising a connection between presence and absence of meaning. Moren walks this unsteady wire and invites others to do so as well. In seeking to connect to the scraps of her grandmother's language and cultural history, she creates a particular genealogy of women. This is not to be understood as forging unifying matriarchal family ties. Not exactly looking for her 'roots', Moren nevertheless cherishes traces of kinship. Her installation, in my view, powerfully unsettles the opposition between 'natural' blood-relations and 'modern' chosen relations. Such opposition, as feminist theologian Anne-Marie Korte points out, has become increasingly problematic.[15] Modern western cultural history has been dominated by a tendency to move beyond origins, ancestry and nature as determinative factors. And yet, modernity's comprehensive processes of emancipation and individualization have produced doubt as well, leading to questions such as: Is there anything left that binds people together? Do democracy and individual human rights offer enough social stability? Do the gains of chosen relations really exceed the loss of status and privilege founded on birth and kinship? Furthermore, the fact that compelling political ideologies have ceased to exist often results in a new reliance on national, ethnic or religious identities. As we see in many parts of the world, including the western world, this frequently leads to social tensions and violent conflicts. Lastly, Korte notes the rapidly increasing knowledge of the genetic code and practices of genetic engineering as yet another factor, derived from the life sciences, that questions the ban on origins and descent. 'Nobody wants to be predestined to diseases and disabilities, but, paradoxically, we want to know, and therefore will know more and more about our origins and destiny in order to arm ourselves against this type of fate'.[16]

These various tendencies converge on what Korte refers to as a postmodern interest in genealogy. In contrast to the view that our continuity with the past would hinge on tradition, understood as our ancestry's heritage to us, postmodern genealogy is focussed on tracking down the traces in the past that form our own background. In a theological context, the interest in stories of origin and descent is expressed in the rediscovery of the book of Genesis, where relations of families, generations and nations come into existence 'from virtually nothing, just hoping for the best and God's blessing'. Just like the flourishing of geneological research and other cultural

---

[15] A.-M. Korte, "Van generatie op generatie. Bloedverwantschap in de religieuze verbeelding", in A.-M. Korte, F. Vosman, Th. de Wit (eds.), *De ordening van het verlangen. Vriendschap, verwantschap en (homo)seksualiteit in joodse en christelijke tradities* (Zoetermeer: Meinema 1999), 68-86.

[16] Ibid., 72.

expressions of family affinities, this recent attraction to the stories of Genesis displays western culture's focus on the personal domain.[17] Many people, as Korte notes, experience the private domain as their 'real' or 'authentic' life in an otherwise excessively fragmented and complex world.

Using her family history and her relationship with her grandmother as a point of departure, no doubt Moren's *la_alma* is also affected by this postmodern interest in genealogy. Moren did not open Alma's box, however, to establish a pedigree for herself or to write a family saga. The fiction of comprehensiveness, linearity, and authenticity thus created would entirely contravene *la_alma*'s experimental form of writing history. Furthermore, the embededness of the lives of Moren's ancestors in the global developments of the nineteenth and twentieth centuries attest to the strong interlacing of the personal and the political. Yet I believe *la_alma* is about kinship, not only in the sense of the family ties between Lisa Moren and her grandmother but also as the congeniality between strangers that comes into existence through the viewer's active involvement in the piece. What is taking place in both Moren's patient word search with Alma and the interactivity of *la_alma* modeled on it is, what I want to call, kinship of soul.

I take 'soul' here in the manner religious studies would approach it, such as advanced by Hans-Peter Hasenfratz.[18] While philosophy would ask 'what is the soul?', psychology 'how does the soul function?', and parapsychology whether an experience of soul corresponds to some objective reality, the phenomenology of religion is likely to wonder about the ways soul appears or manifests itself. In this perspective, soul is not a thing but an *event*. This implies, in my view, an understanding of soul which is dynamic, relational, and manifestst itself as manifests an unexpected event rather than as something available on demand. Hasenfratz' description of soul, based on a selection of texts from 'the immediate or wider surroundings of what we call "our culture"', supplements this with some other aspects. Not only does this description support the event character of the soul, but it also explains that soul thus involves a power that occurs to people as a 'revelation of both physical life and life beyond the physical'. In other words, soul is a force that is active in the body, the mind or psyche, and life after death. Thus the idea of the soul as the person's immortal and immaterial essence has to give way to soul as a principle of life with material as well as spiritual manifestations.

---

[17] Think of websites like MyFamily.com which offers a sentimental journey into one's extended family heritage as well as attractive merchandise.

[18] See H.-P. Hasenfratz, *Die Seele. Einführung in ein religiöses Grundphänomen* (Zürich: Theologischer Verlag, 1986), 14-36.

la_alma's soul, then, appears as a nourishing life force, cautiously and creatively inspiring the bridging of gaps of memory, communication, and interpretation between people, times, and continents. Even between life and death, as we sometimes experience the presence of a dead person through our memories of them, just as Lisa Moren's grandmother is somehow represented in the installation. Theologically speaking, soul thus would be a force of transcendence in the sense once lucidly described by Carter Heyward.

> To transcend means, literally, to cross over. To bridge. To make connections. To burst free of particular locations. A truly transcendent God knows the bounds of no human life or religion. Such a God is not contained within holy scriptures or religious credal formulations. No one person, no group of people, has a hot line to a god who is actually transcendent, for God is too constantly, too actively, moving, crossing over from my life to yours, and from ours to theirs, to become our source of special privilege.[19]

Whether we relate this life force of transcending to the divine, like Heyward, or, as Moren did, to 'the physical instinct' of talking and communicating, its fragile and momentary character cannot be ignored. Rather than the solid construction of the Brooklyn Bridge it resembles the unsteady foot-bridge of *la_alma*. Its piles do not rest on firm ground but on faith: at the beginning of the video we see someone flicking through a small cardboard book, in which only the word 'faith' really stands out. Faith in tiny foot-bridges: that they may hold out just long enough to enable crossing over.

Epilogue

After finishing my article I sent it to several persons who actually saw *la_alma*, asking them whether in their opinion my essay made any sense, given their experience of *la_alma*. Two of the responses I received by Davina Grunstein and Cyriaco Pereira were so important that I think they should be given the last word here. Both address the *tactile* character of Moren's installation, the very issue I had to leave aside, but which nevertheless appears as crucial for the interpretation of *la_alma*.

From D. Grunstein's e-mail (12 Jan 2001):

> I remember not being sure while I was touching the book what was creating the movement in the images. Was it me who was directing the images and causing these changes, or were the changes programmed in? Each touch didn't seem to be met with an equal change in imagery. I think this sensation of a gap between cause and effect may have been really important to the story of *la_alma*. It

---

[19] C. Heyward, *Our Passion for Justice. Images of Power, Sexuality, and Liberation* (New York: The Pilgrim Press, 1984), 243-247, 245. See also I. van der Spek, *Eindeloze lichamen. Transcendentieverlangen in de literaire en technologische verbeelding* (Amsterdam: De Balie, 1999).

seems really frustrating to live in a world in which one feels that one is making sense and the reactions of those around you seem to suggest that you are not making sense. (...) This disjunction that I had experienced in the installation between performing an action and not being certain if that action was being met with an appropriate reaction and the question of control, was, I think, an important part of experiencing this story about Alzheimer's disease.

From C. Pereira's e-mail (17 Jan 2001):
My personal remembrance of the work is more tactile. My first experience was a sensual one, of physical activation of events. I think that the gesture of touching the pages was very important. In the beginning the observer tries to create a dialogue and to see if it is a two-way street. We touch the pages and see the video changing, like a behavior prize. But after awhile, when confidence is established, the images begin to make sense. Not a story, but a set of related "invitations" to a certain atmosphere. In this way, it is similar to meeting a person for the first time.

The stories that I read were just as much mine as they are Lisa Moren's, and I think that this is a quality of the book. It was like an 'artificial madeleine.' The semi-opacity of the book connects me to the (almost invisible) figure of her grandmother. The facts and memories are there but, in some way, inaccessible. However, we can have an idea of their deepness. The sickness put her in a dubious situation, at the same time being 'here' *and* in a very foreign country or age. Her world was of constant free associations, as is the one who wishes to communicate with her.

The Need for 'Another World'

Women's Everyday Life and the Embrace of Pain[1]

Kune Biezeveld

Introduction

By urging classical theology to reconsider the way it deals with everyday life - and to stop depreciating or ignoring it - feminist theologians demand a re-evaluation of a number of core theological concepts. In this essay, I will deal with the possible consequences of this revision, specifically as it concerns the conceptual pair *transcendence* and *immanence*. The polarity linked with these terms may well be essential for a focus on everyday life. In particular the idea of 'another world', which is closely linked to the notion of transcendence, may not be displaced. I will put forward the need for a - non-metaphysical - 'other world' as a norm when confronted with the injustice and pain everyday life contains. In what follows, I will first underline the need for a reconsideration of classical theology. Then I will analyse what is involved in the efforts to change its balance. In the following section I will examine the notion of the 'embrace of pain' introduced by Walter Brueggemann to deal with life's injustice and pain.[2] This will lead me to the section where I will suggest a way of maintaining the idea of 'another world'. In the final section I will come to my conclusion. As a former minister in one of the Protestant Churches, I assert: let God be the God of real people.

'This World' and God

In 1980, several years after a new Hymnbook for the Protestant Churches of the Netherlands[3] had been published, the Dutch theologian Joanne Klink made a critical analysis of its texts. She asked the question: 'Do we sing what we believe and do we believe what we are singing?'[4] Apart from such issues as the images of God and

---

[1] I thank Dr. G. Low, Director of the English as a Foreign Language Unit of the University of York, for his help in the final phase of this essay.
[2] W. Brueggemann, "A Shape for Old Testament Theology, II: Embrace of Pain", in *Old Testament Theology* (Minneapolis: Fortress Press, 1997), 22-44, 25. Originally published in *Catholic Biblical Quarterly* 47 (1985), 395-415.
[3] *Liedboek voor de Kerken* ('s-Gravenhage, 1973).
[4] J. Klink, *Hervormd Nederland* 36 (1980) 44, 12; 46, 17; 48, 25. I only address Klink's analysis of the hymns, not her observations on the Psalms.

Jesus, she discussed the description of the religious life that believers are supposed to have and whether this corresponded with their experiences in daily life. Her conclusions were remarkable. In the texts, life was described almost exclusively in terms of immense misery. There is also a huge amount of lamentation. The reason why this had not been noticed so far, according to Klink, was because the lamentation is drowned by overwhelmingly positive exclamations of faith experiences. As characteristic of how believers are to experience their lives, she noted the words fear, terror, horror, bewilderment, death, grave, smart, mourning, tears, pain, suffering, agony, affliction, bitterness, despair, fruitlessness, darkness, adversity, calamity, tyranny, slavery, captivity, torture, persecution, insult, shame, sin, and being swept away.

Klink was concerned about how far misery could generally represent the experience of life from the fourth through the twentieth centuries. Is there, for example, no experience of luck, or of 'normal' life? In only six hymns do we find something approaching a morning- or eveningmood, joy about spring or about creation. In about twenty others we come across references to living, labour, strength, health, hearth and home, rest, joy, and love. This, it will be clear, is out of balance with all the misery. In this context, the hymn which mentions normal daily traffic noise is totally incongruous. Klink noted that a hymn does not have to describe our life concretely; in many cases, the shape of life, the primordial experiences which are given words in the church community, can only be expressed in figurative language. This does not explain, however, why the figurative references to everyday life and our living as creatures on earth are so scarce, or why the images of everyday life, when they do appear, are only meant to refer to a 'better home', a 'better life', or a 'better body'. Do we perhaps flee from this normal life and our responsibility for it? Are we forbidden to consider it as the only life there is to live, with heart and soul, with body and mind?

In her analysis, Klink not only questioned the Hymnbook's suggested experience of life, but also its suggested experience of faith. Her general conclusion was that there was an overestimation of faith, with an unreal emphasis on its joyous aspects. Thus in our singing, we ask God to take away our fears and sorrows, to comfort us, to give us rest, to strive for us, to redeem us from all sorts of pain and distress. Where experiences are concerned, we are supposed to have experienced, in order of frequency, liberation, love, protection, grace, guidance, joy, life, light, food, victory, peace, resurrection, presence, comfort, salvation, blessing, help, beatitude, strength, forgiveness, rest, hope, healing, goodness, being born again, being chosen, reconciliation, security, and sense. The key question for Klink was just who really experiences God in this way.

Klink's analysis of the Hymnbook suggests three conclusions about the liturgical language used by the Church to express experiences of life. This language is, firstly, preponderantly negative when life is valued. Secondly, it is too overwhelming where the significance or function of God is concerned. And thirdly, it is remarkably scarce where normal everyday life is concerned. It is not surprising that all three conclusions are adopted by feminist theologians. Maaike de Haardt, in her 1999 study, proposes to take everyday life as a starting point for new explorations of the meaning of God, resulting in a shake-up of the core concepts that theology has traditionally used when discussing God's relation to our lives.[5] In addition to the conceptual pair transcendence and immanence mentioned earlier, she also considers theism and pantheism, monotheism and polytheism, combined with the issue of male/masculine and female/feminine images of God. For De Haardt, the term 'ambiguity' is the best word to describe the essence of everyday life. In this she follows Ruth Page, according to whom ambiguity (or better 'Ambiguity' as a metaphysical picture of the world) has both the meaning of 'polyvalence' and 'openness to change and sensitivity to circumstance'.[6] Further, De Haardt subscribes to the concept of divine immanence and she considers polytheism as promising. This last concept of the Divine may be more just than monotheism when considering the plurality of live.[7] This means that De Haardt is not so much asking for a rebalancing or reordering of the conceptual pairs of concepts, as suggesting a reweight of some of them in today's theology. In any case, she herself opts clearly for notions such as duration, blessing, and sustenance, where the meaning of God is concerned.

With this questioning of traditional categories and the addition of new ones, De Haardt comes close to Klink's analysis and the three conclusions I mentioned above. First, if we accept ambiguity as an essential characterisation of our everyday life (and of the world as a whole), it is impossible to label it adequately with just the negative values that Klink recorded from the Hymnbook. It might be argued that negative values suggest that things could have been otherwise, what is more, that they form the counterpart of a view of God as the supplier of contrasting experiences, in line with Klink's second conclusion. According to this view, God is *outside* this world with all its darkness and pain, and it is due to grace that God sometimes bends down to people on earth to let them experience liberation,

---

[5] M. de Haardt, *"Kom, eet mijn brood"*. *Exemplarische verkenningen naar het goddelijke in het alledaagse* ["Come, Eat My Bread". Exemplary Explorations of the Divine in Everyday Life], (Tilburg, 1999).

[6] R. Page, *Ambiguity and the Presence of God* (London: SCM Press, 1985), 13.

[7] All this follows naturally from her previous publication where she defended the thesis that God has to be seen as immanent in this finite world and in our finite lives, and that every formulation in describing 'another world' inevitably leads to devaluation of this, our only world. See M. de Haardt, *Dichterbij de dood. Feministisch-theologische aanzetten tot een theologie van de dood* [Nearer to Death. Feminist-theological Impulses to a Theology of Death], (Zoetermeer: Boekencentrum, 1993).

blessing, and joy. Seen from the perspective of ambiguity, however, God is very much *in* this world, present in everyday life as a sustainer of it. This latter view overcomes Klink's third conclusion, because it expands the language of faith to make room for everyday life. When seen as connected to God, it becomes self-evident that traffic noise, the spring, flowers, and rain have a place in the hymns to God.

It is not clear whether Klink's critical analysis of the Hymnbook implies the consequences that arise out of De Haardt's proposals. When expressing her conviction that it is a central aim of the Christian tradition to be of significance to people's everyday life, Klink herself may have been thinking of a less radical change of categories. This is not to say that such a far-reaching change is not needed and it is especially this need that I wish to address in this essay. De Haardt offers her (radical) proposals as an invitation for further research on the theological consequences of this new emphasis on everyday life, and it is these consequences that I wish to explore here. I would like to pose three questions in particular:
1. What corrections need to be made to classical theology so as to give every day life an appropriate place in it?
2. Do we need a rebalancing of the pairs of concepts that theology is accustomed to?
3. Do we have to look anew for a real dialectical relation, or must we opt for one side of the balance?

Of all the possible concepts, I intend to focus here on the most problematic and controversial one, namely transcendence. In as much as it is connected with God by those who dislike it, transcendence is seen not only as representing the essential difference between God and the world, (and hence God's absence from the world), but also as having hierarchical connotations which in turn imply a low, dependent status of the world and its people. Seen from a human perspective, transcendence can be used as an invitation to escape from this world to 'another world', and thus can be perceived as an obstacle to accepting the ambiguity of this world. It might be argued on this point that the best solution would be to reject the notion of 'another world', but I wish to argue that there are good reasons to retain it. These derive primarily from the fact that ambiguity can never be a neutral word. It is a word which bears not only on finitude and death, but also on much injustice and pain. By bringing this injustice and particularly pain to the fore, I want to accept De Haardt's invitation to take my part in a new understanding of old concepts, with an eye to naming God's meaning for everyday life.

Delivered or sustained?

If we take everyday life as a starting point for the exploration of the meaning of God or the Divine, various theological implications arise. One important implication can be seen in the distinction between God as sustainer of everyday life and God as liberator, the distinction that immediately brings in the notions of immanence and transcendence. A choice for the meaning of God or the Divine, as the sustainer of daily life, will include an emphasis on the immanence of God, while seeing God as liberator accords with an acceptance of God's transcendence. In her presentation of her own preferences in these issues, De Haardt refers to some similar lines of thinking within feminist theology. The first is a reference to Catharina Halkes, who makes a plea for an emphasis on God's blessing activity at the cost of God's liberating action. The second is a reference to Delores Williams who, as a womanist theologian, considers the notion of survival more suitable than liberation in the context of black women's lives.[8] These two lines of thinking have their own background and contexts. The line De Haardt herself follows is nevertheless distinguishable from both. It is worth briefly examining how her argument differs from theirs.

We may start with Halkes' line of thought in which the new attention to God's blessing activity is paid rather than to God's liberating actions.[9] Halkes' argument is connected with a dispute that has been current in theology since the 1960's and 1970's. It was during this period that there was a reaction against the long-accepted view of Von Rad concerning the relation between creation and 'God's mighty acts in history'. As is well-known, Von Rad was the first to assert that the notion of creation was a marginal concept in the faith of Israel as compared to the notion of salvation via 'historical' events.[10] Von Rad in effect developed the argument begun by Karl Barth in his *Commentary on Romans* (1919; 1922²). In his books Barth reacted against nineteenth-century liberal theology which had sought a harmonious relationship between daily cultural life and Christian faith. This critical contribution to theological debate would become of enormous importance for the struggle of the German Confessing Church in the 1930's against Hitler's national socialism. In this context, a strong connection could easily be made between the fight against the Canaanite fertility cult by the prophets of Israel and the reference by the national

---

[8] De Haardt, *"Kom, eet mijn brood"*, 24f.
[9] C. J.M. Halkes, ... *en alles zal worden herschapen. Gedachten over de heelwording van de schepping in het spanningsveld tussen natuur en cultuur* [... and All Will Be Recreated. Reflections on the Integrity of Creation in the Field of Tension Between Nature and Culture], (Baarn: Ten Have, 1989), 95ff.
[10] G. von Rad, "Das theologische Problem des alttestamentliches Schöpfungsglauben", *Beiheft zur Zeitschrift für die alttestamentliche Wissenschaft* 66 (1936), 138ff.; cf. Id., "The Theological Problem of the Old Testament Doctrine of Creation", in *The Problem of the Hexateuch and Other Essays* (New York: McGraw-Hill, 1966), 131-142.

socialists to the Germanic roots of German culture.

This dialectical theology grew to be enormously influential in both European and American theology. The 'contextual commandment', however, led to a 'marginalisation of creation'[11] within this form of theology, and as a result to a dualistic thinking concerning history and nature, body and soul, monotheism and polytheism, as well as between ethical and cultic categories. The sixties and seventies saw a reaction against what had come to be regarded as an 'out of balance' theology. The first scholar to formulate this was Claus Westermann, a close associate of Von Rad in Heidelberg. In 1968 he published a book in which he made room for blessing as an activity by God to be distinguished from God's acts of salvation in history.[12] According to Westermann, both forms of God's activity have to be kept together in fruitful tension.

This was the start of a new view of Old Testament biblical theology, one in which there was allowance for tensions and polarities. Certainly the gain is, as Brueggemann noted, 'that the contextual, dailiness of life is to be taken as a positive theological datum'.[13] In the same breath, he considers this crucial shift to be a break with the extreme masculinisation of biblical faith.[14] Interestingly, feminist theologians came to much the same conclusion by studying the Wisdom literature, which is extremely rich in detail about everyday life.[15] For Halkes, the main concern towards the issues involved was to break down age-old dualistic thinking, the dualism between nature and culture, and between body and mind, which had had unfavourable consequences for both women and nature. In her view, a new attention to God's blessing activity was the way to rescue nature and body. De Haardt also wishes to break away from dualistic thinking but her concerns are slightly different. She stresses the value of everyday life in and of itself. Everyday life with all its ambiguity cannot be measured as deviation from a fixed norm. It is our one and only life and the context in which the presence of God can be experienced.

---

[11] W. Brueggemann, "The Loss and Recovery of Creation in Old Testament Theology", *Theology Today* 53 (1996), 177-190.

[12] C. Westermann, *Der Segen in der Bibel und im Handeln der Kirche* (München: Chr. Kaiser Verlag, 1968); cf.: *Blessing in the Bible and in the Life of the Church* (Philadelphia: Fortress, 1978); cf. Id., "Creation and History in the Old Testament", in V. Vajta (ed.), *The Gospel and Human Destiny* (Minneapolis: Augsburg, 1971).

[13] Brueggemann, "The Loss and Recovery of Creation", 180.

[14] "While the continuing advocates of the either/or model claim to put God beyond sexuality, in fact, the action celebrated in Yahweh is that of a macho, intrusive God." ('The Loss and Recovery of Creation', 181); cf. W. Brueggemann, *Theology of the Old Testament*, 161.

[15] See, for instance, S. Schroer, "The Book of Sophia", in E. Schüssler Fiorenza (ed.), *Searching the Scriptures* II (New York: SCM Press, 1994), 17-38. Among the first who draw attention to the Wisdom texts we find, remarkably enough, G. von Rad with his *Weisheit in Israel* (Neukirchen-Vluyn: Neukirchener Verlag, 1970).

As far as De Haardt is concerned, the re-balancing by Westermann and others can only be the first step in the revision process. On the one hand, De Haardt refuses to work with ideas such as balance or polar thinking; such ideas are part of the conceptual thinking that feminist theology is trying to break away from. On the other hand, she is presenting a theology which cannot be seen as anything other than an antithesis to the dialectical form. By choosing the concept of God's immanence, she opts for a specific view of this world's reality, including its finitude. Seeing God as a liberating God, albeit in tense connection with God's blessing presence, implies a negative valuation of the world. It is important at this point to note how De Haardt's position differs from that of Delores Williams. As is well known, Williams makes a distinction between a black liberation theology and a womanist survivalist/quality-of-life theology.[16] The best role model to Williams for black female (ex-) slaves are Hagar and Ishmael who, once freed from the house of bondage, were faced with making a life something out of nothing. The main concern for black women was and is quality of life. Though a focus on the quality of life is the reason why De Haardt referred to Williams when exploring the counterbalance of a liberating God, we should not close our eyes to the fact that De Haardt and Williams differ. For Williams, the notion of liberation, or a liberating God, does not belong to a transcendent, 'other-worldly' faith; it simply does not fit with 'this world' in which black ex-slaves are not free at all. 'The question was and still is today, how can oppressed people develop a positive and productive quality of life in a situation where the resources for doing so are not visible?'[17] Here the distinction between liberation and sustenance is not a principal choice between a transcendent or an immanent God, but a conclusion born from everyday experiences. Liberation from injustice is still just as necessary as before.

I consider this to be an important point which has to be uppermost in our efforts to re-balance theology. When considering the meaning of God in everyday life, we cannot give up this idea of the need for liberation. As long as oppression, violence, and injustice are a reality in many people's daily lives, looking for the meaning of God within life cannot neglect them. My concern here, however, is the relation between this side of the issue and that of longing for the concepts of duration and blessing. Halkes and De Haardt argued that duration and blessing changed the balance in theology, so it is of some interest to see how the equation changes if we highlight 'the need for liberation'. Investigating this question might look like going to the other extreme, namely Barth's position. It is meant, however, to be an effort to integrate what I see as an indispensable aspect of a theology which is focused on the meaning of God for everyday life. It is obvious that De Haardt concentrates on justifying the ambiguity of daily life in her theological thinking, and it is this very

---

[16] D. S. Williams, *Sisters in the Wilderness. The Challenge of Womanist God-Talk* (Maryknoll, New York: Orbis Books, 1993), 193ff.
[17] Ibid., 193.

ambiguity which has to be seen in relation to God or the Divine. I agree with her that a too easy connection with ideas of deliverance or a liberating God has to be rejected. A belief in God's liberating acts can imply fleeing from this world to 'another world', but more importantly it does not fit with reality, even with believed reality. This also applies in a non-womanist context; it was, indeed, one of the objections made by Klink in reaction to the Church's over-confident songs. Yet, we are left with the problem of how to deal with the theological tensions that are in play here. Specifically three questions require answering:
1. What are the consequences of a new choice of concepts such as duration, sustenance and blessing?
2. What kind of God belongs to these concepts?
3. What do we do with experiences of injustice and pain? Do we just accept them as belonging to this ambivalent life, or do they provide reasons for protest or for launching appeals against God?

With these questions we remain firmly in the field where we started, namely, Old Testament theology. It concerns the tensions that the Old Testament texts express and which require expression in systematic thinking. I discovered a good way to approach this tension in the term 'embrace of pain'.

Embrace of pain

The term 'embrace of pain' was introduced by Walter Brueggemann in 1985 as a term for 'the full acknowledgment of an experience of pain and the capacity and willingness to make that pain a substantive part of Israel's faith-conversation with its God'.[18] For him, it was a vehicle by which the polarity of the Old Testament texts, or in fact one pole of this polarity, could be expressed. With reference to the terms for this polarity he uses elsewhere, namely, *iconic* and *aniconic*,[19] embrace of pain belongs to the *aniconic* side, which to Brueggemann is the side which represents the voices for change and for transformational activity. In the period following Westermann's plea for a re-introduction of, to use the same term here, the *iconic* side, many different textual voices and interests were revealed. This resulted in an agreement that the concept of polarity was important, though the actual opposition could be labelled in different ways. At present, Old Testament scholars are more willing than in the sixties and seventies to work with the idea of polarity and tension, rather than opting for one side or the other. This is also true of Brueggemann. Having said that, however, he is very much aware of his own theological context, which makes him unflagging in his empathy for the *aniconic*

---

[18] See note 2.
[19] Brueggemann, *Theology of the Old Testament*, 71.

side of the polarity.[20] It is this *aniconic* dimension which relates to my argument in this essay and which, I shall now show, justifies the introduction of the 'embrace of pain'.

To start with, Brueggemann does not impose any constraint on the term 'pain'. 'Pain', for him, refers to any dysfunction in the relationship with God, or in the disorder of creation or society. It may be experienced in both public and private ways. I consider this lack of constraint to be important for a theology that is specifically focused on 'women and everyday life'. It is not by accident that, of all ideas, the embrace of pain was employed by women who created a liturgical setting for the utterance of pain and despair after experiences of sexual abuse. Indeed, in her book *Gegen das Schweigen klagen* (To Lament Against Being Silenced), a book that presents the Psalms of Lament as texts which can give voice to violated women, Ulrike Bail explicitly refers to Brueggemann and uses his ideas.[21]

At this point it is worth exploring Brueggemann's ideas in a little more detail. For Brueggemann, as mentioned above, the embrace of pain belongs to the *aniconic* pole of the possible balance. He has a valid reason for identifying embrace of pain with this side of the polarity. Following Norman K. Gottwald and his sociological approach, Brueggemann makes a distinction between a theology which generates a protest against any closed order on one side, and a 'structure legitimating' theology on the other. In a structure legitimating theology, there are 'orders, limits, and boundaries within which humaness is possible and beyond which there can only be trouble'.[22] This form of theology, which can be found throughout the Old Testament with its emphasis on the covenant as contract, may also be called creation theology. It is closely associated with the creation texts as well as with the Wisdom literature. These texts, according to Brueggemann, also display a (very conservative) social dimension according to which the world is seen as being ordered and in particular governed.

Although Brueggemann is prepared to entertain one aspect of creation theology, that the world is not chaos, he is very unhappy about the other implications and noted that Israel itself broke away from this form of theology . Creation theology is in essence a contractual theology which, when articulated consistently, lacks a human face: 'It is a system of reality that allows no slippage, no graciousness, no room for failure.'[23] The question that Israel more and more began to ask, however,

---

[20] W. Brueggemann, "Bodied Faith and the Body Politic", in *Old Testament Theology. Essays on Structure, Theme, and Text* (ed. by Patrick D. Miller; Minneapolis: Fortress Press, 1992), 67-94, 71ff.

[21] U. Bail, *Gegen das Schweigen klagen* [To Lament Against Being Silenced]. *Eine intertextuelle Studie zu den Klagepsalmen Ps 6 und Ps 55 und der Erzählung von der Vergewaltigung Tamars* (Gütersloh: Chr. Kaiser/Gütersloher Verlagshaus, 1998), 62f.

[22] Brueggemann, "A Shape for Old Testament Theology, I: Structure Legitimation", in *Old Testament Theology*, 1-21, 15.

[23] Ibid., 17.

was how to deal with that part of created reality which does not properly submit to, or is subordinated with difficulty to, the political or divine regime that is legitimated. It is in this critical question that Brueggemann considers the embrace of pain to be the key element. In fact, the question of pain can be seen as one of the main pillars of Old Testament faith, taking the form of protest against the contractual theology in which pain need not occur, or is viewed as a failure to be corrected. Therefore, the issue of pain affects not only the people of Israel or its poets, but also its God. Indeed, it is a crucial issue in Israel's portrayal of God. The lament-speeches by which Israel pushes the relationship with its God to the boundaries of unacceptability, meant that Yahweh is no longer free to be a trouble-free God who presides over untroubled legitimating structures. Israel's laments force a re-characterisation of God, such that God now has to listen to people's complaints.[24] Textually, this resulted in a reference to the Exodus story which is a story about a God who forms new history around the reality of pain.

Brueggemann himself did not focus on a reconciliation of Westermann's views with his own. He is certainly well aware of the significant efforts made by scholars like Westermann to integrate the natural processes of death, birth, and growth as simply part of experiences of life into a well-balanced theology. At the end, however, a well-balanced theology is not his objective. When urged to choose, he chooses in favour of those who are denied the beauty of life and are crushed by the order.[25]

I would like to begin the attempt to create a broader synthesis by looking again at De Haardt's position, namely, the urgent need for the other side of the polarity. Although De Haardt's choice will also be in favour of those 'who are denied the beauty of life and are crushed by the order', she makes her way via the concept of ambiguity. Of course, she will distance herself from any theology which can be associated with structure legitimazation. For her, the recognition of the fundamental ambiguity of the world is the only way to free theology - and life - from the straightjacket of traditional patriarchal concepts. On this point I totally agree with her. My question, however, is whether the term ambiguity can be used in such an open way. When meant to be a contrasting term to 'order', the word with which it matches will be 'disorder', or even 'chaos'. In other words, my question concerns the boundaries of this ambiguity and its relation to the notion of the embrace of pain. In my opinion, the term ambiguity, used this way, is in danger of being an empty

---

[24] Brueggemann, "The Rhetoric of Hurt and Hope. Ethics Odd and Crucial", in *Old Testament Theology*, 45-66, 49.
[25] Brueggemann, "A Convergence in Recent Old Testament Theology", in *Old Testament Theology*, 95-110, 104.

term which cannot encompass injustice, precisely what Brueggemann intended to include.

At this point, however, the question arises as to whether we, when convinced of the need for another world, are obliged to follow Brueggemann back to the liberation pole. The problem is that Brueggemann's emphasis on liberation resulted in a narrow focus and only took account of 'lived experience' where it involved pain complaints. Humans undergo, as I stated with Klink and De Haardt in sections 2 and 3, a broad range of experiences. So the question becomes whether it is possible to integrate the views of Westermann and De Haardt with those of Brueggemann. There seem to be two possible routes out this impasse. Firstly, a range of arguments can be put forward against Brueggemann's valuation of creation theology as method for legitimating divine or social order. The main objection is that creation theology is in fact less legitimating than Brueggemann suggests and does allow for a measure of disorder and pain.[26] It is true that in the already mentioned feminist interest in Wisdom texts, this last aspect gets full attention too. Secondly, and perhaps even more important, both the concepts of creation and Wisdom integrate the polarity by representing themselves as sustaining and liberating at once. Instead of following the usual contrast between Exodus and Genesis, our eyes can be opened to the explosive, liberating character of the first chapters of Genesis, as well as to the creation character of Exodus.[27] And, as far as Wisdom is concerned, does not the Wisdom of Solomon state that, throughout the course of history, human beings 'were saved by wisdom' (9:18)?[28]

Here, I would like to move beyond the notion of thinking in terms of polar opposites and keep together both sustenance and liberation. In this way, the notion of embrace of pain does not remove us from everyday life. We are simply saying that reality appears to be less ordered or governed than one would like or hope it to be. At the same time, however, I want to avoid the danger of reverting to legitimating theology. For Brueggemann, Israel's appeal to God was a breaking away from such a theology. From that moment on, God could no longer be seen as colluding with this ambivalent and often violent world full of injustice. This is why, in Christian theology, the doctrine of creation could never become a self-evident part of people's faith. By rejecting Marcion, however, theology made it clear that it would never do without the doctrine of creation either. This is precisely the argument reintroduced by Westermann and all those feminist theologians who are

---

[26] G. van Ek, *Mens en maatschappij tussen chaos en kosmos* [*Man and society between chaos and cosmos. An investigation of the fundamental principles of social criticism in the wisdom literature of the ancient Near East and specially in ancient Israel*] Diss. Utrecht 1997.

[27] J. Richard Middleton, "Is Creation Inherently Conservative? A Dialogue with Walter Brueggemann", *Harvard Theological Review* 87 (1994) 3, 257-277.

[28] Cf. E. A. Johnson, *She Who Is. The Mystery of God in Feminist Theological Discourse* (New York: Crossroad, 1993), 89.

concerned with this issue. Although I agree with the Westermann position, it is important not to lose the notion of the embrace of pain, simply because of everyday life. Strange as it may sound, I think we therefore need a reckoning with 'another world'.

The need for 'Another World'

In one of his essays, the Dutch philosopher of religion H.J. Adriaanse, when trying to express what religion is about, refers to a remarkable story told by Franz Werfel. It is a story about an old maidservant Teta Linek.[29] When there is a sudden death in the family she serves, Teta proves to be the only one capable of dealing with it. She keeps watch over the body of the son who has been killed, indefatigably counting her rosary. The father of the boy has already disappeared, drunk and asleep somewhere in the house. A friend takes up vigil by the bed, but he cannot endure it. The next morning, he has to admit that the only one who truly dealt with the death was the 'mindless old maid' Teta. Only for her did death have a place in the order of being, while the friend, representing modern people without imagination, could only see decomposition. For Adriaanse, the story by Werfel serves to illustrate what religion can do. Here, he follows the sociologist of religion Niklas Luhmann who defines religion as the use of an external reference point. This can be named transcendence. Transcendence describes what is seen *as it were* 'from a point outside the world'.[30] So, in religion, the world, which is single, is in a certain sense doubled. For Adriaanse, this approach to religion gives the key to understanding the story. Teta, by counting her rosary, was able to look at the dead body differently.

I will take this possible interpretation of the Teta story to develop some closing thoughts on the subject of my essay. The first thing to notice is that transcendence for Luhmann - and Adriaanse - is seen as essentially the same as religion. Religion *is* 'making use of transcendence'. For me, the main question to address is whether this use of transcendence is compatible with the embrace of pain, without, of course, pushing us back to an inherently low valuation of everyday life. To answer this question, I shall read the Werfel story anew, but this time from De Haardt's perspective. How, we may ask, would De Haardt interpret Teta's behaviour?[31] To a certain extent, she would agree with Adriaanse. Although she might, at first,

---

[29] F. Werfel, *Der veruntreute Himmel. Die Geschichte einer Magd*. See H.J. Adriaanse, *Vom Christentum aus. Aufsätze und Vorträge zur Religionsphilosophie* (Kampen: Kok, 1995), 47f.
[30] Ibid., 51ff.
[31] In an other context I compared De Haardt's position with that of Adriaanse, and I used for this the story by Werfel. See K. E. Biezeveld, "God in Everyday Life. Re-thinking Transcendence and the Immanent God", in H. A. Krop, Arie L. Molendijk, H. de Vries (eds.), *Post-Theism. Reframing the Judeo-Christian Tradition* (*Festschrift* for H.J. Adriaanse, Leuven: Peeters, 2000), 479-491.

assume that Teta would deny death, she would, I think, come in the end to the opposite view. Teta is the only person who faces the death of the boy and accepts it. She is able to give death a place within her reality. That, De Haardt would presumably say, is what we are asked to do; and that is what we *can* do, strengthened by the presence of God in the midst of our contingent life. So, there is in fact a correspondence between Adriaanse's and De Haardt's position. At the same time, however, the difference between the two needs to be pointed out. Why, exactly, is it that Teta is capable of dealing with the sudden death of the boy? Adriaanse would say that counting her rosary enables her to look at his death from a different perspective; she sees more than the decomposing body. Thus, Teta transcends the banality of life and is no longer imprisoned by appearance. De Haardt, however, would not accept this 'looking from another perspective'. She would say that the only way to endure keeping vigil over the dead body is to accept the finiteness of our lives. While the two men fled from the deathbed, Teta was able to stay the night, counting her rosary. She experienced the presence of God, just as she had in all those other moments of her life when she was cooking, cleaning, and working hard to make life liveable. For Teta, God was integrated into her life, even if 'we' would call it a *banal* life.

The main result of reading from De Haardt's perspective is an emphasis on the notion of immanence. This feminist interpretation is totally in line with recent philosophical development. Here transcendence has been deprived of its metaphysical load and immanence is in a certain sense made absolute. The world does not need an origin outside itself anymore. One may wonder, however, whether it is useful to retain the bipolarity of transcendence and immanence. Are there any grounds left for keeping it? Is there still anything that can be called immanence? Historically, the dualism between the two concepts came into existence with the Gnostic disjunction of creation and salvation. From that time on, the ground of being and the principle of salvation were separated as respectively 'immanent' and 'transcendent'. While Christian theology tried to overcome the disjunction, repeatedly referring to the Church's condemnation of the Gnostics and Marcion, and holding onto the unity of God the Creator and God the Saviour, it never succeeded in getting rid of its Gnostic heritage. The theme of this essay - and this volume - is a good illustration of this fact.

At this point it is worth considering some of the implications of returning to the notion of transcendence. Is any dealing with the concept of transcendence no more than a rearguard action? The article on transcendence in *Religion in Geschichte und Gegenwart*, in which the remarkable history of this term is presented, states at the end that transcendence has now become a fundamental idea with critical potential, to be used in a world without codable norms. When the world does not want to be restricted to what is factual or objective, it needs a 'critical' idea which forces people to keep questioning reality.[32] There is a remarkable concurrence here with the very start of the concept of transcendence, that is, before Gnostic dualism came into existence. According to the *RGG*-article, the birth of the concept can be seen in Parmenides' distinction between thinking and observing, which returned in Plato's separation of the phenomenal world and the world of ideas. After Plato's posing of the idea of the Good beyond the world of the ideas, this concept of ideas beyond being came to be thought of as having a metaphysical load. A connection between this highest Idea and the one God was 'easy' to make, because in the meantime Xenophanes had criticised the world of the myths which presented the gods as playing their roles *in* this phenomenal world. From here on the history of transcendence became, as is well known, an alliance between Greek philosophy and Jewish and Christian theology.

My question is: Now that we face again a non-metaphysical transcendence, can we return to the birth of the concept, that is, to the distinction between thinking and observing? Is it possible to provide a link with the critical potential which transcendence in our time is supposed to have? Can we imagine a non-metaphysical, or better, a metaphorical, 'other world' as a tool for questioning life? Let us return once again to Werfel's story. According to Adriaanse, Teta's ability to look from an external perspective made it possible to see more than the observable decomposition. Here, the critical potential of transcendence results in the endurance of a vigil, with Teta realising that nothing can be changed in face of death. In other situations, the critical potential can result in a protest or a fight whenever one is faced with a situation which has to be changed. This possible alternative view of the notion of transcendence, offers, I suggest, a way of maintaining the term's power, without having to accept its negative implications.

Conclusion

Let me, as a conclusion, summarise what this essay has put forward. Firstly, it was pointed out that De Haardt's agenda is determined by her intention to free everyday life in all its richness and ambivalence from the inherently negative evaluation which results from a transcendent perspective. Consequently, she uses ambiguity in a neutral way. I have argued that the notion of the embrace of pain constitutes a reason to retain the concepts of a norm and a critical potential. Both can be seen to be implied by the notion of transcendence, which is itself closely linked to the meaning of God. The embrace of pain is ultimately an appeal to a God who is at once the creator of the world and the addressee of people's lamentations. In this way, the religious notion of transcendence implies as critical a potential as the

---

[32] H. Blumenberg, "Tranzendenz und Immanenz", *Religion in Geschichte und Gegenwart* 1962³, VI, 990-997.

secular form of the concept.

To end I would like to return to the critique by Klink of the Churches' Hymnbook that I discussed at the start of the essay. In light of the above analysis, what do we say about the negative descriptions of people's daily lives which so upset Klink? We cannot deny that we, when talking about the embrace of pain, end up with at least a part of the negative connotations Klink exposed. I hope that this theological tour has made one thing clear: wherever daily life is described in the language of faith, it concerns real people. It concerns black ex-slaves who still have reason to identify themselves with Hagar and Ishmael. It concerns violated women who want an ear for their lamentations. It concerns many, many others. When they come to sing of God's liberating acts, we surely live in 'another world'.

A Mixed Blessing

Differently Abled Women and Experiences of Transcendence

Jacqueline Kool

An island?
This article discusses the experiences of 'differently abled women', women with disabilities or a chronic disease. How is it that they express their relationship between their everyday reality and their experiences of transcendence?[1] And how does this relationship relate to the social context surrounding these women?

And what about a book about 'common bodies' that includes an article about women with no arms or with chronic pain fatigue, women who read with their fingers or speak with their hands, women who move on wheels or with crutches? Are these bodies common bodies? Both yes and no. My story focuses on exactly this ambivalence and I will argue that both answers are legitimate. To paraphrase Orwell, all people are different, but some are still more different than others. First I would like to introduce two telling situations.

The other day I attended a large conference which addressed the possibilities and limitations of higher education for people with function limitations. Various national politicians participated in a forum. They heard many stories about the ambitions of young people and their difficulties in realizing them in a disabling environment such as education. The politicians were touched by the 'courage and pain' they encountered and made it very clear that this day had been an eye-opener for them. 'It is so important that you inform us, show us who you are and what your lives look like', was their response. In the year 2001, the world of people with a disability or a disease apparently still lies outside the view of 'normal people'. However conspicuous disabled people may be with their sign interpreters, wheelchairs and braces, they are still largely invisible.

Yet another story. During a preparatory discussion for this volume, the question arose whether my story would not be too much of an island, whether the experience of differently abled women would not be isolated too much. I was asked to engage

---

[1] I use transcendence in an active meaning either as (a desire for) crossing and climbing boundaries both physically and otherwise, or as the unexpected and inconceivable breaking through in existence. In doing so, I follow I. van der Spek, *Eindeloze lichamen. Trancendentieverlangen in de literaire en technologische verbeelding* (Amsterdam: De Balie, 1999), 9 and 11.

more in the existing discussions in theological women's studies. This set a train of thoughts in motion. Of course I do not want my contribution to be an island but at the same time I ask myself: is it not just reality that to some extent the story of differently abled women is an isolated story? With my limited energy, I had been travelling for seven and a half hours for this meeting of just two hours. A wheelchair journey from Utrecht to Amsterdam turned out not to be that simple and I had to wait outside for 45 minutes before a solution had been thought up for the fact that the meeting had been planned in a building with a large flight of steps outside. There really is some gap, then, between the everyday realities of women with disabilities and women without them.

The social arena
The position of women with disabilities in society is far from self-evident. We are usually absent in social discussions and figures and all too often live a life in the margins of society.[2] This has both material and immaterial causes, such as the physical design of society as well as people's mentality and way of seeing. The common perception of the disabled is usually very negative and stereotyped. That is why, in addition to social mechanisms of exclusion and inaccessible buildings, the public domain is an arena of struggle for differently abled women. The world looks with able eyes, seeing the disabled as dependent, pitiful wretches, thus concluding that living with a disability means only pain and misery. The common perspective is still an able perspective.

In the movement of people/women with disabilities, such images are being protested in order to create room for the lived experience and a positive appreciation of people with a disability. This is supported by the terminology that is being used. Disability or limitation is not primarily interpreted as an individual physical condition, but as an interaction between individuals and society. Instead of labelling people as disabled, terms are used such as 'disabling environments', 'differently abled bodies', and 'physically challenged'. People without a disability become 'temporarily able-bodied bodies'. But language, no matter how important it is, does not simply bridge the gap between people with and without a disability. In the reality of everyday existence we are continuously confronted with our 'being different'. And the social assessment of women with disabilities as 'lesser people' still emanates from every nook and cranny, as we will see.

---

[2] Women with disabilities usually do not exist in studies: "in most studies of the social situation of people with a disability it is not deemed relevant to distinguish between the sexes, while in studies focusing on differences in the social situations of men and women the aspect of 'able-bodied/disabled' is never addressed." See F. Fortuin, "De resultaten van het onderzoek 'Vrouwzijn en gehandicapt", by NiMaWo 1993, Lecture for the Vrouwen Alliantie, Utrecht, 21 november 1990, 12.

Women with disabilities experience that in social perception they are first seen as disabled and then as women. Health obviously precedes gender.[3] This may explain why women with disabilities are usually absent and even experience exclusion from feminist circles, such as feminist theological and women's religious movements.[4] The American scholar Anita Silvers analyses this phenomenon in the feminist movement, trying to build a bridge between women with disabilities and women without them. She argues in favor of including women with disabilities. When women name traditionally feminine values such as caring, fertility, nurturing and pleasuring as the highest virtues, women with disabilities can feel badly imprisoned. The same is the case when feminists consider values such as independence, wholeness, and the ability to care for and control oneself as the highest attainable good. It seems as if women with disabilities represent everything from which feminist women want to distance themselves. We usually depend on other people's care, have less education, are not financially independent and for the outside world rather embody suffering and defectiveness, not the wholeness praised by feminist theologians.

Often interests conflict with each other, such as in the areas of providing and asking for care, in antenatal diagnostics and in the issue of parenthood and disability. This explains experiences of dislikes and hostility. Or, in contrast, of misplaced care or concern, and paternalism. Silvers, on the other hand, argues in favor of diversity in the women's movement, that it must become an innovative place for women 'where their distinctive social functions and interactions are equally accessible to all who wish to take their place as women'.[5] Women with disabilities are a touchstone for the women's movement because they are more vulnerable and can be a measure of the completeness of the feminist reform: to what extent do paternalism and exclusion still play a role in feminism itself? Silver emphasizes both the differences and the common ground between women with disabilities and without them.

The rediscovery of the body

One of those common interests could be the current boom in thinking about corporeality. Much has been and is being written about the body, espacially by female theologians[6]. This theological writing is, on the one hand, a reaction to the religious and cultural tradition that identified women with their bodies, justifying women's position as second-class citizens. On the other hand, the attention to the

---

[3] Emancipatieraad, *Beeldvorming, gender en handicap* (Den Haag, 1997).
[4] See for example: E. Elshout et al., "Roundtable Discussion. Women with Disabilities, A Challenge to Feminist Theology", *Journal of Feminist Studies in Religion* 10 (1994) 2, 99-134.
[5] A. Silvers, *Women & Disability*. Lecture University of Groningen, 7 May 1997, 12.
[6] For an overview and explanation of the attention for corporeality within theological women's studies see: A.-M. Korte, "Het lichaam een zegen? De nieuwe fascinatie voor het lijfelijk bestaan", *Sofia. Nieuwsbrief Vrouwenstudies Theologie* 3 (1996) 3.

body in women's theological writing is a manifest criticism of the huge amount of attention paid to the body in our current culture. This culture shows an endless stream of bodies, preferably female ones, indicating that the outward appearance of the body has pre-eminently become a status symbol. It is particularly the view that the body can be made and controlled that is criticized by female authors. Yet physical existence is taken very seriously by these authors. They seek to describe what it means to have a body. The question is: which bodies are the subject of our analyses of the meaning of 'the body'?

Valerie Saiving rightly pointed out that ageing or sick bodies hardly have a place in feminist theory. She concludes that understanding the unity of the various stages of physical existence has a life-confirming power.[7] This raises the question to which extent differently abled women identify themselves with and could benefit from the ongoing discussions about corporeality, and what our contributions to these debates could be. These questions can only be partially answered. There are only a few female theologians with a disability participating in such discussions.[8] Furthermore, the objective of these publications varies. A signaficant number of female theologians aim to claim the female body as women and to positively value traditional female values and qualities.[9] The book *I am my Body* by Elisabeth Moltmann-Wendel may be illustrative.[10] Moltmann wants to re-value the body in opposition to religious and socio- cultural attitudes that are hostile towards the body. Her central thesis is that we should not see our body as something that we *have* and with which we act, but as ourself. We *are* our body, our body is nature, which we should treat carefully and learn to listen to. If we bless our body, it will be good to us. It is the Christian theological concept itself that God became body which contains the affirmative and sanctifying effects for our physical being.

---

[7] V.C. Saiving, "Our Bodies/Our Selves. Reflections on Sickness, Aging, and Death", *Journal of Feminist Studies in Religion* 4 (1988) 2, 117-127.

[8] This is another reason why I find it important to publish this story in a volume on common bodies. Differently abled women are so often absent in ongoing discussions; we do not have the proper education, are not invited, the maternal conditions are lacking, or the common exposés turn out to provide only very limited inspiration to our thinking. Therefore, publications and discussions by differently abled women usually take place within their own circle.

[9] Examples can be found in A.-M. Korte, "In de geest van het lichaam. Lichamelijkheid als hermeneutische categorie binnen feministische theologie", in J. Jäger-Sommer (red.), *God opnieuw gedacht. Verantwoordelijkheid voor de schepping in feministisch perspectief* (Baarn: Ten Have, 1995), 231-252.

[10] E. Moltmann-Wendel, *Mijn lichaam ben ik. De herontdekking van de lichamelijkheid* (Baarn: Ten Have, 1994). [Original title: *Mein Korper bin ich/Neue Wege zur Leiblichkeit* (Gütersloh: Gütersloher Verlagshaus, 1994)].

In this way Moltmann paints a romantic picture of the body as the last piece of unspoilled nature over against a rationalized and cold world. She offers an organic or holistic view of the body as a counterpart to the body that can be made, emphasizing the life cycle of growth-bloom-decay-death. We have to admit that Moltmann does pay attention to illness and old age and tries to avoid old clichés in which suffering is made meaningful. However, she only deals with it briefly and somewhat vaguely. In fact, she gives herself away in her introduction. 'But subjects such as disability, incest, rape, which are only touched on here, require a separate study.'[11] Such a combination and choice of words do not inviteme, as a woman with a disability, to keep on reading. Illness and disability move almost automatically towards a theme of suffering.

If I compare Moltmann's project with the experiences of differently abled women, the book offers little comfort. The authors Karin Spaink and Renate Dorrestein emphasize that a certain distinction between an I and a body is essential to people who fall ill. It provides room to the experience that there is more and that you are more than your (sick and sore) body. Whereas Moltmann sends the message 'Not only my body is ill; I am ill,'[12] Dorrestein says 'I am not CFS, I only have it.'[13] And what about the body as unspoilled nature that we have to listen to so that it will bless us? Spaink makes short work of this view. She writes, 'Listening to your body, give me a break? If I really did that, it would be a full day's job. What I need to learn is to not pay attention to it. Closer inspection always makes me feel something strange. My body is a driveling chatterbox, a garrulous aunt who incessantly wants to draw my attention with loud clothes and clanging jewelry.'[14]

To women whose lives imply aids such as wheelchairs and braces, hearing prostheses, spinal column fixations and hip pins, the image of the body as unspoilled nature has a slightly comical ring about it. Moreover, such a view of the body all too often leads to the celebration and sanctification of female biology, including menstruation, pregnancy, confinement, and of traditionally female values such as caring, nurturing, and protecting, as for example, in Goddess spirituality. Earlier I pointed out that this revelation results in differently abled women feeling that they are confined in many ways. Womb-dancing in a wheelchair offers little attraction to me. An 'organic' view of corporeality obscures the fact that suffering as a result of disability and illness usually has social causes. Illness and disability are related not just with tragedy but with injustice as well. Illness can be caused by a polluted environment, bad labour conditions, or medical mistakes. Furthermore, suffering in the event of illness or disability is generally not caused by the function limitation

---

[11] Moltmann-Wendel, *Mijn lichaam ben ik*, 17.
[12] Ibid., 52.
[13] R. Dorrestein, *Heden ik* (Amsterdam: Contact, 1993), 117.
[14] K. Spaink, *Vallende vrouw. Autobiografie van een-lichaam* (Amsterdam: Van Gennep, 1993), 97.

itself but by the isolation and exclusion which are its social consequences.[15]

Female theologians striving to avoid a romanticized view of the body will put more emphasis on the meaning of suffering, as we see for example in Moltmann's work. Annelies van Heijst addresses this topic in her book *Leesbaar lichaam*, in which she analyzes two novels she considers to be modern women's stories of suffering. In this way, she wants to uncover a hidden repertoire and knowledge about life and body, which are usually invisible in our speedy society that is focused on beauty and health.[16] The Korean theologian Chung Hyun Kyung also offers room for the experience of the female body and the specific knowledge yielded through the angle of suffering, struggle and pain. It is specifically in the context of oppression and suffering of Asian women that she wants to name their life-giving power.[17] Kyung speaks of the epistemology of the broken body.

It seems obvious that this 'angle of suffering' would offer a better perspective to women with disabilities, because they usually live in a context in which struggle and suffering are familiar concepts. Yet it turns out that women with disabilities are wary of consenting to this. After all, it is the outside world that all too easily interprets our existence primarily as suffering, even though our own experience of life does not match this view. The stories of women with disabilities show, however, that suffering cannot be easily put aside. Women's own story may be located in the very intermingling of experiences of happiness, pleasure, struggle, and suffering.[18] Kyung's project does make sense to differently abled women considering its form, that is to say, drawing on life-giving power in a context of oppression. We will see this again later on.

Hermeneutics of the (un)common body

Women with disabilities do not always identify themselves with the theoretical quests of female theologians. Yet both their projects are kindred. Apparently, we are looking for the meaning of our embodiment both to ourselves and in relation to the world and our vision of that world. After all, when we take the experiences we have with and in our body seriously, the body yields knowledge. It is a vital key to our

---

[15] See E. Elshout, *Het gehandicapte lichaam: Een schokkend beeld*. Lecture Kerk & Wereld Driebergen 1 Oct. 1994, 10.
[16] A. van Heijst, *Leesbaar Lichaam. Verhalen van lijden bij Blaman en Dorrestein* (Kampen: Kok Agora, 1993).
[17] Chung Hyun Kyung, *The Struggle to be the Sun Again. Introducing Asian Women's Theology* (Maryknoll, NY: Orbis books, 1990).
[18] See J. Kool, "Genieten of lijden? Gezondsheidscultuur en het afwijkende lichaam", *Mara* 9 (1995) 2; en Id., "Heelheid onder de loep", *Ophef*, 2 (1995) 2/3.

understanding of reality and the making of meaning.[19] Anne-Marie Korte speaks of a 'hermeneutics of the body'. She aims at an archaeology of the female body in order to make room for an autonomous physical experience of women. It highlights that our experience of being embodied is by definition ambivalent or even paradoxical. People have very contradictory experiences with respect to their bodies and there is always a certain tension between an 'I' and our bodies. Korte wants to face these ambivalences and name them because they form our thinking.[20]

This archaeology of the female body, in which there is room for paradoxes and tensions, also invites differently abled women to recount their particular stories. When the body is conceived as a source of meaning and knowledge, it seems logical that the ill or disabled body brings forth its own knowledge distinct from common knowledge. This is exactly what Van Heijst contends, while female theologians with disabilities, such as the American Nancy Eiesland and Elly Elshout from the Netherlands, seem to subscribe to it as well. The specific knowledge generated by the 'uncommon body' is therefore 'uncommon knowledge'. It completes or rewrites the common body images. Hence the disabled body is at odds with that common physical reality, creating an effect of disruption. Elshout presents the disabled body as a shocking counter-image of the image of wholeness, in the religious context often represented as liberating with respect to the dominant social images of the ideal body. Since the disabled body is 'different' and by definition does not meet the constructed ideal of flawlessness and attractiveness, it shocks and has a transformative power.[21] There is a gap between the body that is ill or is falling ill, the body that is old or that is ageing and, on the other hand, 'our' common existence and our view of the body.

What this specific knowledge offered by the 'uncommon' body looks like will be discussed later. For the moment, emphasis is on the other, the individuality of the experience of living in a disabled body. It looks like this experience is an 'island' after all. This brings us close to the common notion that people with disabilities are 'deviant', 'different', and that people without disabilities cannot imagine a life with a disability or illness, preferring to keep this image at bay as much as possible. There are common bodies and uncommon bodies and consequently there are common lives and uncommon lives.

---

[19] See in this context also: M A. May, *A Body Knows. A Theopoetics of Death and Resurrection*, (New York: Continuum, 1995).

[20] A.-M. Korte, "In de geest van het lichaam" and "Kennis van het vlees. Feminisme, spiritualiteit en de lichamen van vrouwen", in A.-M. Korte and L. Wilkens (red.), *Andere gezichten, andere geluiden. Vrouwenstudies in theologie en godsdienstwetenschappen*, (Gorinchem: Narratio, 1997).

[21] Elshout, *Het gehandicapte lichaam*. Elshout does not present this image as having no connection with other feminist theory developments; she links her story to M. Daly's *Gyn/Ecology*.

The big difference between this common social judgement and the view of women with disabilities in naming 'specialness' is, of course, its valuation. Elshout and others give a positive meaning to this specialness: it offers its own opportunities for gaining experience and knowledge from which others could learn, instead of interpreting it as a 'lesser life'.

However, the question about the specialness of life with disabilities has another aspect, which is also of particular importance in relation to the theme of this volume. However special this life may seem in comparison to the common life, for those who live in such an uncommon body the daily existence with a disability or illness is as usual and ordinary as that of everyone else. 'Bodies are forgetful', Karin Spaink once said, referring to the very experience that the body quickly becomes accustomed to a changing situation, that life just goes on and is 'just your life'. When she clambers aboard a bus using her hands and crutches she says, for instance: 'What you see is not fumbling; I just do what is easiest for me, like everyone else.'[22]

Ordinary or special?

I would like to go deeper into the issue of the specialness or the ordinariness of life with a disability. With respect to the daily relationship with our body, the experiences of differently abled women are twofold. On the one hand, women every day experience themselves as the physical objects of others' control and abuse in a disproportionate manner. Many women with disabilities endure more medical care and social service systems that further own and control their lives. On the other hand, due to negative social representations, women with disabilities in particular have to take great pains to build both a positive self-image and a life that fits in with our experiences. Sometimes there is a reciprocity between this process and the social representations to which one conforms. After all, we are just as governed by common views as anyone else. Furthermore, the 'unfortunate wretch who is brave enough to cope' offers a strong identity. But often women will dissociate themselves from these images because they do not offer room for a human being of flesh and blood and do not fit in with lived experience. A theological elaboration of this theme can be found in Nancy Eiesland's book *The Disabled God*. The title already shows that Eiesland connects disability with transcendence/God. Eiesland makes an interesting contribution to the subject, though there are some problems too, as I will show later. Her book starts with the statement that, 'Living with a disability is difficult. Acknowledging this is not a defeat, I have learned, but a hard-won accomplishment in learning to live a life that is not disabled.'[23] The crux lies in the

---

[22] Spaink, *Vallende vrouw*, 40.
[23] N. Eiesland, *The Disabled God. Toward a Liberatory Theology of Disability* (Nashville: Abingdon Press, 1994), 13.

last words, atmitting that a life with a disability is not easy does not mean that life is possessed by disability and illness. Neither does it mean that everything in life referring to the disability/illness is only negative. In Eiesland's words, ' The telescoping of our lives into simplistic categorisations of good and bad, pain and pleasure, denies that the lives of people with disabilities, like all ordinary lives, are shot through with unexpected grace, overwhelming joy, and love returned. Life is simply a mixed blessing.'[24]

This is what Eiesland wants to describe: the dignity and mercy of those unconventional lives, but also their repugnancies or disillusions. We see the same in Elly Elshout's writings. In her texts, she stresses the ability of women with disabilities to give concepts such as struggle, vulnerability, and dealing with limits, a place in daily life. They are particularly alive to the balance between limitations and possibilities, and of the importance of compromising.[25]

In texts of differently abled women and in conversations we have with each other, the question of ordinariness or specialness often turns out to play a complicated role. After all, in a world that all too easily pictures you as different and pitiful, you have every interest in showing that you are 'just as ordinary as anyone else'. At the same time there is no escape from the experience that your life makes different demands and that your social position makes it impossible to act as if nothing was the matter. I only need to refer to the story about the train and flight of stairs with which I began this article. Eiesland illustrates this ambivalence with the story of Diane DeVries, born without legs and with half arms.[26] The doctor who delivers her faints and her grandmother cries out that she is the devil's child. But De Vries and her father call the disability 'just something that happens'. She sees her own body not as imperfection but as compact, streamlined, healthy and, admittedly, different. However, she is well aware, due to the many painful and sometimes blatantly hostile confrontations, that the world does not always share her view. Nevertheless, DeVries keeps seeing herself as 'different and ordinary'.

The author/poet Nancy Mairs who has Multiple Sclerose is also active in this field. With her work she wants to 'reclaim human experience, insofar as I can find it embodied in my own experience, from the morass of secrecy and shame into which Christian and pre-Christian social taboos have plunged it, to rescue and restore God's good creation, 'to keep as close to the bone of my experience as I can.'[27] In this way illness and disability become part of ordinary life, without shunning or alleviating the chaos and fear of the body. In fact, the realism Mairs displays makes it impossible to turn her into a hero or saint. 'Suffering', she contends, 'has few heroes, least of all those who wish to live ordinary lives.' To her,

---

[24] Ibid., 13.
[25] E. Elshout "Het gehandicapte lichaam", *Praktische Theologie* 1 (1996), 26.
[26] Eiesland, *The Disabled God*, 33 ff.
[27] Ibid., 44.

life is filled with 'blessings and curses', while sometimes the distinction between them fades. Eiesland analyses how the real lived experiences of Mairs and DeVries 'highlight physical contingency as a frequent source of creativity and of common and uncommon experiences of interrelationship'.[28]

Mairs and DeVries then identify disabilities as part of ordinary life while at the same time testifying to the differences between people with disabilities and people without them. They challenge the false and oppressing explanations of those differences. Resistance plays an important role in the stories of both women, on the one hand as a battle against injustice and, on the other, because they tell the truth about their experiences, however complex they may be.

The Disabled God

Eiesland's analysis of Mairs and DeVries leads us to her theology, enabling us to consider more carefully how differently abled women put transcendence into words. Eiesland connects the individual stories of women to the larger story of the civil rights movement of people with disabilities in the US, through what she calls 'a liberatory theology of disability'. She describes how she had always considered the notion Divine Revelation as really universe-shocking. But something very different happened in her life: she started to see the image of God in a 'sip-puff wheelchair' and in the image of those who are judged as 'not feasible', 'unemployable', 'with a questionable quality of life'. 'Here was God for me,' she writes.[29] In this image of God, which she helds in common with otherdisabled people, God is not almighty, not pitiful, but 'a survivor, unpitying and forthright'. The ensuing liberatory theology of disability finds its basis in the bodies, the experiences, the (hidden) history and the knowledge of people with disabilities. This theology's starting point from resistance means solidarity between people with disabilities and other marginalized groups.

It is an explicitly Christian and biblical theology. Eiesland sees revelation in those biblical texts that transcend the able-bodied perspective and in which people with disabilities are theological subjects and historical actors. They contain stories and images that enable subversive thinking and resistance. To Eiesland, Jesus Christ as the Disabled God, is such a revelation image. She wants to use the church's symbolic devices, but to transform them as well. Traditional Christian theology, because of its symbols and praxis reify the oppression and exclusion of people with disabilities and in this way undermine their self-empowerment and liberation. Symbols are needed that touch people both with and without disabilities, calling all people to conversion, and changing the relationship between both groups.

---

[28] Ibid., 47.
[29] Ibid., 89.

The image of the crucified and resurrected Christ as the 'Disabled God' aligns with the goals Eiesland sets for transforming symbols. It is an image that fits with tradition yet has an innovative twist as well. By naming Christ disabled, wholeness and disability are no longer mutually exclusive, as in common perception. After all, the resurrected Christ, with his violated and maimed body, has always been the image of wholeness in the tradition. By reclaiming this image and explicitly calling it 'disabled', Eiesland connects it with the life experience of people with disabilities and with the social reality of people being made disabled (by discrimination and by poverty and violence). The image also questions the use of 'normal' bodies as a basis for the study of religion and religious praxis and rituals. The theological implications of the Disabled God reach even further. The resurrected Christ embodies damaged hands, feet, and sides, and is, with this damaged body also the Imago Dei. 'Our bodies', Eiesland says, 'participate in the Imago Dei, not despite of our impairments and contingencies, but through them.'[30] Disability is not only not contradictory to human-divine integrity, it even becomes a new model of wholeness in a symbol of solidarity. It incites personal and social transformation. After all, God does not appear as a ruler, as a man or as a suffering servant, but as a survivor, unself pitying, vulnerable yet powerful, as one who wants to be touched regardless of the taboo on disabled bodies. This God is present wherever people are fighting for an ordinary life which has meaning and dignity.

In this image of God, the experience that is essential to Eiesland returns; that bodies, life itself, are a complex mixed blessing. This image reflects a God with joy and pain who calls's to interdependence. Eiesland considers it a hopeful image, not because it wipes away all human contingencies and transcends physical being, but because of the liberating realism it displays: our bodily boundaries and limitations are accepted and acknowledged as the truth of human existence. It entails the recognition that even our non-conventional bodies, which often let us down, are worthy of living and that so-called curses can sometimes be blessings.

The disabled body as object

Eiesland's project in which 'unconventional bodies' become images of the divine, can enhance women's individuality, our value and our lived experience. Furthermore, it makes room for a socio-political view on disability and for resistance. The Disabled God could have a surprising and disruptive impact on liturgy and preaching. Besides these positive aspects, however, I also see some drawbacks in this image. First, the Disabled God is explicitly Christian and christocentric. Consequently, it will only have value for those people who feel positively involved in Christianity and the image of the crucified Christ. Eiesland assumes that the Disabled God is affirmative to women and marginalized groups, but I wonder if in theological women's studies such a strong christocentric image

---

[30] Ibid., 101.

would not be alienating rather than transformative, at least in a western and white context. There is still another, perhaps even more fundamental aspect that I am concerned about. Eiesland turns the resurrected Jesus into a Disabled God who, with his violations and pain, embodies the divine and/or God. In this way being disabled becomes a symbol of the divine. Earlier in her book she does something similar through her use of Nancy Mairs's concept of the body in trouble as a metaphor of life. In this respect, Eiesland does not stand alone. Female theologians with disabilities, and female theologians who think about physical discomfort and ageing, seem to take a remarkably easy step in representing the (disabled) body through an abstract image that symbolizes life, the Church, or the women's movement. Earlier, Elly Elshout represented the disabled body as a metaphor of the religious community or the church of women. She offers it as a counter image to the biblical image in Paul's letters, in which the healthy body is the Church's image. And maybe the images of Annelies van Heijst's organic body and Valerie Saiving's ageing body function or act as counter images to the idealized, healthy and young body and are in keeping with this approach.

They are dedicated efforts to positively consider and revaluate the different or not-healthy body. But because the body is first elevated to metaphor or symbol and subsequently connected to transcendence, the body and its concrete experience are made abstract. In my view, experience is weakened in this way, and the specific knowledge it produces, that is to say, its critical function, is lost. The body remains an object. The physical is transcended, as it were, and not taken seriously in itself, or left alone. It seems as if the transcendence of the disabled body - or even polishing it with divinity - must legitimize a positive valuation of differently abled people. This reminds me of Susan Sontag's criticism in her book, *Illness as Metaphor*.[31] She argues that over and over again we are inclined to assign meanings to the sick body in order to be able to give it sense or meaning. The sick are burdened with this because, together with their illness, they become the symbol of something else, whether negative (for example, of evil or lack of willpower) or positive (for example, of vulnerability and a fighting spirit).

In a later publication, Eiesland makes a first attempt at a more exciting image. Starting from the experience of life in an unpredictable body, she introduces the concept of 'risk'. 'Being at risk is the fundamental experience of human life', and from there we must arrive at a risky ethical and theological imagination.[32] This appears to be an initial move to a less abstract vision of the body.

---

[31] S. Sontag, *Illness as Metaphor* (New York: Farrar, Straus and Giroux, 1988).

[32] N. Eiesland, "Things not seen: women with disabilities, oppression and practical theology", in D. M. Ackermann & R. Bons-Storm (eds.), *Liberating Faith Practices. Feminist Practical Theology, in Context* (Louvain: Peeters 1998), 123-127.

Passionate equanimity

A different image of transcendence in relation to differently abled women emerges in the book *Grace and Grit* by Ken Wilber and Treya Killam Wilber. While Eiesland connects the image of God to an abstract disability, in Ken and Treya Wilber's story the experiences of the body are not abandoned, rather, they are the vehicle and image of what I call 'experiences of transcendence'. The authors themselves speak of a 'contemplative or meditative spirituality'.

The book is about the growth of insight and love during the life and death of Treya, who dies of cancer at the age of 40. Shortly after their marriage Killam Wilber discovers she has breast cancer. It is the beginning of a five year struggle for her life during which she undergoes the entire gamut of possible treatments from both regular and alternative medicine. She soon discovers how charged and riddled with meanings cancer is. Everyone immediately has an opinion abtou her cancer; she doesn't follow a healthy lifestyle, she has suppressed her feelings, carries to much anger around, has worked too hard, and so on. Slowly she develops her own way of dealing with these opinions of others and learns to distinguish between the disease and the illness. The disease is the cancer, which demands enough of her as it is. The illness is the whole of images and judgements culture assigns to cancer and which only make the disease more difficult to bear. Therefore the resistance alluded to in the title of the book is twofold: on the one hand, it is the fight for health and, on the other, it is the fight against all those false images and judgements. At the same time her conviction grows that her life is good and worthwhile in itself.

In her process, meditation and spiritual exercise occupy an increasingly important place. The book shows, using fragments from Killam Wilber's journal, how she tries to use her illness and the changes occuring in her body, for inner growth and transformation. Killam Wilber learns that if she is to be able to give a place to her body and everything that happens inside, she must not ignore, transcend or turn off her body. On the contrary, the road she chooses is one of full experience and acceptance of her body. By descending into the body, through means of meditation, among other things, Killam Wilber learns to arrive in the here and now. Experiences of pleasure, pain, desire and fear all take place in the body. Killam Wilber practices more and more to observe these experiences and to accept and love whatever there is, be it pain or pleasure. At the same time, she sees that she is not ruled by these experiences, and that she can distance herself from them. Everything in the body changes continuously, thus not only indicating our limitedness and vulnerability, but also our strength and our ability to change and transcend boundaries. To Killam Wilber, this process taking place with regard to her body is illustrative of the spiritual attitude towards life. She moves between surrendering to what is and a fight for life, between being and doing.

The body is also important in the experience of spirituality because spirituality directly relates to the senses. Killam Wilber's eyes, ears, mouth and hands make her

experience something that is amazing to her, and through which she transcends and frees the limited 'I'. Seeing mountains and flowers, playing with dogs, a caress, all these experiences need touch. Furthermore, the body brings Killam Wilber's spirituality down to earth, to the reality of everyday existence. She describes beautifully how taking pills, administering morning enemas, and her physical exercises intertwine with her spiritual exercises and meditations. In other words, spirituality 'persists', straight through the drivel and whining of her body. The point of departure of her spirituality is the ordinary, not sitting on a mountain somewhere far away. On the one hand, this is difficult for Killam Wilber. On the other hand, she experiences it as an enrichment as it brings her closer to the world around her.
As she puts it in a speech,

> 'Learning to make friends with cancer, learning to make friends with the possibility of an early and perhaps painful death, has taught me a great deal about making friends with myself, as I am, and a great deal about making friends with life, as it is. I know now that there are a lot of things I can't change. I can't force life to make sense or be fair. This growing acceptance of life as it is, with all the sorrow, the pain, the suffering, and the tragedy, has brought me a kind of peace. I find that I feel ever more connected with all beings who suffer, in a really genuine way. I find a more open sense of compassion,' (...) Because I can no longer ignore death, I pay more attention to life.'[33]

All in all, Killam Wilber seems to conceive of the body as a kind of training ground for themes that play a central role in spirituality. Moving between surrender and fighting spirit. Equanimously accepting everything of (physical) existence and learning to love it. Having faith. The experience of being closely interwoven with our body next to the experience of not coinciding with it. Being involved with others. This experience of one's own body also means distancing oneself from cultural or religious codes of the female body, which may lead to an autonomous physical experience. She eventually summarizes this acquired attitude to life with the beautiful term 'passionate equanimity'.

Transcendence into the body
By way of Eiesland's more prophetic line, focused on naming and resisting injustice, and Killam Wilber's more mystical, primarily inward-looking line, we arrive at a special interpretation of transcendence. Transcendence is never separate

---

[33] T. K. Wilber, *Grace and Grit. Spirituality and Healing in the Life and Death of Treya Killam Wilber* (Boston: Shambala Publications, 1991), 360.

from everyday physical existence. It is only obtainable in and through the body. The pivotal point is the body acting as a crossroads of experiences, of pain, pleasure, repugnance, enjoyment, strength and vulnerability, which are either existing side-by-side or intermixed. A simple assessment of experiences such as good or bad, pain or pleasure, is therefore not tenable. Life itself is a 'mixed blessing'. In the work of various authors we see a new physical image emerging which reviews old myths about the natural body by positing the 'extension' of the body with technical means that are essential to existence: wheelchair, crutch, and artificial hip.

This brings us back to the question of whether this image of transcendence of women with disabilities is different from the stories of other women, does it really find itself on an island? I want to recall Korte's explorations of body as a hermeneutic category, referring to the experiences of ambivalence and paradox. I think that differently abled women can identify themselves with this but nevertheless make an essential next move too. They do not remain caught in a feeling of paradox but rather transcend it. The theologian Adele B. McCollum says very concisely, 'Overcoming barriers and locating freedom in physical restrictions constitute my idea of transcendence. In other words, it is the body which provides the location and possibility for transcendence.'[34] Physical challenges provide concrete experiences of living without certainty. After all, those who live in an unconventional body often have no idea where they stand from day to day. This creates a challenge to traditional ideas of transcendence which rely on non-material a priori/a posteriori beginnings and endings.

It is not only, as Korte indicates, that we experience ambivalence because we do not coincide with our body. When we fully descend into this physical experience, live through it to the core since we have no choice, we are faced with a fundamental experience of life, that is to say, an experience of insecurity, of risk, of no truth and nothing given or absolute. And straight through it women describe in varying ways the feeling that, if everything in fact is in jeopardy all the time, life is as good as it gets. Thus openness is being created to the experience that this life is *my* life, that it is a life in relationship with others, with 'God' or a deepest 'Self', that it is unique and meaningful, even if it may often be one big chaos. Room for resistance against social misconceptions and for compassion. It is a life from the strength that the vulnerability of existence is apparently capable of generating. As McCollum says in a Zen-like manner, 'A broken teacup is not a flawed example of a teacup but a perfect example of a broken teacup.'[35] Physical existence can train us in an almost mystical attitude of letting go while at the same time experiencing to the fullest. The differently abled women that write about this appear to be much less inhibited than other female theologians in calling their (physical) experiences religious or transcendent. It was also pleasant to find much humour in the work of many authors.

---

[34] Elshout, "Roundtable Discussion", 127.
[35] McCollum, "Roundtable Discussion", 129.

A wonderful example was given by Nancy Mairs. A friend asked her: 'Do you ever say to yourself, why me, Lord?' 'No, I don't', I told him, 'because whenever I try, the only response I can think of is: why not? If I could make a cosmic deal, who would I put in my place? What in my life would I give up in exchange for sound limbs and a thrilling rush of energy? No one. Nothing. I might as well do the job myself. Now that I am getting the hang of it.'[36]

---

[36] N. Mairs, *Plaintext* (Tucson: University of Arizona, 1986), 20.

"I Have Only One Body!"

The Conflict between 'Love' and Integrity in Everyday Practices

Riet Bons-Storm

> "How do we juggle the demands of parenting, relationships, vocation, and activism without doing violence to ourselves?" [1]

> "As women, we need to examine the ways in which our world can be truly different. I am speaking here of the necessity for reassessing the quality of all the aspects of our lives and of our work, and of how we move toward and through them." [2]

Introduction

A good friend of mine always answers when I ask her how she is: "Exhausted." She is no exception. I recognize the experience in my own life. One of the women I interviewed in my research concerning the life and faith development of elderly women [3] says:

> All my life I wanted to respond to challenges and test myself: Can I do what I want to do? I wanted to give shape to my feeling of responsibility in caring for others... I worked in the church, in women's work, my mother required a lot of attention, and I had three children. I got divorced, which cut deeply into my being. After many years I became very tired, living out of that enormous feeling of being responsible. I was so tired that even peace and justice did not mean anything to me anymore. I went on because I did not know how to get out of all of it. I couldn't even be angry anymore. My doctor said: 'Mrs. A., I wonder, are you actually still living?'.

All around us in Western/Northern society we see women who experience themselves as very busy. Many of them have a job outside the home. As members of the labour-force, as professional women they still are relatively new in the game of the labour-

---

[1] The Canadian feminist psychologist G. Kropf Nafziger in a catalogue, announcing her course 'Feminist Mothering' in *The Leaven Center. A catalogue of Fall/Winter 2000 programs* (Lansing, Mi.: The Leaven Center, 2000).
[2] A. Lorde, *Sister Outsider* (Freedom, CA: The Crossing Press, 1984), 55.
[3] R. Bons-Storm, *Kracht en Kruis. Pastoraat met oudere vrouwen* (Kampen: Kok, 2000).

market. Doing their job they have to prove that they can do it well.[4] Many women feel that partners, spouses, friends, children, even grandchildren or elderly parents appeal for their attention and their supportMany good causes also ask for their solidarity and support. Women often feel responsible and so are apt to become confused by clashing responsibilities. Appointments crowd their days and make their nights short and full of worries. A growing inner conviction that they are overextended clashes with their feelings of responsibility for others and their desire to relax and have time for themselves. The body can only be in one place at a time. Moving requires a choice: to whom or to what will the embodied person go? Protesting overextensed bodes cause emotional and physical stress. It is necessary to explore the factors that possibly induce this feeling of the bodily and spiritual exhaustion of many women, feminists included, in everyday life, as well as ways to reduce it.

Everyday life stands for a mixture of various meanings. On the one hand, it means the common, repetitive happenings concerning the most basic needs of human beings, body, mind and soul. It stands for the thousand little and big things to be done to keep a family, a workplace, one's own life going. On the other hand, everyday life means the place for our 'practices'. Rebecca Chopp states "..a practice is a pattern of meaning and action, that is both culturally constructed and individually activated...Practices involve full embodied actors."[5] This means that everyday life contains an endless amount of choices: what do we do with our time and why? Responding involves the actual movement of our bodies.

One could expect that decades of emancipation and feminist thinking would make a difference. They do, but not much; not enough to shape all women, socialized in patriarchal culture, into people that feel reasonably free to use their time and energy according to their own choices. To translate feminist thinking into feminist practices proves to be difficult. Feminist practices would be practices defined by women themselves in their everyday lives, not defined by the definitions and expectations of others. Rosi Braidotti quotes Betty Friedan saying,

> Although the women's movement has changed the lives of us all and was more important than we could dream, and although our daughters take their individuality for granted, they, and we, experience that it is not so easy to live

---

[4] The fragility of the situation of working mothers becomes clear in debates about their 'rights' or 'privileges'. The politically earned right to have maternity leave easily becomes a 'privilege' coveted by workers who do not have children.

[5] R. S. Chopp, *Saving Work. Feminist Practices of Theological Education* (Louisville, Ky: Westminster John Knox, 1995), 15-16.

(with or without husband and children), only on the basis of that first feminist action-program.[6]

A feminist practical-theological perspective

Practical theology focuses on the actual lives, faith and doubts of people in their contexts. While dogmatic and systematic theologies construct theories about what there is to believe, or - as some theologians would state, about what people have to believe - a practical theologian is concerned about what people actually can believe in a particular situation. Practical theology is about the *Wirkungsgeschichte* of doctrines and of liturgical and pastoral decisions in the lives of people. As such, the practical theologian starts her reflection at the crossroads of two hermeneutical circles: on the one hand, the quest for meanings of biblical and Christian traditions, on the other hand, the quest for meanings of a particular situation in history and their impact on people in their various conditions and contexts. The meeting point of these circles gives food for thought about practices, practices of a faithful, grace-ful life.[7] How can women, reared in a Christian tradition, especially in a Western middle class situation, live a 'grace-full' life given the turmoil of the various expectations in our culture about how a woman has to spend her time?

To be, to exist, means to have a certain, finite amount of time. Every day has only 24 hours, every life has only a limited number of years. To be is to divide that allotted finite time into embodied practices. Who and/or what dictates the use of our time?

Restraining scripts

As a practical theologian, I meet women, suffering from exhaustion on the crossroads of several traditions. 'Tradition' means here what is given to them in their socialization and more or less, conscious upbringing and growing up in a particular place and point in history. On the one hand, they live by a Christian tradition, as they received it during their socialization and as they themselves constructed it on the basis - and often within the parameters - of this socialization. On the other hand, they live by what they were given to understand and came to understand about themselves through dominant culture in their society, for instance the meanings of being a woman and middle class in the 21st century in Western Europe. At the meeting point of these 'traditions' they construct their actual practices. One could say that these 'traditions' come to them as 'scripts'[8], directions for a role. A role can be seen as a certain

---

[6] R. Braidotti, *Beelden van de Leegte. Vrouwen in de hedendaagse filosofie* (Kampen: Kok Agora, 1991), 181; B. Friedan, *De Tweede Fase* (Utrecht/Antwerpen: Veen, 1982), 24-25.

[7] R. Bons-Storm, *Kritisch bezig zijn met pastoraat* ('s-Gravenhage: Boekencentrum, 1991).

[8] What I call 'a script' is similar to what Joan Laird calls 'a social-cultural narrative'. According to Laird the social-cultural narrative is an implicit or explicit narrative that orders society, defines the roles for men and women in their various positions, and mirrors the avowed values of society. J. Laird in M. McGoldrick a.o.(eds.), *Women and Families. A Framework for Family Therapy* (New York: Norton, 1991), 430.

configuration of practices, on the one hand prescribed by a script, on the other hand interpreted by an actor. A script can be understood as 'experienced ideology', it is ideology translated in directives for actual behaviour. A script, handed over in socialization, does not have absolute power. The context in which a person is socialized, the voices of other scripts confirming or contradicting each other, and also the strength of a person's character in resisting scripts, make the directions of scripts more or less compulsive for a person.

Although a library of sophisticated feminist thinking exists about the ideological hazards for women in Western society, I contend that feminist thinking does not take seriously enough the power of directives of the dominant scripts for women's daily practices. A script still has controlling power if consciously or unconsciously a person still fears the punishment (disapproval, rejection) - of significant others. Therefore it is necessary to look again at these scripts, see where they reinforce each other, and look for the possibilities for other directives for women's daily practices.

As I shall concentrate on women reared in a Christian tradition, I may assume that the script of dominant Christian theologies influenced them. I call a theology 'dominant' if it has shaped the doctrines and is considered important in the theological education in a mainline church. Dominant theologies with their emphasis on God the Almighty Father are deeply influenced by patriarchal ideology. Women recieve this script from early childhood. As children, it gave them a general frame of reference, a certain place in a universe governed by God.

In Western middleclass society, Freudian ideas have become common knowledge. However, not the whole of sophisticated psychoanalytic theories, but rather general ideas about human development as girls or boys, these ideas implicity or explicitly influenced women while growing up, providing meaning and interpretations of themselves. Freud's ideas of the dominance of the Male pervaded psychoanalysis in its many ramifications.

In modern society, economy, in the sense of efforts to obstain personal wealth, is a leading factor in shaping lives of people. As a product of modernity-induced emancipation women and men are considered alike: a woman is supposed to be able to achieve wealth and status like a man.

Growing up in Western middleclass society, nearly all women have heard to a certain extent, the counterscript of feminism. This script gives new meanings to women and to their relationships with others.

In this article I shall explore how Western middleclass women can give meaning to themselves and their relationships while living in the confusion of these scripts, scripts that can be considered as the main scripts of their lives.

The virtue of pain: the theological script

In this script, the most important directive is: "Love God and thy neighbour." The "as thyself" that follows usally does not get the same emphasis as the command to love the neighbour (St. Matthew, 22, vs 39). Although this commandment is given to men and women alike, women more than men are the ones who are supposed to embody this love through attention and care for others, more than men. According to Christian tradition one's love for God becomes manifest in one's love for others. This theological thought makes the commandment to love one's neighbour even more powerful. Moreover, 'the neighbour' is usually understood as 'any other person', as everybody except the self. The command to love one's enemies (St. Matthew 5, vs 44; St. Luke 6, vs 27 and 35) makes certain that absolutely nobody is excluded.

For many women reared in the Christian tradition, this command to love all others translates. translates itself in feeling responsible for the well being of others, with bodily care being an important aspect. Looking after the needs of others, being with them, made women the guardians of nearness and intimacy. However, the implicit command to love all others in distress and to care for them can lead to exhaustion.

Being exhausted is like pain, it is the absence of wellbeing. Christian tradition associates pain with virtue. Thus pain has the possibility to redeem, just as Jesus' pain ultimately redeemed human sin. Without pain, no redemption. The experience of being exhausted sometimes takes on a certain sadomasochistic hue in watch some women cling to their overextended and crowded lives.

I think it is plausible that the role directions of the patriarchal theological script become even more demanding in times of stress and disaster, because of the promptings of an 'apocalyptic script'. This script interprets history as an increasing number of disasters that reveal the true nature of this world, ending with a final catastrophe in which Truth will be revealed and a new era of Divine Truth shall reign.[9] I contend that the promptings of an apocalyptic script, the idea of difficult times, culminating in an apocalypse, give women a stimulus to endure an exhausting life, hoping that the good works of love and dedication will eventually come to light and show their effects. Then, but not now, tears will be wiped of, sickness and death will disappear. For the time being, 'good' women have to work for a better world, in which human beings are given attention and care.

Christian women are made to believe that it is God who sends them towards others in order to 'love' others.

---

[9] Catherine Keller understands the apocalyptic script as "a text, disseminated through a complex history of interpretations of that text, and acted out in multifarious secular and subliminal practices." C. Keller, *Apocalypse Now and Then. A feminist Guide to the End of the World* (Boston: Beacon Press, 1996), 11.

The 'natural' bond of love: Freudian psychologies

Western women are influenced by the script, hidden in mainstream psychologies, that are more or less psychoanalytic. Childcare and education are riddled with vague psychoanalytic notions. The representations of women in those psychologies provide role directions for women, all the more so when they are presented as descriptions of women's actual and inevitable nature. Woman is depicted as determined by her body to pine for emotional relationships through bodily nearness to her father, and later (if all goes well) to her husband and eventually to her son. This inclination to emotionladen nearness constitutes her identity as woman. Where men value separationprimary separation being from the mother, women are inclined to value intimacy. In *Das Unbehagen der Kultur* (1929) Freud assumes a primary hostility between people, aggression evidenced by in every human relationship. The only non-aggressive relationship can be found between the mother and the male child. Thus only a mother is able and willing, by nature, to constitute an intimate, non-aggressive bond, 'love', towards another person. In a cold world, governed by separation, woman as the 'natural mother' has to bring warmth and affection. But the Father condemns woman's loving nearness as a suffocating intimacy. She is always at fault. She loves too much or not enough.

Mainstream psychologies send women into this world frustrated by ambivalence. On the one hand, they have to fulfil the role of dutiful daughter, lover, wife and mother, shaping basic trust through intimacy they bodily provide. They have to be with others as female bodies. They are assumed to pine for Motherhood. They are assumed to be 'emotional' by nature and by that very fact not 'logical' enough to make important decisions themselves. On the other hand, they have to beware of intimacy that is too intimate and against the will of the Ultimate Norm, represented implicitly, although explicity in Lacanian psychology as 'Father'. Punishment by the 'Father' consists of being condemned as unnatural, neurotic, or mad. If a child causes trouble, wets its bed, is aggressive or too withdrawn, general opinion assumes that the mother was either too absent or too close to the child. The result is that many women choose, although 'choose' may be the wrong word, as the 'choice' is mainly unconscious, to remain on the 'safe side' and be true to their assumed nature, being there for others, caring for others, but taking heed of the law of the Father as best they can.[10]

The laws of success: the market script

In the Market script the highest aim to pursue is the growth of profit. Everything, human beings included, can be a commodity on the market. The value of a human being depends on her/his aptness to be a merchant, a commodity, or a deliverer of

---

[10] R. Bons-Storm, "Cherchéz la Mere", *Fier*, July/August 1998.

products for the market. The big goal is to earn more money, and money means power. One's gifts and possibilities are named 'personality capital'.

In this script, relationships are governed by competition. Even if teamwork is required, this nearly always has a temporary character and is directed to 'a product'. Assertiveness and aggression are inevitable, as is individualism. Every person is responsible to use his/her assets in the best possible way to reach personal success, not necessarily considering the wellbeing of others. In the market-script this is not called 'egoism' and is not deemed immoral. Aiming at one's own success, gain or profit seems simply necessary, the only option in a world full of competition. Traditional relationships and their demands on time and emotional and bodily availability loose their impact. Society shows a stuctured separateness.

In Western middleclass society women hear the message that everyone who tries can earn, if not wealth, then at least a comfortable living, earning enough money to provide for herself. If she does not do this, she is either lazy or stupid. Unlike in previous decades, nowadays girls have many of the same opportunities in schools as boys. Girls enter life after school expecting to be able to compete on the market. However, Western society is still deeply influenced by patriarchal ideas, coming to people through, for instance, theological and psychological scripts. Girls/women hear the message: your ultimate role is motherhood, either to your biological children or to people who are unable to care for themselves.

Thought through to its ultimate consequences, the market-model of modernity implies a society without families and children. Everyone must be independent, free for the demands of the market in order to guarantee his/her economic existence. The market subject is ultimately a single individual, 'unhindered' by relationship, marriage and family. Correspondingly, the ultimate market society is a childless society - unless the children grow up with mobile, single fathers and mothers."[11]

The Market script condemns and ignores the weak and vulnerable, but creates many overworked people, their bodies damaged by stress. In the Market script the body is either a commodity or a means to earn more money/power. The body itself and its limitations are seldom taken seriously. Exhaustion and escape towards short but intense amusements damage the body and make people unwell. Unwell people need care, and, as patriarchy undergirds the Market, women are given the role to go to the weak, unhappy, and sick, and care for them.

Just like in the psychological script, in the Market script Western middleclass women end up in an ambivalent position. On the one hand, being a woman during a time in which they are exhausted to be 'equal to men', they have to adhere to the roledirections of the professional, money making person, to be financially independent and unencumbered by the demands of relationships with partner or children. On the

---

[11] U. Beck, *Risk Society. Towards a New Modernity* (London: Sage, 1992), 116 and S. Irwin in E. B. Silva and C. Smart (eds.), *The New Family?* (London: Sage, 1999), 37.

other hand, while the ideology of patriarchy still reigns strongly, they feel the tug of the demands of being with others in care and intimacy, in the circle of their family and friends, with colleagues and unspecified 'neighbours'.

Meeting counter-scripts

I described three scripts that make it difficult for women to take time for themselves. As the scripts are influenced by patriarchal ideas about 'Woman', it is very hard for a woman of flesh and blood to choose a role, and with it a division of her time that fits her possibilities as she experiences and understands them herself. The dominant scripts in Western society direct women to ignore the signals of the body. A strong motivation to do one's best and to transcend the limits of the body are generally appreciated. Sometimes, of course, when a special occasion asks for it, one has to ignore the aches and pains and do something, stay active, care for somebody or something that one feels committed to. So we need an ethical reasoning to look for directions to discern when one has to ignore the signals of exhaustion and when one has to take heed of them, not only to live a more 'grace-full' life ourselves, but also as a political act that destroys the power of scripts that ignore women's wellbeing and subject quality.

It can be assumed that a Western middleclass woman indeed has heard other scripts, counter-scripts, scripts that, for example, can be called 'feminist'. Susan Frank Parsons states, "A feminist is one who takes seriously the practical course of women's lives, the analysis and critique of these conditions of life, and the ways in which women's lives may become more fulfilling."[12] In this cold world full of separation, competition, and aggression there are feminist authors who try to compose alternative scripts for women that act as counter-scripts to the patriarchal scripts described above. The values that determine these new roles are connection, attention, care, and friendship.

With the help of the newly composed scripts, emancipated, feminist women are supposed to be able to construct their own roles, choosing their own practices. However, many situations in women's everyday lives require choices that 'rush ahead of consciousness'.[13] Whatever their choices, they will feel a certain ambivalence, feeling themselves caught in the middle of different roles. Many become tired and confused. Patriarchal ideology may in some instances be fraying at the edges, allowing some elitewomen to play their own chosen roles, assuming, of course, that they speak in their Master's voice, patriarchy's power is still very strong.

---

[12] S. Frank Parsons, *Feminism and Christian Ethics* (Cambridge: Cambridge University Press, 1996), 8.

[13] See S. Arber and J. Ginn, "The mirage of gender equality. Occupational success in the labour market and within marriage", *British Journal of Sociology* 46 (1995) 1, 21-43.

Do the attempts to give women new scripts - honouring women's subject quality - help women to limit the time given to others and to feel less guilty when giving time to themselves?

Feminist connection ethics and their hazards

Mary Grey, representing a prominent strand in feminist theology, contends that relationality is the 'raw stuff' of the world.[14] She states explicitly,

> The metaphor of connectedness has become central to the women's movement and for Christian feminist spirituality... We speak now of 'mutuality-in-relation', of overcoming relationships based on hierarchical dominance/submission patterns with relationships of reciprocity, interdependence and mutuality... 'Compassionate empathy' is seen to inspire a new way of being in the world, even if the dangers of falling into a new essentialism and universalism must be avoided."[15]

Beverly Wildung Harrison's *Making the Connections*[16], Catherine Keller's *From a Broken Web*[17], and the entire oeuvre of I. Carter Heyward emphasize an ethics of connection in mutuality.

A hazard of feminist connection ethics is that its values are similar to the values ascribed to Woman/women in patriarchal ideology. Although feminist authors like Mary Grey do not contend that 'connection' and 'care' originate in the physical characteristics of the female, the link to women's socialization as people who are physically able to become mothers is very strong. In 1960's, when an ethics of care, based on the nature of women was strong in dominant psychologies, Frances Gillespy Wickes pointed to the negative side of an ethics of care with an ontological basis. She wanted to dispel the 'participation mystique'. In a male-dominated society and culture women do not easily discern where their own interests are different from the interest of other people. Only if one understands the difference between identification and interdependence can one see how interdependence can enhance women's selfhood. Interdependence can imply knowing where one's boundaries are, the boundaries of one's body and its integrity, of one's realm of interest, and of one's possibilities. Interdependence is always also related to the boundaries, the integrity, and the interests of others.[18] Feminist theological ethics do not usually take heed of the

---

[14] M. Grey, *Redeeming the Dream* (London: SPCK, 1989), 31.
[15] M. Grey, *The Wisdom of Fools? Seeking Revelation for Today* (London: SPCK, 1992), 59.
[16] B. Wildung Harrison, *Making the Connections. Essays in Feminist Social Ethics* (Boston: Beacon Press, 1985).
[17] C. Keller, *From a Broken Web. Separation, Sexism, and Self* (Boston: Beacon Press, 1986).
[18] F. Gillespy Wickes, *The Inner World of Choice* (New York: Harper & Row, 1963).

boundaries of people. Carter Heyward's book *When Boundaries Betray us* [19] makes it clear how difficult it is to get boundaries for feminists who have relationship, mutuality, and friendship as their highest values. It is not unthinkable that feminist connectionethics have the possibility to affirm the directions of patriarchal scripts that declare women to be the guardians of humanity's physical and emotional wellbeing. 'The good life' leading to justice is understood as connecting with others, even to become friends in unlikely coalitions.[20]

One could suppose that 'mutuality' keeps 'caring relationality' in balance. However, mutuality means that I and the other are involved. If a (feminist) woman values equality, she will not force the other to take heed of her, to enter a relationship of any kind with her. Although she can take the initiative, she is dependent on the other regarding the onset and the course of the relationship. Is it the one or the other, the unlikely other, perhaps even the enemy, that sets the pace, the contents, the quality, the intensity and the boundaries of the relationship? Theoretically it is possible to state, "They do it together." In everyday life this becomes much more difficult. I suspect that many women who are deeply influenced by the various scripts that give her the responsibility for the wellbeing of any other and declare that by nature, by God's will or for the sake of justice she is equipped to give attention, care and love, forbidden to put her own interests to the forefront, is inclined to let herself be directed by the needs of the other.

This is bound to happen even more easily if the call for solidarity is involved. In many cases where solidarity is requested, the needs of the other direct the relationship more than the needs of the one. Mutuality-in-solidarity need not always be a well-balanced relationship, but nevertheless we need direction to help a person discern where, for the sake of her own survival as a healthy person, she can make an end to any relationship, even to any call to solidarity.

The body at the crossroads

It is clear that a script for women's roles, based on the values of connection, care, and solidarity, has its hazards because it originated as a counter-script in a patriarchal culture. Modernity reached Western women, sometimes clothed in feminist dress, and taught them to trust their own counsel and make their own choices, while the public mind or consciousness, internally ingrained into women, expected them to follow the directions of patriarchal scripts. The frame of reference of many women is still coloured by patriarchal scripts, as described above. The pain these scripts often create

---

[19] C. Heyward, *When Boundaries Betray Us. Beyond Illusions of What is Ethical in Therapy and Life* (San Fransisco: Harper San Fransisco, 1993).
[20] In the feminist ethics of Mary Hunt 'friendship' and 'unlikely coalitions' are leading concepts. M. Hunt, *Fierce Tenderness* (New York: Crossroad, 1991).

is felt in women's bodies in their everyday lives. Can the body play a role as a setter of boundaries, mentioned by Frances Gillespy Wickes?

Sometimes 'the body' appears in the discourse of connection, relationality, mutuality and solidarity. Mary Grey speaks of "the embodiment of mutuality."[21] Grey's argument emphasizes the importance of embodied practices, making theological assumptions concrete in daily life. However, she speaks rather idealistically about the possibilities to do so. Catherine Keller suggests that to give body to chosen theological-ethical ideas can be very difficult. She puts the theological idea of the community as the Body of Christ: members of one another... grieving with each other's griefs, delighting in each other's joys (1 Cor. 12, vs 26), over and against the daily reality. Keller writes, "But contrary to the Master narrative, it is we - in solitude and solidarity - who must resume the bodies which Babylon violates and numbs."[22] Women have to embody their ideas in the midst of Babylon, where bodies, including a woman's own particular body, suffer and become numb, no longer feeling pain, but incapable of resilience.

Concentration on the actual body, the 'common body' and its particularities and limitations, may help us to escape from the exhaustion and confusion. Kathy Davis states, "While there has been a wealth of feminist scholarship devoted to exploring the particularities of embodiment, recent feminist theory on the body has displayed a marked ambivalence towards the material body and a tendency to privilege the body as a metaphor... Bodies are not simply abstractions, however, but are embedded in the immediacies of everyday, lived experiences."[23] I am aware of the risk of essentialism, taking the body as an acultural substance. We know the body as locus of interaction of materiality, discourse and value. Still, it cannot be denied that "the body is simultaneously part of nature and part of culture... we can argue that nature constitutes a limit on human agency, since, as part of a natural environment, we are subject to growth and decay... This limiting boundary is of course both uncertain and flexible, since the limits on human 'natural' capacity constantly change."[24] Knowing that the body is a cultural construct, we nevertheless also have to take the common body, the physicality shared with others, seriously. The common, actual body keeps us in just one place, where we as body-selves exist. "The body is the self's ownmost place... Not that the self lives in the body as in a house, but that *as body the self takes place*" We are "spatially incarnated."[25] Thinking through Keller's thought, the obvious can no longer be ignored. In order to have a caring relationship with somebody we are dependent on the possibility of bridging geographical and emotional distances, which in itself takes time and energy. Every physical body has a certain amount of energy

---

[21] M C. Grey, *Beyond the Dark Night* (London: Cassell, 1997), 11.
[22] C. Keller, *Apocalypse Now and Then* (Boston: Beacon Press, 1996), 221.
[23] K. Davis, *Feminist Perspectives on the Body* (London: SAGE Publications, 1997), 15.
[24] B. S. Turner, *The Body & Society*, Second Edition, (London: Sage Publications, 1996), 197.
[25] Keller, *Apocalypse*, 176.

that marks its operational limits. This amount of energy, typical for a certain body, changes in time, but has its limits, which only can be transgressed at the price of aches and pains, sleeping problems, exhaustion. In a culture, where the Market script prescribes playing the roles of strong and energetic people, and where a strong mind and will are supposed to overcome weaknesses of the body, people are inclined to mirror themselves on the strongest persons and transgress their limits. The body however lets us know when we are exhausted. The body 'speaks' to us as the place of interaction between the physical material of the body, the demands of the various scripts, and the embodied, gendered subject.

Together with Elaine Scarry[26], Paula Cooey takes sentience, the possibility to perceive and feel, as an important feature of the common body. She speaks of the physical body, as far as it can be understood as an idependent of the constructed body, as "creaturely or sentient existence."[27] Sentience is the basis for emotions, which are culturally constructed. Sentience is also the basis of pain. Cooey contends that the "voicing of pain, directly experienced or witnessed, lies at the heart of making, most especially making value."[28] Physical pain and discomfort, the more when they are shared, stimulate the imagination and can be the starting points of change. They can thus be an incentive to take another value, the avoidance of pain but not by numbness, as the leading principle for choices that direct practices.

The starting point of a way to avoid and heal exhaustion by overextension could be to go against the common current and take the pain of exhaustion seriously, acknowledging it in others, listening to their stories, and being courageous enough to tell others about the signals of stress and exhaustion before the body collapses. However, the leading scripts in our society, the Market-script included, will punish people who take their own body and their common bodies seriously. The price to pay could be a negative personal assessment and the loss of a planned and desired career. The scripts of traditional theologies and psychologies ascribe to a woman the urge and the duty to sacrifice herself for the benefit of others. If a woman lets her physical exhaustion put boundaries on her service to others, 'the public' will call her egoistic, self-seeking. In many cases she even will call herself these names, because of the deeply socialized layers of her personality. Her fatigue will be combined with guilty feelings to make her feel worse.

In order to go against the current, one needs companions. One needs to know when one can take one's pains seriously and when, for a good cause, one has to try and transcend one's limits. To try and find an answer to this question, one has to strengthen, I suppose, one's subject-quality and to find companions for exploring

---

[26] E. Scarry, *The Body in Pain* (New York: Oxford University Press, 1985).
[27] P. M. Cooey, *Religious Imagination & the Body* (New York: Oxford University Press, 1994), 16.
[28] Ibid., 60.

dialogue.

The courage to be different together

To acknowledge one's subject-quality means several things among them to know one's own possibilities and impossibilities, one's gifts and limitations. It also means taking physical stress symptoms seriously, while nevertheles discerving one's potential and spedivic comtribution to society. The counter-script of feminism allows women to understand themselves as persons who are more than 'emotional', and who have ideas about the good and the just. One of the elderly women in my research[29] says, "Probably, as human beings, we have some specific task ... I do not know exactly what the task is, but there is a mission for me. We are all different...." This 90year-old woman makes explicit in a way what many women feel, that 'we have a task, corresponding to our gifts and limitations. We know not exactly what this task is, but we try to find out. My task is probably different from the task of others.' It is not necessary to understand this 'task' as some heroic mission, rather, it is sufficient to know- (and knowledge is necessary in my view) to try and look for something that can be done, as it corresponds with our special gifts. This task is limited, it can never be something universal, like making the world just and peaceful. A double awareness is needed: awareness of the world in which we live and to know what is to be done, and awareness of our gifts and limitations.

More often than not, it is others who know us, rather than we ourselves, who see what our possibilities and limitations are. We need dialogue with others to find out what there is to be done, what we can do, and how to do it. In order to explore this further, Margaret Walker's book *Moral Understanding. A Feminist Study in Ethics*[30] can assist us. She states, "Morality allows and requires people to understand themselves as bearers of particular identities and actors in various relationships. People learn to understand each other this way and to express their understandings through *practices of responsibility* in which they assign, accept, or deflect responsibilities for different things" (italics by Walker).[31] It is important to note that sometimes one has to deflect responsibilities. Practices of responsibility and accountability are the outcome of ongoing dialogue between people who are aware of who and what they are. People who are (doubly) aware form communities where stories are shared about experiences of pain and joy and the moral choices involved. Morality is, in this way, placed by Walker in and not above the actual social and personal lives of people.

---

[29] Bons-Storm, *Kracht en Kruis*, 48.
[30] M. Walker, *Moral Understanding. A Feminist Study in Ethics* (New York/London: Routledge, 1998).
[31] Ibid., 9.

A helpful concept of Walker's is "charting responsibilities"[32]: that is, to draft "geographies of responsibility"[33] in order to know who can be held accountable for what. Without such a chart one cannot know the limits of one's responsibilities. In a community of dialogue, where stories are told and moral practices sought, it is possible to discern where responsibilities end, where they overlap, and what the areas are for which nobody feels responsible.

In communities of moral dialogue, values are explored. A common leading value can be sought, testing it in stories of experiences of pain, oppression, liberation and joy. Moral deliberation becomes more exciting and serious where communities touch each other, as they do in the intricate mesh of the social world. The common good becomes articulated for a wider range of people. Here, as already in the case of moral deliberations in a smaller group, integrity becomes important. "The idea of integrity covers two basic terms: wholeness and uprightness", as Van Es states. "In ideal circumstances integrity requires that one's words and deeds reflect a coherent and relatively stable set of values and principles to which one is authentically committed."[34] I would like to add the importance of integrity of the body. The body is too important an asset to be damaged. In addition to integrity of body and personality, mutual respect and mutual trust are of great significance.

I find these communities in some 'Women and faith' groups and in groups of feminist theological scholars like the OPP[35] (which mutually promotes the working for one's PhD and scholarly achievements in general), where the members try to discover the particularity of the gifts and possibilities of one another and also try to inspire one another to achieve high scholarship without jealousy or heavy demands on each other.

Theological directions for grace filled practices
A religious faith gives directions for practices. Many women, however, feel the burden of an inheritance of a patriarchal theology that instructs them how to believe and how to act. Thus there is much theological thinking done trying to escape the strict directions of patriarchal ideology and script. The starting point of such thinking is the acknowledgement that one does not need to be a respected, university educated male theologian in order to make one's thoughts about the Divine and Its relation to humanity explicit and communicable. In other words, one has to acknowledge one's subject-quality, even when the dominant scripts dictate that a life of obedience and

---

[32] Ibid., 77.
[33] Ibid., 79.
[34] R. van Es, *Negotiating Ethics. On ethics in negotiation and negotiation in ethics* (Delft: Eburon, 1996), 251.
[35] OPP = Onderlinge Promotie Promoting, i.e. Dissertation Support Group.

servitude is appropriate. Having acknowledged one's subject-quality, one then finds the courage to choose what in a tradition can be accepted as grace-filled, and what is not. This does not deny that one can at the same time choose to believe that one is chosen, with love and acceptance, by the Divine.

Trying to understand the Christian tradition in which I was reared, I choose the idea of a Divine, standing for justice, for the well being of the little ones, the widow and orphan, the marginalized and weak. This roughly shapes my commitments. Integrity means being true to these commitments. I have to struggle to believe that the Divine, Who made me in Her/His image, values my body and its integrity as much as S/He values my soul. In a community of dialogue I shall have to discover exactly which field of care as well as resistance to injustice will be my avowed assignment, appropriate to my gifts, and my limitations, not the least of which are the limitations of my physical energy, in the specific situation of my various commitments to partner, children, grandchildren, friends and colleagues.

The Divine, standing for justice and the well being of everybody, is, according to various religious traditions, including the Christian tradition, truly gracious: S/He accepts people as they are, not on account of their endeavours and accomplishments. The longing for such a Divine and the acceptance that S/He can be supposed to be there for us can help to strengthen our acceptance of limitations, while opening our eyes to our gifts and possibilities. Susan Frank Parsons states that hope for reconstruction of a morality that comes not from 'above', measuring all people by the same standards, is grounded in a looser definition of who and what is human, in recognizing diversity and a dynamic view of the Divine. She writes of "…a God who surprises and upsets by moving in and around the margins of society to stir up forms of resistance."[36] If we confirm others in their quest for integrity, forsaking the quest for perfection and of being all things to all people, rather letting ourselves be accepted with grace, there will be time for laughter, song and dance with others, and even, sometimes, private solitude.

Can women relax?

In my quest for grace filled living I have tried to understand why women, although their conditions may vary, can to a certain extent feel themselves driven into states of physical exhaustion. I argued that a multiple awareness of existing scripts, of their own gifts and limitations, and taking the body seriously, is necessary. I also argued that a community of dialogue, where integrity of body and soul is affirmed, may help a woman to understand when she has to say 'yes' and when 'no' to any request or task, even to a call to solidarity.

But why do the voices of patriarchal scripts still have the power to influence our practices, openly or surreptitiously, leading many women to exhaustion and feelings

---

[36] Frank Parsons, *Feminism and Christian Ethics*, 92.

of ambivalence and guilt?

The answer may lie in our current situatetnessof Late Modernism on the brink of Postmodernism. The highest value in Modernism is order, an authority that comes into being by obedience to the highest authority, which goes by many names including God, Nature, F/father, Money-Multiplied. Disobedience to the highest Ordering Principle takes the form of 'disturbing the peace', which is understood as being inconvenient and requiring such punishments as ridiculize, marginalisation, rejection, or worse. "So we love order, even order that is based on illusion and self-deception. When we say we want peace, we mean we want order... The order of our lives is built on our potential for violence" states the ethicist Hauerwas.[37] The fear of disorder, of being different from a norm set by a figure of authority, can still be found in many people. We fear the violence that erupts when we are disobedient, but we also oppress persons who, according to us, disturb the peace by being different from us, deviating from what we think is the right way to act. Sometimes this right way is the way of an Authority outside, sometimes this right way is the way we ourselves have chosen to live within the parameters of the will of Authority.

Staying with the example of communities of 'Women and faith' groups or the OPP, it is clear that these communities exist on the margins of the dominant structures of church and university. Members of 'Women and faith' groups and the OPP have to raise their voices to be heard and to be acknowledged. The patriarchal system in church and university is too alive and kicking to listen to women who do not speak in their Master's voice. Thusthe aim of many a feminist scholar has to be to heed not only the quality of her publications, but also the quantity. She has to compete. And that demands much of her time.

Can women, can feminist women, relax? No. Not really. Not yet.

---

[37] S. Hauerwas, *The Peacable Kingdom* (Notre Dame, Ind.: University of Notre Dame Press, 1983), 144.

Reciprocity and Grace in the Golden Rule

Proverbial Wisdom as Source for Intercultural Dialogue and Moral Theology

Grietje Dresen

Introduction

After a school committee meeting some other mothers and I came to talk about our relationship to the Roman Catholic Church. This was not a regular topic at school committee meetings, but they knew it concerned me. One mother said she didn't see anything in Roman Catholic faith anymore. The last straw for her was the weekly prayer, right before Holy Communion, with the phrase: 'Lord, I am not worthy...' Her entire Catholic education, and her resistance to it, were condensed in this formula. Somewhat later we came to talk about the awful things that can happen to children these days, for example one mother worked as a nurse in a children's hospital. In that context the first mother said she believed that if some such terrible thing were to happen to one's own child, one would be given 'strength according to one's cross' (strength to bear, *kracht naar kruis*, in Dutch). The spontaneity and conviction with which she uttered that traditional religious saying touched me. That much she retained of her Catholic background, I thought. If one has a saying like that ready at hand and really feels that way, then surely that is a great treasure, whether one uses it in a religious sense or not.

This article is about the living ethos expressed in current moral or religious proverbs. As a moral theologian I find this - often barely conscious - ethos fascinating. The ethical systems within philosophy and theology often lack connection with a lived ethos, or worse, can even conceal and cripple that ethos through their complexity and mutual incompatibility. Of course moral theology and moral philosophy can not do without systematic reflection; but any reflection worth the name, whether historical, analytical or hermeneutical, that wishes to retain its relevance to human life and society, should begin and end with lived practice, in this case lived morality. Proverbs are of course not the only, and hardly the most vital place of encounter with morality. As I shall illustrate shortly, they constitute a preliminary phase of ethics: ethics of the common-or-garden variety. As such, however, current and morally relevant proverbs provide useful insight into the tried and tested 'emotional economy'[1] of cultures, an insight that can clarify both the ethos of a particular culture and the dialogue between cultures.

This article attempts such a clarification in various ways. In the first part, which is mainly historical, I shall explain why proverbs as expression of everyday wisdom fell out of favour intellectually, and were devalued to the level of popular or pedagogical clichés. The conclusion of the first t - and that of the second part - reflects my firm conviction that in this day and age moral theology cannot afford to bypass (moral) pedagogy. For the sake of clarifying what can still inspire us and bind us together, people need to learn, preferably at the earliest possible age, to talk to one another about what is important to them and why. Therefore I conclude this first part with a proposal to use current proverbs as a point of departure for intercultural philosophical discussion at schools. In the second part of this article I reflect more substantially and hermeneutically on the way in which proverbial wisdom could be relevant for theology, i.e. on the way a seemingly sober proverb can disclose everyday experiences of care and gracious love. In this part I consider more closely a proverb that occurs in many cultures: the so-called Golden Rule. Using Paul Ricoeur's layered interpretation of the Golden Rule in *Oneself as Another*, I intend to show how complex - both intuitive and concrete, as well as reflectively refined and abstract - the insight in a seemingly simple proverb as the Golden Rule can be.

I Proverbs as expression of everyday ethos and source for intercultural dialogue

In the example given at the beginning of this article, the Dutch expression 'strength according to one's cross' was used quite incidentally. In this incidental fashion, we use more proverbs than we realise. Sayings of this kind constitute the deposit of everyday life experiences, but owe their transmission to their catchy, stylised form. They constitute a condensed and - in the case of living proverbs - recognisable expression of how, in a particular culture, emotions are cultivated, forms of behaviour appreciated and existential experiences located within the framework of a particular understanding of humane nature, the world, and God.[2] Insofar as proverbs constitute the deposit of a culture's reflection on human action and the *condition humaine*, including conceptions of good and evil, happiness and unhappiness, they may be regarded as a non-academic form of ethics. Proverbs have their roots in daily life, but they also have a trans-cultural aspect. Many expressions

---

[1] The term derives from the sociological oeuvre of Norbert Elias.
[2] Cf. P. Berger & T. Luckman, *The Social Construction of Reality* (New York: Anchor Books, 1966), 87; C. Geertz, *The Interpretation of Cultures* (New York: Basic Books, 1973), and Id., "Common Sense as a Cultural System", *Antioch Review* 35 (1975), 5-26.

recur in comparable formulations in various languages and cultures.[3]

To the insight that proverbs interpret the ethos of a people (and in the case of illiterate peoples even constitute a unique source) we owe the most extensive and well-financed projects for collecting and documenting proverbs. Missionaries and missions were eager to employ local proverbs as a point of contact for the communication of the Christian message.[4] In this article my interest is not missionary (at least not in the traditional sense), but ethical. I am interested both in living proverbs as an expression of everyday ethos, and in the question of which attitude to life and what values might be transmitted through proverbs. Even more relevant for moral theology is the intercultural aspect of proverbs, that is to say, the question whether and how widely prevalent proverbs could serve as a starting point for intercultural dialogue, and as a pointer in the quest for 'universally' shared moral assumptions.

Before submitting these questions to closer scrutiny, I must consider a phenomenon that, in literate Europe, influences the reception and appreciation of proverbs. Due to the proliferation of worldviews (as a result of social differentiation and the prevalence and accessibility of *written* texts) and a typically Western, enlightened preference for individuality and originality, the use of proverbs has lost much of its power. That is not to say that proverbs have become totally extinct in pluriform and 'developed' countries, but the repertoire has been drastically depleted[5], and the use of proverbs is easily experienced as old-fashioned or preachy.

Enlightened disdain for proverbs as cliché

Let me illustrate the above statement by means of the example with which I began. The woman who so naturally used the expression *strength according to one's cross* undoubtedly picked it up from her Catholic upbringing. I doubt whether young people know the expression. And to many people it will sound like a moral cliché - to the elderly because of its association with the traditional glorification of suffering, to young people because of their unfamiliarity with glorified suffering. The same applies to other Christian sayings involving the concept of the cross, like *'Ieder huisje heeft zijn kruisje* ('each house has its cross') However, it cannot be said that the insight verbalised through this proverb could have no meaning in our

---

[3] Cf. H. V. Cordry, *The Multicultural Dictionary of Proverbs* (Jefferson N.C. & London: McFarland & Comp., 1997); *The Prentice Hall Encyclopedia of World Proverbs*, ed. W. Mieder, (Englewood Cliffs, N.J: Prentice Hall, 1986).
[4] There are already more than 1000 written collections of African proverbs. Since 1994, the African Proverbs Project has coordinated the research. This project stimulates research and the publication of books, bibliographies, and electronic information (on CD-Rom and the Internet). Information and links via http:/www.afriprov.org.
[5] See for details W. Mieder, "Paremiological Minimum and Cultural Literacy", in W. Mieder (ed.), *Wise Words. Essays on the Proverb* (New York & London: Garland, 1994), 297-316, passim.

time. Thus the French philosopher Luc Ferry begins his best-seller *L'homme-Dieu* with a story from the (no less popular) Tibetan Book of the Dead, in which a comparable insight is expressed.[6] Apparently, what can no longer be said through a traditional proverb can be said in the form of a Buddhist tale. Why did the verbalisation of insights through proverbs fall out of favour to the extent that it did?

Historical research into the distribution of proverbs in Europe has shown that, in *learned* circles, the use of proverbs has declined noticeably since the second half of the seventeenth century.[7] Before that time even great authors like Villon, Cervantes, Rabelais, Chaucer and Shakespeare, repeatedly refer to the moral wisdom of proverbs. Under the influence of Romanticism in particular, a change set in first and foremost among intellectuals and in literature. In Romanticism an explicit preference for individuality and originality emerged, especially as far as the expression of emotions and existential experiences was concerned. Proverbs were increasingly regarded as something rather coarse, belonging to the culture of the simple and unlearned. In intellectual circles there emerged, as a kind of substitute, great enthusiasm for aphorisms, pointed sayings by means of which many 18th and 19th century philosophers gave expression to their individual wit. These aphorisms were subsequently collected in many forms. Thus they in turn began to play the role of proverbs for the intellectual elite. During the second half of the nineteenth century another predilection - now for the utterances of famous men - was added to this.

In Europe, and certainly in the Netherlands, nearly everyone is by now literate. The literate masses are familiar with the aforementioned aphorisms and quotations in the form of the (now likewise disparaged) 'Success Diary' sayings. As a matter of fact, Success Diaries rarely include vernacular proverbs. Proverbs can be found on decorated tiles in pubs or toilets, in paremiological studies and dictionaries, and in schoolbooks and other lowly valued literary genres. More common are *variations* on proverbs that serve as headlines or attention grabbers in newspapers or other

---

[6] A young woman, obsessed with the wish that her deceased son should come to life again, approaches the Buddha for help. Compassionately, he says: 'There is but one remedy for the unhappiness oppressing you. Go to the city and get me a mustard seed from a home in which nobody has ever died...' The conclusion is predictable. There are more than enough mustard seeds, but in every house where the woman calls, she hears a story about the heartache that had struck the inhabitants. When she returns to the Buddha, she is already on the Way: She has learned that no one is spared suffering. It is that insight, and into the source of suffering (attachment to transient things), which softens the suffering and constitutes the beginning of enlightenment. L. Ferry, *De God-mens of de zin van het leven* (Amsterdam: Ambo, 1998), 9-10.

[7] I follow the extensive article of an authority in the field, James Obelkevich: "Proverbs and Social History", in Mieder (ed.), *Wise Words*, 211-252.

forms of public communication. Graffiti artists, for example, display a certain preference for such distorted proverbs.[8] Apparently, young people are still familiar with quite a few sayings, but they prefer to use them in new ways so that a shift of meaning occurs. Young people employ familiar but distorted proverbs in order to give their own texts more rhetorical force - more authority, legitimacy or intensity; the distortion of the old saying and its surprise effect is used to draw attention to one's very own, new text.[9] But from where, then, are these old sayings picked up, if they are out of favour in the 'higher' culture?

Mother tongue

The sporadic research[10] mapping the distribution of proverbs in Western societies suggests that, in an *urban* context, it is especially women who use them, for pedagogical purposes informally, in daily life, or formalised, within individual or group instruction.[11] The use of proverbs in these contexts seems to have a predominantly - but not exclusively - moral-pedagogical function.[12] By means of proverbs, values and codes of conduct are mnemonically inscribed, carved into the memory. In this context, proverbs often represent a 'motherly' wisdom.[13] In a pedagogical context there is less of the intellectual disdain for the moralistic quality of proverbs. After all, everyday interaction and education cannot but consist for a great part in the exchange of moral 'clichés'. Moreover, educators tend to revert unconsciously to the example of those who brought them up. Until recently, that example came especially from the mother, simply because she was the one who was most often present. Even if a mother rarely uses proverbs *explicitly*, children will still tend to remember from among the proverbs they are taught later - for instance in school - those that link up with what they already know: the ones that, as it were,

---

[8] J. Nierenberg, "Proverbs in Graffiti. Taunting Traditional Wisdom", in Mieder (ed.), *Wise Words*, 543-561.
[9] Thus is the conclusion of Nierenberg, "Proverbs in Graffiti", 558.
[10] Over the past two decades, the interest in proverbs as in popular culture has increased. Since 1984, the journal *Proverbium. Yearbook of International Proverb Scholarship* is published (completed with *Supplement Series* since 1998).
[11] Obelkevich, "Proverbs and Social History", 216. That this could be different in agrarian contexts is deduced especially from the fact that in agrarian cultures many (often warning) proverbs about women circulate. However, this undeniable phenomenon does not have to mean that in those contexts men use proverbs more regularly than do women. Probably women use gender-neutral agrarian proverbs at least as frequently. The fact that fewer proverbs have been passed down with an *anti-male* bias could point to the conclusion that women, for whatever reason, are less inclined to create such a paremiological corpus of warnings against men. Or (and this seems more likely) that such a corpus *did* exist, but has not been preserved in written form; for instance because particular sayings were not recognised as current ones, or because the collectors did not have access to female communities.
[12] Ibid., 217.
[13] Cf. the examples reported in Mieder, "Paremiological Minimum", 299 and 303-304.

'click' with their conscience.

Indeed, many proverbs only acquire meaning at a mature age, or in the context of some special occurrence,[14] because the proverbs themselves derive from comparable life situations. Thus a proverb like *'Een mens lijdt nog het meest door het lijden dat hij vreest'* ('People suffer most from the suffering they fear') can lie dormant in the sub-conscious for decades, and then suddenly, in a concrete situation, provide insight into one's own anxiety. Something similar probably applies to all 'religious' proverbs, that is to say, all those proverbs that testify to an active and positive trust in a power that transcends the human actor (like *I do my best, God does the rest*), and even more so at a time when trusting faith in God is no longer taken for granted.

Proverbs as point of departure in intercultural philosophical education

However, these last comments are not meant to suggest that it would therefore be senseless to learn religious or 'sapiential' proverbs at an early age. On the contrary, the 'empty' experiential knowledge, formulated by others and inscribed in memory in the form of a proverb, cannot only be *filled with meaning* at a later stage, but can also *itself* offer meaning in the course of that process, just as other, at first uncomprehended ritual forms and actions do. At those moments when fitting words are sought for extreme experiences, experiences like grief, jealousy or intense longing, the meaning thus offered by a proverb can provide something to hold on to, a meaning that might otherwise have been discovered only after much searching. Therefore I hope that the teaching of proverbs will not be sacrificed because of the relentless march of modernisation in schooling. I even see new and interesting possibilities for the use of proverbs in education; not so much in language education, but in religious or philosophical ('view of life') education, especially at schools attended by students of diverse cultural and religious backgrounds.

It could be interesting, precisely in such culturally mixed schools, to let children from the senior primary or junior secondary levels discuss well known moral and sapiential proverbs from their cultures. They could, for instance, first interview their parents (or grandparents) as a homework assignment. Probably they would have to bring along basic lists of proverbs from their cultural background, compiled with the help of immigrant language teachers.[15] The provision of lists does of course have a directing influence, but that need not be an objection, since the aim is not representative paremiological research, but to create an opportunity for (inter-generational

---

[14] Cf. T. B. Rogers, "Psychological Approaches to Proverbs. A Treatise on the Import of Context" in Mieder (ed.), *Wise Words*, 159-181.

[15] Research has shown that people are incapable of collecting many proverbs 'dry', i.e. outside of their contexts. However, this does not reveal much about the number of proverbs they actively know or would possibly use in situations calling for them. Cf. Mieder, "Paremiological Minimum", 300.

and inter-cultural) dialogue on the meaning of proverbs that children understand and appreciate. In the 'interviews', they could search for the proverbs that their parents still know, might possibly use, and, most of all, do appreciate, i.e. recognise as expressions of their (often barely conscious) view of life. Reports of the interviews and the children's reactions on them could then be the occasion for further discussion in class: Do the children grasp what a particular proverb intends to convey? Can they explicate it in their own words? Can they relate it to concrete situations? Is the idea contained in it recognisable to them or not, and if not, why not? Which proverbs recur, albeit sometimes in variations, in different cultures?[16]

In the second part of the present article I focus on the actual content of a proverb that would certainly be included in any such inventory: the Golden Rule. In the Netherlands the Golden Rule attained the status of a colloquial proverb only in the negative formulation: *Do not do unto others what you do not wish done to you.* This negatively formulated version is sometimes called the *Silver* Rule.[17] But whether golden or silver, the adjective makes clear that we are dealing with a rule that is regarded as extremely valuable. In *The Declaration of a Global Ethic*, compiled by Hans Küng, it is even claimed that this rule - whether in positive or negative form - 'should be the irrevocable, unconditional norm for all areas of life, for families and communities, for races, nations and religions'.[18] What makes the Golden Rule so golden?

II The Golden Rule. Everyday ethos of mutuality, pre-ethical experience of gift

The Golden Rule in the negatively formulated version already appears in the sayings of Confucius who lived in the sixth century before Christ.[19] A variation on the rule can be found in the Tao Te Ching, from the fourth century before Christ, in which the even more ancient Taoist tradition found written expression.[20] Here I limit

---

[16] Cf. Rogers, "Psychological Approaches", 170-171, for an example of such a discussion of proverbs in an educational (but not explicitly multi-cultural) setting; referring to J. Pasamanick, "Talk *Does* Cook Rice. Proverb Abstraction Through Social Interaction", *International Journal of the Sociology of Language*, 44 (1983), 5-25.
[17] E.g by J. Topel in "The Tarnished Golden Rule (Luke 6:31): The Inescapable Radicalness of Christian Ethics", *Theological Studies* 59 (1998) 3, 475-485.
[18] *The Declaration of a Global Ethic. Studies in Interreligious Dialogue* 3 (1993) 2, 101-113, 106. The Declaration was submitted to the Parliament of the World's Religions in Chicago, 1993.
[19] Cf. J. Wattles, *The Golden Rule* (New York & Oxford: Oxford University Press, 1996), ch. 2. Around the same time, the underlying idea of the Rule was formulated - and passed on through oral transmission - in the Hindu and Buddhist traditions; the central concept of *Dharma* or ordinance of life rests upon a comparable notion. In Vedic writings this thought appears even earlier.
[20] Topel, "The Tarnished Golden Rule", 482.

myself, due to my poor knowledge of other traditions, to (recent) Western interpretations of the rule. So this is no round-table discussion. My exploration is meant as an example of hermeneutical reflection on proverbs and, as such, as a contribution to a contextual moral theology that is both culturally and interculturally sophisticated, i.e., capable both of incorporating everyday concerns and of putting them into comparative perspective.

An ethos of reciprocity

In *Oneself as Another* Paul Ricoeur implicitly corrects the principle of mutuality based on exchange (or even retaliation) that Albrecht Dihle[21] pointed to as origin of the Rule.[22] Ricoeur refers to the Golden Rule in his theory of the moral self. In that theory Ricoeur distinguishes between three phases or levels of moral reasoning. The first and central phase is a substantial exploration of the good, in which three dimensions can in turn be distinguished: the question concerning the good life, the question of the good life *with and for others*, and the question of the good life *in community* (the classical *bonum commune*) expressed in institutional terms. These first, 'substantial' dimensions of the good must be tested and purified with reference to (far more procedurally elaborated and institutionally expressed) criteria of the right and the just. This critically tested determination of the good and the right must then, in the third phase, be applied in a concrete situation with the help of practical wisdom or *phronèsis*. The Golden Rule plays an important role especially in the second dimension of the first phase, that is to say, in determining what the good life with and for others is. Ricoeur quotes both the negatively formulated rule of the Jewish tradition[23], and the positive formulation in Lk. 6:31 and Mt. 7:12, and assumes continuity between these two. He localises this continuity in the formal structure of reciprocity in both formulas. In both cases he perceives a resemblance between the principle of the Golden (or Silver) Rule, and the formulation of the commandment to love one's neighbour in Lev. 19:18 and Mt. 22:39 (and parallels).

However, in *Oneself as Another*, where he seeks to develop an autonomous philosophical discourse, he gives special attention to the background of the aforementioned formal structure of reciprocity, and concentrates less on the possible

---

[21] A. Dihle, *Die Goldene Regel. Eine Einführung in die Geschichte der antiken und frühchristlichen Vulgärethik* (Göttingen: VandenHoeck & Ruprecht, 1962), 110.

[22] P. Ricoeur, *Oneself as Another* (Chicago & London: Univ. of Chicago Press, 1992). Transl. of *Soi-même comme un autre* (Paris: Editions du Seuil, 1990). Cf. Ricoeur's explicit discussion of Dihle's classical thesis in P. Ricoeur, *Liebe und Gerechtigkeit/Amour et Justice* (Tübingen: Mohr, 1990), 50-51. Ricoeur and Dihle refer to the same traditions, namely the classical-philosophical, Jewish and Christian traditions of the Rule.

[23] Thus in the book Tobit (4:15) and in the influential Jewish Bible exegetes Hillel en Philo, both from the first century.

theological significance of the resemblance with the commandment of love. The latter he interprets, not as a peculiarity of *content*, but in terms of a meta-ethical 'economy of the gift', in which 'love is connected to the "naming of God".'[24] Such an economy of the gift transcends the (autonomous) determination of the good and the right, but without disqualifying it. It is precisely this strict distinction between an autonomous *dynamic of reciprocity* and a biblically inspired *dynamic of abundance* that has elicited criticism, as we shall see.

Ricoeur places the mutuality or symmetry that the Golden Rule assumes against the background of a more original dissymmetry: the (grammatically retained) dissymmetry between the one who causes to undergo, and the one who undergoes. This dissymmetry includes, among other things, the dissymmetry of violence, of destructive ways of acting towards others. The negative formulation of the Golden Rule calls for an end to this violence in a way reminiscent of the negative commandments in the Law ('Thou shalt not...'), but formulated on the basis of an everyday context of kinship and care. Thus the Golden Rule - 'one of those received notions that the philosopher does not have to invent, but to clarify and justify'[25] - fulfils a transitional function between a concrete and substantial ethos of care and concern (*solicitude*), and a more abstract formulation of norms in the form of a law.[26] As such the Golden Rule also mediates between a more substantial, eudaemonistic tradition in ethics, and the more formalistic tradition since Kant. In order to illustrate this mediating function, Ricoeur elaborates on Kant's critique of the insufficiently formal character of the Golden Rule and on Kant's transformation of the Rule into his categorical imperatives. The Kantian imperatives[27] call for reciprocity in relation to a supposed, generalised other. The call to reciprocity in the Golden Rule, however, originated as the answer to a concrete dissymmetry - an answer emanating from a material ethos of care and concern. In the rule of 'abstract' reciprocity, we discern the echo of that solicitude that is familiar with the concrete differences and the mutual dependence between people, but also with the potential of violence between them.[28]

Ricoeur is, first of all, interested in the Golden Rule as expression of an 'ethical sense', a 'benevolent spontaneity'[29] connected with self-respect, which precisely in

---

[24] Ricoeur, *Oneself as Another*, 25.
[25] Ibid., 219.
[26] See esp. the paragraph VIII,2, *Solicitude and the Norm*, 218 ff.
[27] 'Act in such a way that the maxim of your will can always hold at the same time as a principle of general legislation' and 'Act in such a way that you always treat humanity, whether in your own person or in the person of another, never simply as a means, but always at the same time as an end'.
[28] Ricoeur, *Oneself as Another*, 226-227. Cf. S. Benhabib, "The Generalized and the Concrete Other. The Kohlberg - Gilligan Controversy and Moral Theory" in Id., *Situating the Self. Gender, Community and Postmodernism in Contemporary Ethics* (Cambridge, Polity, 1992), 148-177.
[29] Ricoeur, *Oneself as Another*, 190.

an asymmetrical situation can recognise the claim of the other. This ethical sense originates in the elementary, sensory-affective sensitivity to the neediness and suffering of the other that Ricoeur calls solicitude.[30] The Golden Rule is an expression of this caring ethos, but formulated at a more abstract or even (in the Kantian imperatives) universalised level, which must in turn be institutionally expressed, and prudently concretised. Thus ultimately the Golden Rule plays a role in all three phases that Ricoeur distinguishes and relates to one another in *Oneself as Another*. It is precisely the way in which the Rule translates a caring ethos into an abstract maxim, still to be institutionally expressed,[31] which subsequently, in its concretisation and application, calls for 'ethical sense' and practical wisdom[32], that constitutes the 'transitional structure' of the Golden Rule in Ricoeur's interpretation.

A hermeneutical interpretation can thus transform the convictions contained in common proverbs such as the Golden Rule into 'considered convictions', testifying to what Rawls calls 'reflective equilibrium'.[33]

Reciprocity and gift

As indicated earlier, Ricoeur's aim in *Oneself as Another* is to develop an autonomous philosophical discourse. He does elaborate on the Golden Rule as it was formulated in Judaism and Christianity, but he seeks to interpret the ethos of care and the structure of reciprocity within it, in a non-religious explanatory model. That is why he does not specify the relation of the Rule to the Jewish and Christian commandment of love, as indeed he does in other texts.[34] So particularly in his famous address *Liebe und Gerechtigkeit*, Ricoeur explicitly considers biblical *agapè* as taking its meaning from a religious 'economy of the gift', and situates it over against the ethos of reciprocity he displays within the Golden Rule. In *Oneself as Another*, however, Ricoeur explicitly abstains from a theological discourse of love, because it is supposed not to add anything *material* to the argumentation.[35]

In a fascinating article on Ricoeur's interpretation of the Golden Rule, the Christoph Theobald questions Ricoeur's banishing of theology in *Oneself as Another*. Theobald's questions intrigued me, although I do appreciate Ricoeur's

---

[30] Ibid., 191-192.
[31] See e.g. ibid., 226-227.
[32] Thus - referring to the Golden Rule - ibid., 265-266.
[33] Ibid., 288 (cf. 226-227).
[34] Cf. P. Ricoeur, *Liebe und Gerechtigkeit/Amour et Justice*; and Id., "The Golden Rule. Exegetical and Theological Perplexities", *New Testament Studies* 36 (1990), 393-397. In *Oneself as Another* the commandment of love is only referred to incidentally (cf. 194; 219; 351) as an invitation from the everyday ethical domain that has not yet been turned into law, and that - thus formulated - never *can* become law.
[35] Ricoeur, *Oneself as Another* 25.

striving for an autonomous philosophical argumentation, which is indispensable in an 'hermeneutical age of reason'[36]. However, like Theobald, I find it important to attempt to find *within* such an argumentation, the words for a 'poetics of *agapè*', for the significance of the *experience* of love as a gift.

Theobald points out that in those texts where Ricoeur does explicitly consider the relation between the Golden Rule (as structure of mutuality) and the commandment of love (as 'economy of the gift'), he assumes a certain discontinuity between the two. Theobald wonders, however, whether there is not perhaps a more fundamental continuity hidden behind the apparent discontinuity, insofar as such an economy of the gift might be operative precisely in the ethos of care from which the Golden Rule derives.[37] Theobald sees this dimension operative especially where Ricoeur speaks of 'the paradox of the exchange at the very place of the irreplaceable': in the willingness to take the perspective of the other without denying his or her uniqueness.[38] If the different levels on which the Golden Rule is functioning are interrelated (as Ricoeur shows), then why should philosophy and theology be so strictly separated according to a supposed boundary between autonomous philosophy and a discourse of the gift, as Theobald asks. Why should philosophy, for the sake of its autonomy, exclude a 'poetics of *agapè*'?[39] Are 'the gestures and words of the latter not also accessible for philosophy *as* philosophy'?[40]

Like Ricoeur, Theobald does reserve the *faithful naming* of the experience of gift (i.e. grace) for theology; a theology that for the sake of a God who transcends all singular convictions, cannot evade philosophical argumentation. He is convinced though that a philosophical recognition of the *function* of the experience of gift within a phenomenology of conscience need not lead to crypto-theology within philosophy, but, on the contrary, could contribute to a better understanding of the ethical dimension of solicitude or (more precisely) of the capacity and willingness to step into another's shoes - the dimension in which, according to Ricoeur, the Golden Rule originates.[41] A philosophy that does not hesitate to name and specify

---

[36] Ibid..
[37] C. Theobald, "La règle d'or chez Paul Ricoeur. Une interrogation théologique", in J. Greisch (ed.), *Paul Ricoeur. L'herméneutique à l'école de la phénoménologie* (Paris: Beauchesne, 1995), 139-158, 151. The article has been illuminating in my reading of Ricoeur.
[38] Ricoeur, *Oneself as Another*, 193-194 [cf. footnote 32 there].
[39] The paraphrase 'poetics of *agapè*' refers to Ricoeurs definition and location of a discourse of *agapè* in *Liebe und Gerechtigkeit*, 12-13 ff and 20-21 ff; cf. *Oneself as Another*, 25.
[40] Theobald, "La règle d'or",151.
[41] Ibid., 156. A comparable argument, concerning the significance of the capacity for empathy and listening as a *condition* for the functioning of more abstract, procedural theories of justice (e.g. the ideal of non-dominating communication in Habermas' theory of communicative action, and the [willingness to accept the] veil of ignorance in Rawls' *Theory of Justice*) is formulated by ethicists of care as a complement to these more procedurally functioning theories of justice. Cf. Benhabib, *Situating the Self*, and I.M. Young, "Asymmetrical Reciprocity. On Moral Respect,

this dimension could make an important contribution to the political, agnostic debate that seeks the roots for tolerance and sense of community *within* the various religions or 'views of life', as Theobald argues. Not in order to find, in these views of life, an ultimate foundation for that society as a rightful institution - for such foundation should not be sought in God, but in the institutions themselves, in the way justice is organised in them –, but rather to leave philosophical room for a hidden God, i.e. to leave room for a way to think of God as 'hidden, but simultaneously showing in the moral spontaneity of human conscience'.[42]

The Golden Rule can be seen as the expression of such a moral spontaneity in which 'God' is hidden, precisely in the layered interpretation Ricoeur gives to it. Theobald himself tries, as a complement to Ricoeur's conscious option for philosophical agnosticism in *Oneself as Another*, to name theologically the place where we might find God in the context of the evangelical Golden Rule. In doing so, he focuses not so much on the specific meaning of the Golden Rule in Luke's Sermon on the Plain, but on the so-called fulfilment formula in Mt. 5:17, to which Matthew's version of the Golden Rule in 7:12 refers ('Always treat others as you would like them to treat you: that is the Law and the Prophets'). In Theobald's view, the fulfilment of Law and Prophets, of which Matthew speaks here, is connected with the theme of substitution, which plays such an important role in Matthew[43]

With reference to the context and interpretation of the Golden Rule, he speaks of a 'Messianic drama', and connects this drama both with the theme of substitution in Matthew and with the dynamic that Ricoeur calls the 'paradox of the exchange at the very place of the irreplaceable'. The evangelical Golden Rule is not new[44], according to Theobald, but perhaps the context of the fulfilment formula and of Luke's Sermon on the Plain provides it with a (literally and figuratively) superabundant dimension. 'This capacity or this power [to take the perspective of the other while recognising his or her uniqueness, *GD*] is the true place of fulfilment, of which the total and "overflowing" dimension discloses itself in the commandment of love and of love for one's enemies, which lie hidden in the Golden Rule.'[45] In the context of the Gospel, what is at stake here is not primarily an exhortation to do the nearly impossible, but an *appeal to what has already been*

Wonder and Enlarged Thought", in Id., *Intersecting Voices. Dilemmas of Gender, Political Philosophy, and Policy* (Princeton N.J.: Princeton University Press, 1997), 38-59.

[42] Theobald, "La règle d'or", 158; see also 157.

[43] Thus e.g. in Mt. 25:31-46, in the way Jesus calls for the performance of Jewish works of righteousness.

[44] In "The Tarnished Golden Rule", the Luke scholar J. Topel exerts himself (as did others before him) to show that the evangelical version of the Golden Rule is new, closely related to the evangelical love commandment.

[45] Theobald, "La règle d'or", 154.

given. Theobald writes, 'Matthew seems to lean on the memory - mediated by the Son of Man - of having been in the situation of the other oneself, and having benefited from the sympathy of another, in order to rouse that "always greater" capacity for putting oneself in the place of another.'[46]

What is at stake theologically, in this 'drama of messianic fulfilment', is not the rather tragic tension between the norm and the complexity of everyday life[47], nor the question of autonomy versus heteronomy in moral judgement, but the question of whether and how the experience of God's abundance - the experience of *grace* - can be translated into a kind of human action and judgement in which this abundance shows[48].

The experience of grace in everyday life

The evangelical, positively formulated Rule has not become a current proverb in Dutch. Does this mean that there is no room for the experience of grace in the everyday ethos of Dutch society? I think - or hope - nothing is further from the truth. Let me explain this by returning to the pedagogical context in which my interest in the Golden Rule originated[49]. After all, proverbs are kept alive especially in pedagogical contexts, as we have seen.

To the supposed universality of the Golden Rule, it is often objected that the Golden Rule is in fact not a common proverb in all cultures. The ethical ground-rule put forward in it implies - as Ricoeur explains - an individual process of conscience formation. To be sure, the procedure as such does imply a capacity for empathy or sympathy, as Ricoeur and Theobald have shown, but the train of thought itself has an individual point of departure, and is realised individually and internally. In cultures where actions are primarily determined and judged by community life and by concrete - if not external - codes of behaviour, a proverb such as the Golden Rule will therefore be less likely to emerge, or to take deep root.[50]

This correction is probably to the point as a criticism of the supposed universality of the Golden Rule. However, in so-called modern, complex societies, moral formation will always have to proceed via a process of individual conscience formation (even if it is granted that this process is influenced from the outside, by parents and social environment). In modern societies individuals are not borne by a single,

---

[46] Ibid..
[47] Ibid., 155 Theobald is referring here to Ricoeur's commentary on the theme of *Antigone*.
[48] Comparable to the way in which Mt. 5:17-48 calls for doing more than just the required righteousness; ibid., 155-156.
[49] The same applies for Wattle's interest in the Golden Rule, cf. *The Golden Rule*, Preface, vi.
[50] Thus my inquiry on the relevant discussion list [proverbs-list@afriprov.org] yielded no African versions of the Golden Rule as such [my thanks to J.G. Healey M.M. and D. Sybertz M.M.], and the CD-Rom *African Proverbs* does not have *Golden Rule* as a keyword. All this need not imply, however, that the proverb does not occur - probably it does in more concrete and figurative versions.

closed community, and thus have to face the demands of their own lives for themselves. Precisely in those societies where diverse cultures are united and must live, talk and deal with one another, fixed ethical codes that cannot be argumentatively illuminated by the speakers themselves may well have violent repercussions in social intercourse and ethical debate. As a mother of young, but rather streetwise children, living and attending school in a multicultural neighbourhood, I notice that if I explain to my children the rules I set for them, I often fall back upon simple variations of the Golden Rule, such as 'You wouldn't like that, would you?' or 'What if everyone were to do that?' (which is actually a simple variant of the first categorical imperative). Precisely because of this relying on the Golden Rule myself, I became interested in the currency of this and other proverbs in other cultures.

However, at the same time, I note that at such moments I do indeed revert to variants of the negatively formulated Rule. That is quite natural in the context, for the rules concern bans: don't tease other; don't make a mess in the park, etc. Calling on children to do well would be going a little bit far. Does that mean that the experience of grace and the dynamic of gift based upon it, which Theobald reveals to be the very heart of the evangelical Rule, cannot come to life in a pedagogical context? I think this is far from the truth. Not only can even young children truly feel concern or compassion for another (another child in pain, for instance)[51], but they want to express their concern or their love explicitly, and preferably as tangibly as possible, by giving something.

This is not the place for an extensive account of how children's capacity for empathy and love can be *smothered* if they grow up in constraining circumstances. However, a society that does not do the utmost to prevent or to ease such constraining circumstances loses any basis on which to speak of 'norms and values'. Theobald saw the capacity for empathy and love of neighbour in Matthew's 'lean on the memory - mediated by the Son of Man - of having been in the situation of the other oneself, and having benefited from the sympathy of another'.[52] I do not want to suggest that the experience of God's love is reserved for those to whom others have already done well. God's love must be greater and more just. But I do think we should read this dynamic of the exchange of places as an appeal not to hinder the conditions for developing the ability to love (to feel and to give love), and to do our best to let children's capacity for love grow to its full potential. In a pedagogical context, children live, first and most fundamentally, by the grace of another. If that other does not evoke the capacity for exchanging places through his or her love and care, the expressions of reciprocity and gift offered by Scripture and tradition -

---

[51] Cf. P. D. Hastings et al., "The Development of Concern for Others in Children with Behavior Problems", *Developmental Psychology* 36 (2000) 5, 531-546 (and references there).
[52] See note 46.

including proverbs like the Golden Rule - run the risk of remaining mere dead letters.

Respect is a gift - not a given

Both in developmental psychology[53] and in recent discussions on care ethics, great emphasis is laid on this intergenerational transmission of (the capacity for) vicarious emotional responding and perspective-taking skills. In the past these skills were mainly handed down in matrilineal transmission, from mothers to daughters. Empathy, concern for others, and the capacity for affective perspective taking were looked upon as female skills. In present and future times, however, it is and will be more and more important that both women and men develop these qualities. The complexity of our modern, multicultural societies demand of men and women capable of good listening, empathy and care taking, not only in private life, but also in the public domain and in institutional settings.

Like Ricoeur, the feminist political philosopher Iris Marion Young stresses the *asymmetrical* character of the reciprocity implied in most social contacts and in moral and political dilemmas. But unlike Ricoeur (whose work she does not quote), she does not see much in changing perspectives. In order to communicate and deal fairly with one another, we need not so much adopt the position of the other, she argues, for doing so we risk overlooking the particularity of the other. The concept of asymmetrical reciprocity she develops supposes the willingness to really *listen* to another, in order to let the other express her *own* point of view. This openness or 'wonder' (as Young calls it, following Luce Irigaray) she parallels with the practice of giving gifts. As in gift-giving, reciprocity in communication is asymmetrical, facilitated through our *willingness* to communicate, i.e. to listen and to speak out.[54]

I find this concept of asymmetrical reciprocity developed by Young - and already adopted by feminist theorists of care[55] - to be of value because of its stressing real openness towards the other. However, it does not cover the vital aspect of conscience formation by learning to see *oneself* as another, nor the social and institutional levels of moral reasoning that Ricoeur incorporates in his threefold model in *Oneself as Another*. In Ricoeur's model, too, the observation of asymmetry is crucial for each step to be made; but for him, the willingness to change perspectives as formulated in the Golden Rule also offers a clue for determining the righteousness of individual decisions and of social institutions. Above all, the differentiating interpretation of the Golden Rule by Ricoeur, completed by Theobald's motivational reading of the theme of substitution and vicarious responding in Matthew, also

---

[53] E.g. N. Eisenberg et al.,"The Relations of Parental Characteristics and Practices to Children's Vicarious Emotional Responding", *Child Development* 62 (1991), 1393-1408.

[54] Young, "Asymmetrical Reciprocity", 41 and 54 ff.

[55] E.g. S.L. Sevenhuijsen, *De plaats van de zorg. Over de relevantie van zorgethiek voor sociaal beleid* (Utrecht: Universiteit Utrecht, 2000), 14 ff.

accounts for the *origin* of the willingness to listen that Young supposes but does not go into. The willingness to listen *presupposes* respect for the other. And true respect for others is something we have to learn, by being respected ourselves. The experience of being valued ourselves teaches us the worth of being valued, and thus awakes the attitude of respect that is a vital condition for genuine openness towards others.

In a rich study on the principle of reciprocity, the Dutch law philosopher Dorien Pessers states that altruism and respect can be seen as a gift inviting other gifts, 'according the moral rule of do quia mihi datum est: I give to others because once there has been given to me. In the same way altruism can be understood as an ethic of gift giving'.[56] The experience of gift (or, in religious terms, of grace), gained in everyday situations of care and concern, underlies an interpretation of the Golden rule that does not mean to ignore the uniqueness of the other but, on the contrary, aims at true respect for the other as an other self.

Translation: Gerrit Brand

---

[56] D. Pessers, *Liefde, solidariteit en recht. Een interdisciplinair onderzoek naar het wederkerigheidsbeginsel* (Amsterdam: Faculteit der Rechtsgeleerdheid, 1999), 245.

Zu dritt, oder: Das Gebet als eine utopische Erinnerung

Susanne Hennecke

Christen und Heiden

Menschen gehen zu Gott in ihrer Not,
flehen um Hilfe, bitten um Glück und Brot,
um Errettung aus Krankheit, Schuld und Tod.
So tun sie alle, alle, Christen und Heiden

Menschen gehen zu Gott in Seiner Not,
finden ihn arm, geschmäht, ohne Obdach und Brot,
sehn ihn verschlungen von Sünde, Schwachheit und Tod.
Christen stehen bei Gott in seinem Leiden.

Gott geht zu allen Menschen in ihrer Not,
sättigt den Leib und die Seele mit Seinem Brot,
stirbt für Christen und Heiden den Kreuzestod,
und vergibt ihnen beiden.

Dietrich Bonhoeffer in Widerstand und Ergebung

Einleitung

Gehen Menschen heutzutage wirklich noch zu Gott in ihrer Not, geschweige denn zu Gott in Seiner Not? Und erwarten sie gar, daß Gott wirklich zu ihnen kommt in ihrer grenzenlosen, unendlichen Not? Ich wage es nicht, hierüber ein letztes Urteil zu fällen. Doch meine ich, daß die im Gebet vollzogene gläubige Hinwendung zu Gott in der heutigen, ihrem Selbstverständnis nach weitgehend säkularisierten Gesellschaft keinesfalls als alltägliche Selbstverständlichkeit betrachtet werden kann. Auch innerhalb der christlichen Gemeinde ist meiner Beobachtung zufolge die Hinwendung zu Gott, aber auch die Erwartung einer tatsächlichen Hinwendung Gottes zum Menschen problematisch geworden, insbesondere außerhalb des festen liturgischen Rahmens des Gottesdienstes. Gott spricht viele Menschen - Christen und anderswie Gläubige - nicht mehr an, Seine Stimme ist zumindest nicht mehr ohne Weiteres vernehmbar.

In meinem Beitrag gehe ich im folgenden jedenfalls davon aus, daß das Gebet für eine zunehmend größer werdende Gruppe von Menschen, die am Rande oder außerhalb der christlichen Gemeinde stehen, mit Schwierigkeiten verbunden ist. Zum einen ist vielen dieser Menschen das Gottesbild ein Problem geworden. Das im ersten Artikel des christlichen Glaubensbekenntnisses tradierte Bild von Gott als Vater, Allmächtiger und Schöpfer aller Dinge beispielsweise stößt bei vielen Gläubigen auf Unglauben. Diese Schwierigkeit ist inzwischen von vielen Theologen und insbesondere Theologinnen erkannt worden, sodaß zahlreiche neue Gottesbilder bzw. heilsamere Interpretationen der traditionellen Gottesbilder entwickelt werden konnten.[1] Zum anderen besteht meines Erachtens eine Schwierigkeit, die ich als wesentlich eingreifender betrachte als die des problematisch gewordenen Gottesbildes, nämlich die moderne oder auch postmoderne Erfahrung vom Tode Gottes oder jedenfalls die Möglichkeit göttlicher Abwesenheit oder göttlichen Schweigens.

Es stellt sich mir als christlich geprägter Theologin darum die Frage, ob das Gebet unter diesen Umständen überlebensfähig ist. Um diese Frage beantworten zu können, müssen die Theologie und das kirchliche Sprechen meiner Meinung nach - wollen sie sich in der aufgeklärten oder auch postmodernen säkularisierten Gesellschaft auf überzeugende und eigensinnige Weise präsentieren - beiden Schwierigkeiten ins Auge sehen. Denn ihre Nichtbeachtung läßt den zweifelnden, verzweifelten oder hoffnungsvoll suchenden Gläubigen die Wahl zwischen zwei verschiedenen, jedoch ebenso unbefriedigenden Auswegen, nämlich entweder die Fortsetzung des Gebets als ein rein äußerliches Ritual oder der Stillstand des Gebets. Doch besteht angesichts der Erfahrung des Verstummens oder gar des Todes Gottes die Möglichkeit einer dritten Reaktion. Es ist meine These, daß die hoffnungsvoll suchende Christin, der zweifelnde oder verzweifelte Christ sich unter Voraussetzung der Abwesenheit eines erlbidfahrbaren göttlichen Lebenszeilbidchens auf die Suche nach dem Sinn der Gebetshandlung als solcher begeben kann - in der bis auf weiteres unbegründeten Hoffnung, daß die ganze Wirklichkeit Gottes größer ist, als menschliches Vorstellungsvermögen zu fassen vermag und im Vertrauen darauf, daß die Gebetshandlung als solche einem Menschen und auch Gott gut tut.

In meinem Beitrag möchte ich darum näher untersuchen, welchen Sinn und welche Bedeutung die Gebetshandlung als solche haben könnte. Hiermit will gesagt sein, daß ich im folgenden meine Aufmerksamkeit in erster Linie weder auf das Problem des verstummenden oder schweigenden Gottes noch auf das Problem des zweifelnden, verzweifelten oder hoffnungsvoll suchenden Christen oder anderswie

---

[1] Vgl. etwa die Studien von H. Wiersinga, *Geloven bij daglicht. Verlies en toekomst van een traditie* (Baarn: Ten Have, 1992) und S. Mc Fague, *Modellen voor God. Nieuwe theologie in een bedreigde wereld* (Zoetermeer: De Horstink, 1990).

Gläubigen richten werde. Vielmehr werde ich mich bei meinen Forschungen hinsichtlich der Gebetspraxis darauf richten, was diesen Gott und diese Menschen noch miteinander verbinden könnte, d.h. auf die Frage nach der Möglichkeit oder der Unmöglichkeit des gott-menschlichen Verhältnisses als solchem. Mich interessiert also weniger eine bestimmte fromme menschliche Handlung, sondern vielmehr das Durchdenken der Struktur eines bestimmten Verhältnisses, welche mit der Praxis des Gebets gegeben ist.

Zur Ausführung meines Vorhabens orientiere ich mich zunächst an einem Text des Theologen Karl Barth. Sodann werde ich untersuchen, ob und inwiefern Barth den oben genannten Gebetsschwierigkeiten begegnet und inwiefern sein Ansatz noch einmal erweitert und fortgesetzt werden kann. Für dieses Unternehmen werde ich mich an dem Ansatz der französischen Philosophin und Psychoanalytikerin Luce Irigaray orientieren. Irigarays Ansatz ist meiner Meinung nach nämlich hilfreich, um dem Sinn der Gebetshandlung als solcher bzw. die Struktur des im Gebet zum Ausdruck gebrachten gott-menschlichen Verhältnisses noch einmal anders zu artikulieren.[2] Hiermit verbinde ich die Hoffnung, daß die noch suchenden, ewig zweifelnden oder bereits verzweifelten heutigen Christen oder anderswie Gläubigen sich noch einmal aufmachen, um sich in ihrer spezifisch modernen oder postmodernen Situation einen Weg hin zu Gott zu eröffnen.

Karl Barth und das Gebet

Zwar hat Barth keine eigenständige Lehre vom Gebet entwickelt,[3] doch kommt in seinem Oeuvre das Gebet des öfteren zur Sprache.[4] In meiner Darstellung seines Ansatzes werde ich mich im folgenden auf den unvollkommenen, als Teil des theologischen Ethik in Band IV.4 der Kirchlichen Dogmatik geplanten Paragraphen 76 beziehen, der die Überschrift "Die Kinder und ihr Vater" trägt.[5] Thema dieses Paragraphen ist die erste Intention des wohl bekanntesten Gebets der christlichen Gemeinde, "Vater unser im Himmel!". Anhand dieses Ausrufes systematisiert Barth

---

[2] Die Möglichkeit, um Frauen- und Genderstudienfragen mit differenztheoretischen Ansätzen zu kombinieren, sieht A.-M. Korte in der Entwicklung der sogenannten Verwandtschaftsstudien gegeben. Vgl. A.-M. Korte, "Gods geslacht. Gender en verwantschap in vrouwenstudies theologie", *Tijdschrift voor Theologie* 3 (2000), 251-275.

[3] O. Herlyn hat einen Versuch unternommen, die Gedanken Barths zum Gebet zusammenzutragen und zu systematisieren. Vgl. O. Herlyn, *Religion oder Gebet. Karl Barths Bedeutung für ein religionsloses Christentum* (Neukirchen-Vluyn: Neukirchner, 1979).

[4] Vgl. u.a. KD II.1, 574ff., KD III.3, 299ff, KD III.4, 95ff. KD IV.1, 643ff, KD IV.2., 797ff [EVZ], KD IV.4. (Das christliche Leben), §76-78, *Das Vaterunser*, 19-39 [TVZ].

[5] Vgl. K. Barth, "Das christliche Leben", in *Die Kirchliche Dogmatik IV/4*, Fragmente aus dem Nachlaß und Vorlesungen 1959-1961, hrg. von H.-A. Drewes und E. Jüngel (Zürich: TVZ, 1999³).

grundlegende Voraussetzungen des Gebets.[6]

Im einleitenden Paragraphen 74 seines ethischen Entwurfs verdeutlicht Barth zunächst, daß eine theologische Ethik keinesfalls als ein von der Dogmatik loszulösendes menschliches Handeln aufgefaßt werden darf. Vielmehr geht es bei der Frage nach dem "gutzuheißenden Handeln"[7] darum, sowohl die (göttliche) Antwort als auch die (menschliche) Frage im Wort Gottes zu finden. Es geht in einer theologischen Ethik also "um den in seiner Beziehung zum Menschen handelnden Gott und um den in seiner Beziehung zu Gott handelnden Menschen".[8] Hierbei grenzt Barth seine theologische Handlungstheorie[9] gegen zwei mögliche Mißverständnisse ab, nämlich einerseits gegen eine kasuistisch-gesetzliche Ethik, in der die Mittelbarkeit des Verkehrs zwischen Gott und Mensch behauptet wird, und zum anderen gegen eine kairos-Ethik, in der umgekehrt die Unmittelbarkeit der Begegnung zwischen Gott und Mensch im Mittelpunkt steht. Barths handlungstheoretischer Ansatz möchte so eine Alternative bieten und beide - die Unmittelbarkeit und die Mittelbarkeit des gott-menschlichen Austausches - zusammendenken.

Ein wesentliches Kennzeichen dieses Austausches ist Barth zufolge seine asymmetrische Struktur. Es handelt sich keinesfalls um einen Austausch zwischen zwei gleichen Partnern, sondern um die höchst ungleiche Beziehung zwischen einem gnädigen Geber (Gott) und einem gehorsamen Empfänger (Mensch). Gehorsamkeit ist hierbei nicht als sklavische Unterwürfigkeit aufzufassen, sondern ganz konkret als die von menschlichen Subjekten zu vollziehende aktive Anrufung Gottes, die Barth als "Grundsinn alles göttlichen Gebietens" und "Grundsinn alles menschlichen Gehorsams" betrachtet[10]. Beim Gebet handelt es sich mithin um eine Gesprächskonstellation, in der drei Faktoren eine Rolle spielen: Ein Absender (Gott der Vater), ein Empfänger (Mensch) und schließlich der Austausch oder Verkehr zwischen diesen ersten beiden Faktoren selbst (die Anrufung). Alle drei Faktoren werden im Paragraphen 76 eingehender besprochen, wobei der Schwerpunkt auf den dritten Faktor, die Anrufung selbst gelegt wird. Hierbei ist zu beachten, daß die Anrufung keine willkürliche menschliche Handlung, sondern ein konkreter, von Jesus selbst empfohlener Auftrag ist (vgl. Mt 6, 9 und Lk 11, 2).

---

[6] Barth behandelt in diesem unvollendet gebliebenen Entwurf lediglich die ersten drei Intentionen des Vaterunsers.
[7] Vgl. Barth, "Das christliche Leben", 1.
[8] Vgl. Barth, "Das christliche Leben", 2.
[9] Während in KD II die theologische Ethik als eine Lehre von Gottes Gebot als Gottes Tat selber entwickelt wurde, geht es hier im vierten Teil darum, wie Menschen angesichts dieses Gebotes nun auch tatsächlich zu handeln haben.
[10] Vgl. Barth, "Das christliche Leben", 69.

Hinsichtlich des ersten Faktors, der bei diesem Auftrag eine Rolle spielt, der anzurufende Vater im Himmel, betont Barth erstens, daß es sich hierbei um einen ursprünglichen Vokativ handelt. Sogenannte Christen können darum nie objektivierend über, sondern immer nur zwischenpersönlich mit dem Vater sprechen. Das impliziert zweitens, daß es sich bei dem anzurufenden Vater um eine personale Wirklichkeit, ein sprechendes, handelndes Subjekt handelt und drittens, daß es um eine Präzisierung und Konkretisierung des ansonsten leeren, unbestimmten oder zumindest mehrdeutigen Wortes 'Gott' geht. Viertens impliziert die Konkretisierung Gottes als Vater eine kritisch-distanzierte Haltung gegenüber irdischen Vätern. Im Gegensatz zu den Kindern von irdischen Familienoberhäuptern handelt es sich nämlich bei den Kindern des himmlischen Vaters nicht um Blutsverwandte. Zudem handelt es sich fünftens und sechstens beim himmlischen Vater um einen solchen, demgegenüber sich die Kinder abhängig und ehrbietig verhalten dürfen, weil er sich im Gegensatz zu irdischen Vätern als ein schlechthin liebender und gnädiger Vater erweist. Diese Ausführungen zum himmlischen Vater abschließend geht Barth nach, inwiefern der als Vater angerufene Gott auch wirklich und wahrhaftig Gott der Vater ist. Hierbei hält er erstens fest, daß die oben genannten Eigenschaften Gottes nie und nimmer vom angerufenen Subjekt selbst losgelöst werden können. Zweitens betont er, daß die Entscheidung hinsichtlich der Wahrheit und Wirklichkeit des angerufenen Subjekts für sogenannte Christen keine offene Frage, sondern ein von Jesus Christus bereits genommener Beschluß ist. Sogenannte Christen tun schlicht nach, was Jesus ihnen vorgetan hat und kommen auf diese Art und Weise selbst in Beziehung mit Gott: "Er [Christus] nahm sie hinein in die Bewegung seines eigenen Betens. Integrierendes Element seiner Geschichte als Mittler zwischen Gott und Mensch war der Vollzug eben dieser Bewegung".[11] Letztendlich liegt die Möglichkeit der Anrufung Gottes des Vaters darum beschlossenen in der Tatsache, daß Gott der Vater von Jesus Christus ist. Dieser Indikativ, der die Grundlage des Imperativs und damit des Vokativs bildet, ist jedoch keineswegs als eine feststehende These oder Lehre zu betrachten, sondern als ein lebendiger und offener Zugang zur Geschichte Jesu Christi, die ihrerseits als Reflexion des gnädigen Willens des sich erbarmenden Gottes zu betrachten ist.

Hinsichtlich des zweiten Faktors, der beim lebendigen Austausch zwischen Gott und Mensch zu beachten ist, die empfangenden Kinder[12], thematisiert Barth in erster Linie die tatsächliche Möglichkeit einer Anrufung seitens der Kinder Gottes. Hiermit spricht er das Problem des Verhältnisses zwischen Nähe und Distanz an und greift damit meines Erachtens erneut das Thema der Möglichkeit des Zusammendenkens von Mittelbarkeit und Unmittelbarkeit auf. Wenn Menschen

---

[11] Vgl. Barth, "Das christliche Leben", 100.
[12] Hierbei denkt Barth letztendlich nicht nur an die sogenannten Christen, sondern im Anschluß an Phil 2, 11 an alle Menschen, ja an alle Kreatur. Die sogenannten Christen bilden seines Erachtens eine Art kämpfende Minderheit, die eine zukünftige universale Anrufung Gottes antizipiert.

Gott als Vater anrufen unterstellt dies nämlich eine Nähe und Intimität, die auf den ersten Blick einer anderen Unterstellung widerspricht, nämlich die der abgrundtiefen Distanz zwischen Gott und Mensch.[13] Zusammengenommen kann jedoch von einer unmöglichen Möglichkeit des Verhältnisses zwischen Gott und Mensch gesprochen werden. Die Möglichkeit dieses ansonsten unmöglichen Verhältnisses besteht eben darin, daß es nicht ontologisch, sondern ausschließlich durch die freie Gnade Gottes begründet ist. Diese Gnade, das heißt die Möglichkeit einer Unmöglichkeit, ist nach Barths Auffassung in der Geschichte Jesu Christi konkret geworden. Sie hört nimmer auf, freie Gnade zu sein, die in ihrer Zugewandtheit nicht festzulegen ist und bewirkt, daß auch sogenannte christliche Subjekte niemals still stehen können:

> Und auch ihr Stehen - von einem Sitzen oder Liegen in irgendeiner so oder so 'vorhandenen' Christlichkeit kann schon gar keine Rede sein - wird immer nur zwischen zwei Schritten ihres Gehens, ihrer Wanderung [...] Ereignis sein können.[14]

Aus eben diesem Grund wird das Handeln sogenannter christlicher Subjekte niemals Routinesache werden können, sondern immer improvisiert, ungeübt und unerfahren, das heißt kindgemäß bleiben. Schließlich hält Barth fest, daß die sogenannten Christen aufgrund ihrer gemeinschaftlichen Anrufung Gottes als Vater per definitionem in einer Art unnatürlichen Verbindung leben, einer Verbindung die quer durch alle natürlichen oder gesellschaftlichen Gruppenverbände hin existiert. Trotz dieser kollektiven, unnatürlichen Existenzform der sogenannten Christen dürfen reale Trennungen zwischen den verschiedenen Gemeindemitgliedern jedoch nicht ignoriert werden: "Es kann [...] so sein, daß Manche auf Manche warten müssen, bevor sie mit ihnen gemeinsam 'Unser Vater' rufen können".[15]

Der dritte, für meine Forschungen insbesonders relevante Faktor, der in einem Gebet eine Rolle spielt, die gläubige Anrufung selbst, mit der die Kinder Gottes dem Wort und Werk des Vaters Antwort geben, liegt Barth besonders stark am Herzen. Hierbei handelt es sich um eine Bewegung auf Gott zu, die den Kindern in erster Linie um ihrer selbst willen aufgetragen wurde. Der Sinn der Gebetshandlung selbst, der in dieser Bewegung beschlossen liegt, entpuppt sich hierbei als der Vollzug einer Erinnerung. Durch eben diese Handlung erinnern sich die sogenannten Christen nämlich fortwährend an die gott-menschliche Differenz, das heißt an der

---

[13] Vgl. vor allem den *Römerbrief* von K. Barth.
[14] Vgl. Barth, "Das christliche Leben", 125.
[15] Vgl. Barth, "Das christliche Leben", 134.

Menschen Menschsein und an Gottes Gottsein. Durch die Bewegung der Anrufung entsteht so nicht mehr nur von der Seite Gottes, sondern nun auch von der Seite des Menschen her ein lebendiges, dynamisches Verhältnis: "Anrufung zielt also auf eine Erneuerung, vielmehr: auf eine Dynamisierung und Aktualisierung eines statisch gewordenen, eines stagnierenden oder eingefrorenen Verhältnisses zu ihm".[16] Die Anrufung selbst ist mit anderen Worten die von Gott aufgetragene Möglichkeit menschlichen Handelns, um Gott nahe zu sein und die abgrundtiefe Distanz zwischen Gott und Mensch zu überbrücken - eine zugegebenermaßen äußerst zerbrechliche Möglichkeit, da bei den Kindern anders als beim Vater immer die Möglichkeit der Unterbrechung des Gesprächs besteht, die schlimme Wirklichkeit des Stillstandes, des Rastens und damit des Rostens - eines Zustandes, in welchem ihnen der Vater wird, was er in sich und von sich aus so gar nicht ist: ein in stabiler Ferne thronender und so ein fremder, ein unheimlicher, d.h. ein solcher Gott, im Verhältnis zu dem sie sich, weil es ein Verhältnis der Distanz geworden ist, ihrerseits statt in der Heimat in der Ferne und Fremde befinden müssen.[17]

Bei der im Gebet vollzogenen Erinnerung ist deren spezifischer Inhalt zu beachten: Betende Menschen erinnern sich insofern an ihr eigenes Menschsein, als sie sich daran erinnern, daß sie einzig und allein aufgrund der freien Gnade Gottes leben. Beim Beten artikulieren sie zum einen ihre Dankbarkeit dafür. Diese wird nun allerdings nach Barth noch einmal durch das öffentliche Lob übertroffen und schließlich noch einmal durch den schlechthinnigen Lobpreis Gottes, bei dem es nicht mehr nur um eine Erinnerung an das beneficere und benefacere Gottes geht, sondern um eine Erinnerung an den benefactor, an die gnädige Existenz Gottes als solche. Das handlungstheoretische Konzept Barths - und also der Ort der Erinnerung - ist so ganz offensichtlich in einem liturgischen Rahmen eingebettet. Als wesentlicher Inhalt der Erinnerung kann die fundamentale Asymmetrie, die das Verhältnis zwischen Gott und Mensch kennzeichnet, hervorgehoben werden. Beim Beten erinnern sich die Kinder, daß sie sozusagen mit leeren Händen dastehen und nichts miteinander teilen, nichts außer dem, was Gott ihnen in der Bewegung seiner freien Gnade zukommen läßt, d.h. alles, was sie nötig haben. Aus diesem Grunde ist nur das Gebet - der Schrei um Gnade - eine angemessene Form der menschlichen Bewegung auf Gott zu. Göttliche und menschliche Bewegungen korrespondieren somit: Die gnädige Bewegung Gottes zu seinen Kindern befreit diese, um ihrerseits eine Bewegung hin zu Gott zu machen, und in dieser Bewegung schreien sie um nichts anderes als um Gnade.

Die Wirklichkeit dieser doppelten Bewegung ist nach Barth in höchstem Maße verwunderlich, ja man nähert sich hier dem Geheimnis des Bundes, einem Geheimnis,

---

[16] Vgl. Barth, "Das christliche Leben", 137.
[17] Vgl. Barth, "Das christliche Leben", 138.

welches nach einer Randbemerkung Barths nicht kleiner ist als das Geheimnis der Menschwerdung und der Auferstehung Jesu Christi. Es geht in dieser doppelten Bewegung nämlich um die Begegnung mit dem Heiligen Geist, das innere 'vinculum pacis' Gottes, die Verbindung zwischen dem Vater und dem Sohn, welche zugleich eine lebendige, Nähe und Distanz wahrende Verbindung zwischen Gott und seinen Kindern schafft. Diese Gemeinschaft des Heiligen Geistes korrespondiert in diesem Entwurf Barths meines Erachtens gewissermaßen mit der Gnade Gottes in Jesus Christus: in beiden Fällen geht es um die unmögliche Möglichkeit, Nähe und Distanz zwischen Gott und Mensch zusammen zu denken. Mein Vermutung - es ist nicht mehr als eine solche, denn Barth spricht sich leider in diesem unvollkommen gebliebenen Entwurf nicht deutlicher aus - ist hier, daß das 'vinculum pacis' des Heiligen Geistes in diesem Teil der Kirchlichen Dogmatik mehr ist als nur die subjektive Form der objektiv gegebenen Möglichkeit Jesus Christus[18], nämlich eine mehr oder weniger eigenständige Form der Verbindung, die das unmögliche Verhältnis zwischen Gott und seinen Kindern ermöglichen kann. Es handelte sich dann um eine innerbarthianische Korrektur der christologischen 'Engführung', welche das Denken Barths bekanntermaßen allerdings beherrscht.[19]

Abschließend zum Thema der Anrufung möchte ich der Vollständigkeit halber noch einige Überlegungen Barths zum geistlichen Leben als solchem hinzufügen: Dieses Leben ist weder religiös noch geistig, sondern geschieht in der unmittelbaren Konfrontation mit der Anwesenheit Gottes im vermittelnden Werk des Heiligen Geistes. Weder der Mitmensch noch die Probleme der Welt können diese vermittelte Unmittelbarkeit zerstören. Doch handelt es sich beim geistlichen Leben keinesfalls um eine Privatangelegenheit, sondern hat es einen öffentlichen, sozialen, politischen und kosmischen Charakter. Die von der sogenannt christlichen Minderheit vollzogene Anrufung Gottes hat mithin eine auf Universalität antizipierende Dimension, die Barth das prophetische Beten nennt. Barth bezieht ausdrücklich auch Nicht-Christen in die Gemeinschaft des Heiligen Geistes ein:

---

[18] Vgl. hierzu den Paragraphen 16 der *Kirchlichen Dogmatik* "Die Freiheit des Menschen für Gott" (KD I.2).

[19] Zum Ansatz einer innerbarthschen Korrektur der christologischen Konzentration durch das vinculum pacis in der Kirchlichen Dogmatik vgl. D.L. Migliore, "Vinculum pacis - Karl Barth's Theologie des heiligen Geistes", *Evangelische Theologie* 2 (2000), 131-152. Migliore weist in diesem Beitrag auch darauf hin, daß das Denken einer trinitarischen Analogie gerade auch die Geschlechterhierarchisierung in der Theologie Barths revidieren könnte. Erste Überlegungen zur Relativierung der dialektischen Struktur des Barthschen Denkens durch das Denken einer (triangulären) Differenz finden sich auch bereits in S. Hennecke, "Hij leve hoog. Dick Boer als docent en zo", in S. Hennecke/R. Reeling Brouwer (red.), *Afdalingen. Werkstukken en vriendendiensten bij het afscheid van Dick Boer* (Gorinchen: Narratio, 1999)

'Unser Vater' können diese Leute dann wohl nicht rufen, ohne dabei auch die einzubeziehen, mit denen sie noch nicht in dieser Verbundenheit der Erkenntnis und des Bekenntnisses leben, weil Jesus Christus ihnen noch fremd ist - nicht in Absonderung also von dem ganzen überwältigend großen Heer der sie umgebenden Halbgläubigen, Irrgläubigen, Abergläubigen, Ungläubigen.[20]

Ein letzter wichtiger Aspekt des geistlichen Lebens ist neben der Erinnerung und der prophetischen Antizipation schließlich die göttliche Transformation. Hiermit stellt Barth die Wahrung der fundamentalen Asymmetrie im gott-menschlichem Austausch des geistlichen Lebens nun auch von Seiten Gottes her sicher. Der Begriff der göttlichen Transformation geht davon aus, daß die menschlich-subjektive Seite der Anrufung, die betende Zuwendung zu Gott, niemals von der objektiv-göttlichen Dimension, der Erhörung des Gebetes, losgelöst werden kann. Ja, es ist dem kommunikativen Wesen Gottes per definitionem ein Bedürfnis, Antwort zu geben, eine Annahme, die es dem Anrufenden überhaupt erst ermöglicht, ein Gebet als sinnvoll zu erfahren. Ein Gebet kann nämlich nie und nimmer auf ein Selbstgespräch oder, wie Schleiermacher meinte, auf menschliche Selbsthilfe reduziert werden. Vielmehr läßt Gott sich im Gebet ansprechen, eine gnädige Herablassung, die allerdings nie und nimmer von seiner Freiheit und Souveränität getrennt werden kann.

Um die fundamentale Asymmetrie im gott-menschlichen Verhältnis zu gewährleisten und trotzdem beide für das Gebet wesentliche Bewegungen, die erhörende Bewegung Gottes und die anrufende Bewegung des Menschen, zu integrieren, führt Barth den oben genannten Begriff der Transformation ein. Hiermit will gesagt sein, daß das Flehen der Kinder bei der Erhörung des gnädigen Gottes auf ein anderes, eine höheres Niveau gehoben wird:

> Gerade daß er sie in dieser ihrer Dürftigkeit nicht verachtet, sich vielmehr von ihr rühren und bewegen läßt, gerade sein göttliches Erhören wird also immer darin bestehen, daß er sie, indem er ihr [der Anrufung; S.H.] entspricht, unendlich viel besser versteht, als sie sich selbst verstehen, und so auch ihrer Anrufung in einem unendlich viel besseren Sinn Raum gibt als in dem, in welchem sie selbst ihn auch im besten Fall anrufen mögen [...] Er erhört sie 'überschwenglich', d.h. so, daß sie ihre Anrufung, so wie sie aus ihrem Herzen, Verstand und Mund hervorging, nachträglich gewiß nur in höchster Verwunderung über die gnädige Transformation, in der er ihr entspricht, in der er sie offenbar entgegengenommen hat, wiedererkennen können.[21]

---

[20] Vgl. Barth, "Das christliche Leben", 163.
[21] Vgl. Barth, "Das christliche Leben", 174.

Die Erfüllung des Gebetes, so darf zu guter Letzt festgehalten werden, findet sich gerade nicht in einem kongruenten göttlichen Entgegenkommen, sondern in der göttlichen 'Korrektur'.[22] Gott hört sozusagen trotz der 'falsche[n] Nebentöne' im menschlichen Getön seine eigene, reine Stimme.[23]

Zwischenbemerkungen

Zusammenfaßend läßt sich feststellen, daß Barth den Sinn des Gebets und damit die Grundbestimmungen des geistlichen Lebens mit den Begriffen 'Erinnerung an eine Asymmetrie', 'prophetische Antizipation' und 'göttliche Transformation' umschreibt. In meinem Beitrag werde ich mich im folgenden auf den ersten Begriff konzentrieren, die Erinnerung an eine Asymmetrie.

Die in diesem Beitrag zu diskutierende Frage ist nun meines Erachtens, ob sich dasjenige, was Barth als einen wesentlichen Sinn des Gebets herausarbeitete, nämlich die Erinnerung an einen asymmetrischen Unterschied, bei dem Nähe und Distanz einander nicht ausschließen, in einem anderen, säkularisiertem Kontext, in dem die Anwesenheit und das Sprechen Gottes nicht mehr als Selbstverständlichkeit betrachtet werden kann, erneut und auch erneuert artikulieren läßt. Der handlungstheoretische Ansatz Barths bietet für eine solche Fragestellung meines Erachtens insofern Anknüpfungspunkte, als er die Frage nach der Wahrheit und Wirklichkeit Gottes nicht ignoriert, die Last der Antwort auf diese Frage jedoch nun aber gewissermaßen auf die Schultern einer dritten Person neben der Person des göttlichen Vaters und der Person des empfangenden Menschenkindes legt, nämlich auf die Schultern Jesu Christi. Zudem bietet Barths Ansatz insofern einen Anknüpfungspunkt für heutige zweifelnde, verzweifelte oder suchende Gläubige als in ihm der Schwerpunkt auf die Frage nach der unmöglichen Möglichkeit der Anrufung selbst gelegt wird, das heißt auf eine dem Menschen durch die Gemeinschaft des Heiligen Geistes ermöglichte und also mögliche eigene gläubige Aktivität.

Als zunehmende Schwierigkeit zeichnet sich meines Erachtens die Akzeptanz der im Barthschen Denken positiv gedachten Hierarchie zwischen den beiden Gesprächspartnern ab. Es ist die Frage, ob eine derartige (wenn auch gut gemeinte) Hierarchiebildung in der ihrem Selbstbewußtsein nach modernen oder postmodernen Gesellschaft, die entweder von einer fundamentalen Gleichheit oder einem nicht-hierarchischen Unterschied zwischen Unterhandlungspartnern ausgeht, überhaupt noch Überzeugungskraft ausstrahlt. Die bei Barth unterstellte heilsame Hierarchie zwischen den Gesprächspartnern bildet um so mehr eine Provokation, als das moderne oder postmoderne Selbstbewußtsein nicht immer als gelungene Spiegelung der faktischen Lebensverhältnisse betrachtet werden kann: Hierarchische Beziehungen

---

[22] Vgl. Barth, "Das christliche Leben", 176.
[23] Vgl. Barth, "Das christliche Leben", 177.

im allgemeinen und gerade auch patriarchale Beziehungen im besonderen gehören durchaus zur Lebenswirklichkeit vieler moderner oder postmoderner Gläubigen, sodaß bei der Anrufung des wohlmeinenden freundlichen Vatergottes immer wieder kritisch geprüft werden muß, ob sie den von Barth sehr wohl intendierten befreienden Charakter nicht durchaus auch einmal verlieren könnte und statt dessen zur Legitimation hierarchischer und insbesondere patriarchaler Verhältnisse mißbraucht werden kann.

Die im folgenden zu untersuchende Frage ist darum meines Erachtens, ob es unter diesen Umständen möglich ist, sich die für das Gebet wesentliche Erinnerung an ein asymmetrisches Verhältnis - das heißt auch an die unmögliche Möglichkeit einer Nähe in Distanz - so vor Augen zu halten, daß sie ihren wirklich gnädigen Charakter nicht verliert, sondern dieser vielmehr auf neue Art in einem anderen, nämlich säkularisierten Kontext zum Leuchten kommen kann. Zugleich muß der Frage nachgegangen werden, inwiefern nicht auch neue, unter säkularisierten Umständen überzeugendere Gottesbilder für den zweifelnden, verzweifelten Gläubigen oder die hoffnungsvoll suchende sogenannte Christin hilfreich sein können, um sich aufs Neue in ihrer Bewegung auf Gott hin aufzumachen. Um diese Frage nach der Möglichkeit einer Neuinterpretation und Neu-Einbildung der sogenannt christlichen Gebetshandlung unter säkularisierten Vorzeichen ausführlicher behandeln zu können, werde ich im folgenden einige Betrachtungen der französischen Psychoanalytikerin und Philosophin Luce Irigaray vorstellen.

Luce Irigaray und das plazentare Verhältnis

Die französische Philosophin und Psychoanalytikerin Luce Irigaray betrachtet religiöse Phänomene in erster Linie aus religionskritischer Perspektive, das heißt sie enthüllt diese und erforscht die ihnen zugrundeliegende Materialität. In zweiter Linie geht es ihr jedoch auch um die Produktion einer alternativen religiösen Ordnung. Bei der von Irigaray beabsichtigten religiösen Neuproduktion handelt es sich um nichts weniger als um den Versuch der Errichtung einer sexuell differenzierten Religion und Kultur, die sich kritisch gegenüber dem dominanten patriarchalen christlichen Umfeld und dessen ebenso patriarchalen säkularen psychoanalytischen und philosophischen Varianten verhält. Der für die Theoriebildung Irigarays zentrale Begriff der sexuellen Differenz meint einen bisher noch nicht gedachten, nicht-hierarchischen, unableitbaren Unterschied zwischen den Geschlechtern. Hierbei ist als Besonderheit des Differenzdenkens Irigarays festzuhalten, daß es ein Verhältnis durchdenken möchte, bei dem sich nicht alles um zwei Pole dreht - um den des Mannes und den der Frau -, sondern in dem darüber hinausgehend das Verhältnis zwischen den beiden Polen als ein eigenständiger Faktor artikuliert werden kann, ein Faktor, der von Irigaray Zwischenraum genannt wird.[24]

---

[24] Andere von Irigaray verwendete Ausdrücke zur Bezeichnung oder zur Beschreibung des Zwischenraums sind etwa: Dazwischen, Rest, zwischen, dritter Term, Spiel, Transport, Begehren.

Der Irigaraysche Differenzbegriff meint mithin ein trianguläres Verhältnis.

Im Folgenden werde ich mich auf einen bestimmten Aspekt der Relgionskritik Irigarays konzentrieren, nämlich auf die Kritik des christlichen Glaubens an Gott den Vater. Hierbei orientiere ich mich in erster Linie an ihrem Beitrag 'La croyance même', werde aber zur Illustration weitere Texte von ihr heranziehen.[25] In 'La croyance même' entwickelt Irigaray die These, daß der Glaube an Gott den Vater als Ersatz für eine ursprüngliche Wirklichkeit zu betrachten ist, nämlich als der Glauben eines Kindes im vorgeburtlichen Zustand an die liebevolle und sorgende Allmächtigkeit der Mutter. Irigaray betrachtet den Glauben an Gott den Vater mit anderen Worten als eine Art phantastische Neuformulierung eines ursprünglichen wirklichen Ereignisses, das sich zwischen Mutter und Fötus im Bauch der Mutter abspielt. Die Erinnerung an diese ursprüngliche Szene, das heißt auch die Erinnerung an die Allmächtigkeit der Mutter, wird also im christlichen Glauben, aber auch in philosophischen und psychoanalytischen Theorien ausgemerzt und vergessen. Aufgrund dieses Vergessens kann die christliche Religion als patriarchal qualifiziert werden.

Nun betrachtet Irigaray das Vergessen in der christliche Religion trotz ihrer scharfen Religionskritik nicht als ein totales Vergessen. Vielmehr findet sich in der christliche Religion ihrer Meinung nach neben dem Vergessen auch eine Erinnerung an die ursprüngliche Szene im Bauch der Mutter. Im folgenden werde ich die ursprüngliche Szene zunächst etwas genauer betrachten und dann darstellen, wie sie nach Irigarays Analyse in mehr oder weniger patriarchalen Glaubenssystemen ersetzt wird. Anschließend werde ich deutlich machen, inwiefern - ganz im Gegensatz zu philosophischen und psychoanalytischen Glaubenssystemen - gerade im christlichen Glauben an Gott den Vater abgesehen von allem Vergessen auch ein Eingedenken oder eine Erinnerung an die ursprüngliche Szene stattfindet.

In 'La croyance même' erläutert Irigaray hinsichtlich der ursprünglichen Szene, daß das Kind im Mutterbauch vor der Geburt sicher geborgen wird, daß die Plazenta es an dieser Stätte umhüllt[26] und daß es mit Hilfe der Nabelschnur versorgt wird. Irigaray betont in ihrer Darstellung, daß die Mutter selbst keinesfalls mit der Plazenta identifiziert werden kann. Diese ist vielmehr als ein Raum-Hülle zu betrachten, die sich zwischen Mutter und Kind befindet und die die Verbindung

---

Vgl. L. Irigaray, *Ethik der sexuellen Differenz* (Frankfurt am Main: Suhrkamp, 1991), insbes.11-20.

[25] Vgl. L. Irigaray, "Der Glaube selbst", in *Genealogie der Geschlechter* (Freiburg i.Br.: Kore, 1989), 25-46, [frz.: *La croyance même*].

[26] Irigaray spricht ausdrücklich von der Plazenta als einer Hülle: "Die Plazenta ist ohne Zweifel die erste Hülle des Kindes selbst". Vgl. Irigaray, "Der Glaube selbst", 62.

zwischen beiden Organismen zustande bringt. Die Plazenta und die Nabelschnur sorgen dafür, daß das Kind mit allem Nötigen versorgt wird, und zwar gratis und im Überfluß und ohne daß das Kind darum bitten müßte. Nach Irigaray spielen also in der ursprünglichen Szene zumindest drei Faktoren eine Rolle, die Mutter, der Fötus, und eine (doppelte) Verbindung, die den Austausch und das Zusammensein zwischen beiden reguliert, nämlich die Plazenta und die Nabelschnur. Beide Verbindungen werden von Irigaray in unterschiedlichen Beiträgen näher beleuchtet.

In einem Interview mit der französischen Biologiedozentin Hélène Rouch präsentiert Irigaray durch das Stellen von Interviewfragen neue Einsichten über die genauen Eigenschaften der Plazenta.[27] Irigarays Ausgangsthese besagt, daß die plazentare Verbindung oder Beziehung eine Alternative zu vorherrschenden Verhaltensmustern wie Kompetenzstreit (Darwin) oder die ewige Wiederkehr immer gleicher Verhaltensmuster (Pavlov) bieten kann. Rouch betont im oben genannten Interview, daß die Plazenta zwar ein Produkt des Embryos ist, daß sie aber eine eigenständige Rolle hat. Zudem ist sie nicht nur mit dem Embryo, sondern zugleich auch mit der mütterlichen Schleimhaut verbunden. Darum kann sie nach Rouch auch als ein Zwischenraum zwischen Mutter und Fötus betrachtet werden. Mit dieser Darstellung der faktischen Verhältnisse im mütterlichen Bauch widerspricht Rouch gängigen psychoanalytischen Vorstellungen, nach denen von einer Verschmelzung zwischen Mutter und Kind in der Gebärmutter gesprochen werden muß. Auch die damit verbundene Annahme, daß das geborene Kind sich immer wieder zu diesem symbiotischen Zustand zurücksehnt, wird mit dieser Darstellung der Tatsachen als ein Produkt (patriarchaler) Phantasie verworfen. In Wirklichkeit geht es im Bauch aber auch nicht um das Gegenteil, das heißt um Aggression in dem Sinne, daß der Fötus ein Fremdkörper im mütterlichen Organismus wäre. In Wirklichkeit, so Rouch, geht es im mütterlichen Bauch gerade um eine von der Plazenta ermöglichte Aufnahme des Fötus in den mütterlichen Organismus und um den gelungenen Austausch zwischen den beiden unterschiedlichen Organismen der Mutter und des Fötus, die einander teilweise fremd sind. Die durch die Plazenta tatsächlich ermöglichte permanente Unterhandlungskultur, die der Einnistung des 'anderen' (Fötus) in das 'eigene' (Mutter) dient, kann keinesfalls als Selbstverständlichkeit betrachtet werden, sondern erfordert neben dem Willen zur Einnistung seitens des Fötus auch die Bereitschaft zur Aufnahme des Fremden seitens der Mutter:

> Er moet integendeel herkenning van de ander, van het niet-zelf, door de moeder zijn, een eerste reactie van haar kant dus, opdat de bestanddelen van de placenta aangemaakt kunnen worden. [...] Alles vindt plaats alsof de moeder altijd al wist dat het embryo (en de placenta dus) ander(s) is, en alsof

---

[27] Vgl. L. Irigaray, "Over de moederlijke orde", in *Ik, jij, wij. Voor een cultuur van het onderscheid* (Kampen: Kok, 1992), 43-50, [frz.: *Je, tu, nous; pour une culture de la différence*].

zij dit aan de placenta liet weten, die dan bestanddelen aanmaakt waardoor het moederlijke organisme in staat wordt gesteld om haar als ander(s) te accepteren.[28]

Der durch die Plazenta produzierte Zwischenraum kann also als ein Raum bezeichnet werden, in dem sowohl die Trennung als auch die Vereinigung bzw. der Austausch zwischen zwei unterschiedlichen Instanzen (hier: Mutter und Fötus) zustande kommt. Insofern ermöglicht die Plazenta die Konstitution eines ursprünglichen Unterschieds im mütterlichen Bauch, bei dem es sich allerdings im Gegensatz zur letztendlich von Irigaray angestrebten sexuellen Differenz um einen hierarchischen Unterschied handelt. Eine vergleichbare Funktion kommt der Nabelschnur zu, wie Irigaray in einem anderen Beitrag, 'Corps-à-corps avec la mère' betont.[29] Auch sie ist eine verbindende Instanz im Bauch der Mutter, die eine hierarchische Beziehung zwischen Mutter und Fötus zustandebringt:

> Das geschah in der ursprünglichen Gebärmutter, der Nährmutter, dem Fruchtwasser, den ersten Umhüllungen, wo sich Kind und Mutter durch die Vermittlung des Blutes als Ganzes erfuhren. Wo Mutter und Kind, natürlich in einer nicht symmetrischen Beziehung, miteinander verbunden sind, vor jeder Trennung und vor der Zerstückelung ihrer Körper.[30]

Die Bedeutung der Nabelschnur wird in 'Corps-à-corps avec la mère' ausführlicher untersucht als in 'La croyance même'. Irigaray betont, daß diese erste Verbindung mit der Mutter nach der Geburt durchgeschnitten wird. Die durch diesen Vorgang entstandene Wunde wird unmittelbar vom Eigennamen des Kindes besetzt, dem Namen des Vaters. Nach der Geburt wird mit anderen Worten anstelle der ursprünglichen mütterlichen symbolischen Ordnung und unter Ignorierung der Geburtsverwundung die um das Gesetz des Vaters zentrierte herrschende patriarchale Ordnung errichtet, ein Vorgang, den Irigaray folgendermaßen beschreibt:

---

[28] Meine Übersetzung dieses Zitats lautet: "Hingegen muß eine Anerkennung des Anderen vom nicht-Selbst, von der Mutter, bestehen, eine erste Reaktion ihrerseits, sodaß die Bestandteile der Plazenta gebildet werden können.[...] Alles findet statt, als ob die Mutter immer schon wußte, daß das Embryo (und also die Plazenta) etwas anderes/anders ist und als ob sie dies die Plazenta wissen ließ, so daß diese dann Bestandteile bilden kann, durch die der mütterliche Organismus in der Lage ist, um sie als ein anderes anzuerkennen." Vgl. Irigaray, "Over de moederlijke orde", 47.
[29] Vgl. L. Irigaray, "Körper an Körper mit der Mutter", in *Genealogie der Geschlechter* (Freiburg i.Br.: Kore, 1989), 25-46, [frz.: *Le corps-à-corps avec la mère*].
[30] Vgl. Irigaray, "Körper an Körper mit der Mutter", 34.

Der Eigenname und sogar schon der Vorname sind immer schon eine Verschiebung im Verhältnis zu dieser ursprünglichen Identität: der Narbe aufgrund der durchtrennten Nabelschnur. Der Eigenname und auch der Vorname gleiten über den Körper wie Bekleidungsstücke, Identitätsstücke - äußerlich.[31]

Die mütterliche Herkunft des Kindes und das Mütterliche überhaupt wird vergessen, ermöglicht aber als etwas Vergessenes die Errichtung des väterlichen Gesetzes:

> ... die Ausschließlichkeit seines Gesetzes schließt diesen Körper, diese erste Behausung, diese erste Liebe, aus. Sie opfert sie, um daraus Stoff für das Imperium seiner Sprache zu machen, die das männliche Geschlecht so stark privilegiert, daß sie es mit dem menschlichen Geschlecht verwechselt.[32]

Doch weist Irigaray in diesem Beitrag ebenfalls auf das erneuernde Potential, das ein Durchdenken der plazentaren Beziehung und des Lebens im Bauch der Mutter insbesondere hinsichtlich der vorherrschenden psychoanalytischen Subjektivitätskonzepte mit sich bringen könnte. Es könnte nämlich zur Entwicklung einer alternativen imaginären und symbolischen Ordnung dienen, die sich am Vergessen des Lebens im Bauch der Mutter nicht schuldig macht. Hierbei handelte es sich um eine noch zu errichtende zukünftige Ordnung, in der sowohl der Unterschied der Geschlechter als auch die Notwendigkeit eines Zwischenraumes respektiert würde. Doch bevor diese zukünftige trianguläre Ordnung errichtet werden kann, müssen erst die bestehenden symbolischen Ordnungen analysiert werden, die nach der Geburt des Kindes bis auf Weiteres errichtet werden.

Nach der in 'La croyance même' dargestellten Analyse Irigarays gibt es verschiedene Ersatzmöglichkeiten für die ursprüngliche Ordnung im Bauch der Mutter. Diese sind jedoch insofern vergleichbar, als es sich im Gegensatz zur ursprünglichen Szene immer um (mehr oder weniger patriarchale) Glaubenssysteme philosophischer, psychoanalytischer oder auch christlicher Art handelt. In 'La croyance même' untersucht Irigaray erst ein berühmtes psychoanalytisches System, das sogenannte Fort-Da-Spiel und dann ein christliches System, den Glauben an Gott den allmächtigen Vater und Schöpfer des Himmels und der Erde.

Erstens soll es nun darum gehen, das psychoanalytische Glaubenssystem zu beschreiben. Zwar führt es zu weit, um im Rahmen dieses Beitrags die Fort-Da-Szene in aller Ausführlichkeit zu besprechen, doch werde ich ihren Inhalt und ihre Bedeutung in der erforderlichen Kürze darstellen.[33] Die Szene wurde vom Vater der

---

[31] Vgl. Irigaray, "Körper an Körper mit der Mutter", 35.
[32] Vgl. Irigaray, "Körper an Körper mit der Mutter", 35.
[33] Für ausführlichere Darstellungen der Fort-Da-Szene verweise ich auf die Beiträge von R. van der Haegen, *In het spoor van seksuele differentie* (Nijmegen: SUN, 1989); A. Halsema, *Dialectiek van de seksuele differentie. De filosofie van Luce Irigaray* (Amsterdam: Boom, 1998); S. Hennecke, *Der*

Psychoanalyse, Sigmund Freud, bei seinem Enkelkind Ernst beobachtet und analysiert. Das kleine Kind Ernst, so die Beobachtung Freuds, ist unter Begleitung der Laute 'o' (fort) und 'a' (da) damit beschäftigt, eine Holzspule wegzuwerfen und diese mit Hilfe eines daran befestigten Bindfadens wieder zu sich zurück zu ziehen. Freud deutet diese Szene als die spielerische Darstellung des Eintritts des kleinen Kindes in die symbolische Ordnung.

Im Gegensatz zur Interpretation Freuds richtet Irigaray ihre interpretative Aufmerksamkeit hinsichtlich dieses Spiels insbesondere auf die Rolle, die die abwesende Mutter (Sophie, die Tochter Freuds) in dieser Szene spielt. Ihrer Meinung ist es nämlich die abwesende Mutter, die mit Hilfe des Spiels herangezogen und auch wieder weggeworfen werden soll. Diese Interpretation ist Irigaray möglich, weil sie wiederum bei einer Interpretation Derridas anschließt, die im Gegensatz zu anderen Interpretationen davon ausgeht, daß der kleine Ernst bei seinem Spiel nicht in seinem Himmelbettchen saß und von daraus die Spule wegwarf und auch wieder heranzog, sondern auf dem Boden außerhalb des Himmelbettchens, von wo aus er die Holzspule mit Hilfe des Fadens durch den Bettschleier in das Himmelbettchen warf und auch wieder zu sich heranzog.[34] So gesehen spielt das Kind nach Irigaray sein Verlangen, um wieder in den Bauch der Mutter zurückzukehren. An die Stelle des Bauches und des Plazenta treten beim ernsthaften Ersatz das Himmelbettchen und der Bettschleier, an die Stelle des Fötus und der Nabelschnur hingegen die Holzspule und der Bindfaden. Doch handelt es sich um einen vermeintlichen Ersatz, denn im Gegensatz zur ursprünglichen Szene geht es in der Fort-Da-Szene nicht um den Empfang einer Gratisversorgung, sondern um den Versuch des Kindes, den Zugang zur Mutter und ihren versorgenden Qualitäten selber in die Hand zu nehmen und zu beherrschen. Beim kindlichen Versuch, sich selber zum Meister über Leben (Geburt) und Tod (Zurückkehr in den Bauch) zu machen, handelt es sich mithin um eine Umkehrung und Pervertierung der Machtverhältnisse. Durch den vorgenommenen Machtgriff werden die Mutter und ihre Qualitäten entweder verworfen (fort) oder assimiliert (da) - eine Alternative, die beim Leben im Bauch nicht bestand. Das Zusammensein an diesem Orte entzog sich nämlich sowohl der Trennung als auch der Verschmelzung. Zuammenfassend läßt sich festhalten, daß Irigaray durch den Vergleich der ursprünglichen mit der psychoanalytischen Szene deren Verschiedenheit ans Licht bringt und daß der Eintritt des Kindes in die sym-

---

vergessene Schleier. Ein theologisches Gespräch zwischen Luce Irigaray und Karl Barth (Gütersloh: Kaiser, 2001) und A.-C. Mulder, *Divine Flesh, Embodied word. Incarnation as a Hermeneutical Key to a Feminist Theologian's Reading of Luce Irigaray's Work* (unpublizierte Dissertation, Amsterdam 2000).
[34] Irigaray verweist auf: J. Derrida, *Die Postkarte. Von Sokrates bis Freud und Jenseits*, Teil 1 (Sendungen) und 2 (Spekulieren - über/auf 'Freud'), (Berlin: Passagenverlag, 1982 und 1987), [frz.: *La carte postale. De Socrate à Freud et au-delà*].

bolische Ordnung auf einem Irrtum und einem Vergessen hinsichtlich der Wirklichkeit des Lebens im Bauch der Mutter begründet ist. Doch gerade weil der Eintritt in die herrschende symbolische Ordnung auf einem Irrtum gegründet ist, kann er als der Eintritt in ein Glaubenssystem bezeichnet werden: was nicht wahr und wirklich ist, kann zumindest geglaubt werden.

Zweitens richtet sich die Aufmerksamkeit Irigarays auf den christlichen Ersatz der ursprünglichen Szene im Bauch der Mutter, der zugleich auch als spezifische Variante des Fort-Da-Spiels betrachtet werden darf. Im (patriarchalen) christlichen Glauben bildet der gläubige Christ, der in Verbindung mit Gott stehen möchte, den Ersatz für den Fötus und die Nabelschnur bzw. für die Holzspule mit dem Bindfaden. Mutter und Plazenta bzw. Himmelbettchen und Bettschleier werden im christlichen Glauben hingegen durch die Hinwendung zu Gott dem allmächtigen Vater und Schöpfer des Himmels und der Erde sowie auch des ersten paradiesischen Raumes zur Beherbergung des Menschengeschlechts, ersetzt. Da die Erinnerung so auf einen allmächtigen gnädigen Vater anstatt auf eine allmächtige versorgende Mutter gerichtet ist, kann von einem Vergessen des ursprünglichen Szene im christlichen Glauben gesprochen werden. Doch ist der christliche Glauben im Gegensatz zum psychoanalytischen Glauben nicht auf einem totalen Vergessen der Mutter und ihrer Qualitäten begründet, sondern wird in ihm die Erinnerung an die ursprüngliche Szene neben allem Vergessen auch am Leben erhalten. Anders als beim Fort-Da-Spielen klingen in ihm beinah vergessene Erinnerungen an die erste Szene wieder auf, und zwar in der gläubigen Anerkennung einer versorgenden, gnädigen Allmacht und durch die Rede von einem ersten paradiesischen Raum, den Gott seinen Geschöpfen bereitet hat. Aufgrund dieser wenn auch entstellten Erinnerung wird der christliche Glauben von Irigaray als nicht total patriarchal qualifiziert. Obwohl sie in 'La croyance même' den Schwerpunkt ihrer Analyse auf die Partizipation des christlichen Glaubens an patriarchalen Glaubenssystemen legt, verdient gerade das utopische Potential dieses Glaubens meines Erachtens mehr Aufmerksamkeit.

Es stellt sich mir an dieser Stelle die Frage, inwiefern nicht gerade auch in der Theologie Barths - konkreter gesagt in seinem handlungstheoretischen Ansatz hinsichtlich der Anrufung - etwas von der Erinnerung des Lebens im Bauch der Mutter aufleuchtet. Mit dieser Fragestellung möchte ich die Möglichkeit einer spezifisch theologischen Neuinterpretation des christlichen (und psychoanalytischen) Glaubenssystems untersuchen.

Das Gebet als eine schöne Erinnerung?!

Es ist meine These, daß die im von Christus aufgetragenen Gebet beschlossene Erinnerung an einen asymmetrischen Unterschied nicht ausschließlich, aber auch als eine Erinnerung an das Leben im Bauch der Mutter aufgefaßt werden kann. Die einem solchen Gebet eigene Erinnerung würde dann eine spezifisch theologische Neuinterpretation des patriarchalen psychoanalytischen, aber auch des patriarchalen christlichen Glaubenssystems ermöglichen, bei der es insbesondere darum geht, das utopische Potential des christlichen Glaubens zu bewahren und zu aktualisieren. Diese These und ihre utopische Implikation sollen im folgenden näher beleuchtet werden.

Zunächst werde ich darstellen, inwiefern das Gebet aus der Perspektive der Barthschen Theorie als eine spezifisch theologische Neuinterpretation des psychoanalytischen Glaubenssystem - in concreto der Fort-Da-Szene - betrachtet werden kann, in der die Erinnerung an das Leben im Bauch der Mutter keinesfalls völlig ausgemerzt worden ist. Während nämlich erstens im Fort-Da-Spiel Nähe und Distanz einander ausschließen, besteht die in Christus enthüllte und vom Heiligen Geist aktualisierte unmögliche Möglichkeit der Anrufung darin, sich eines Verhältnisses zu erinnern, in dem Nähe und Distanz bzw. Mittelbarkeit und Unmittelbarkeit zusammengedacht werden können. Gerade das 'vinculum pacis' des Heiligen Geistes kann meines Erachtens als eine spezifisch utopisch-theologische Erinnerung an die vermittelnde Rolle der Plazenta betrachtet werden, die dafür sorgt, daß zwei einander zum Teil fremde Organismen miteinander in Kontakt kommen und bleiben können. Und während zweitens im Fort-Da-Spiel die ursprüngliche liebevolle versorgende Allmacht der Mutter vergessen und der ursprünglich asymmetrische Unterschied zwischen Mutter und Kind in ein Machtsdenken verdreht wird, das das Anderssein des Anderen ausmerzt, handelt es sich beim Gebet um die Erinnerung an einen asymmetrischen Unterschied, in dem das Anderssein des Anderen, das heißt die Differenz zwischen Gott und Mensch aufrechterhalten wird. Hier bildet das 'vinculum pacis' des Heiligen Geistes sozusagen eine theologische Alternative für den Bindfaden des Fort-Da-Spiels, mit dessen Hilfe eine differenzierte Vermittlung im triangulären Sinne gerade nicht gelingen kann.

Mit dieser Interpretation des Gebets als spezifisch theologischer Neuformulierung und utopischer Erinnerung an das Leben im Bauch der Mutter will ich jedoch nun nicht bestreiten, daß die theologische Handlungstheorie Barths auch Elemente enthält, die die Errichtung einer doch wieder patriarchalen oder anderweitig herrschaftlichen Ordnung unterstützen. Das Gebet richtet sich ja ausdrücklich an einen zwar freundlichen, jedoch explizit männlichen Vatergott, nämlich den Vater Jesu Christi. Auch die Tatsache, daß Barth die himmlische Vaterschaft bewußt als

Kritik irdischer Vaterschaft interpretiert, schließt die Gefahr eines patriarchalen Mißverständnisses des Gebets keineswegs aus. Bei der Anrufung eines freundlichen, sich anti-patriarchal gebärdenden Vatergottes handelt es sich ja trotz alledem um Kompetenzfragen unter Männern, das heißt um eine Ordnung, in der ausschließlich Männer um die höchste Macht ringen. Nun ist die Theorie Irigarays meines Erachtens insofern hilfreich, als sie die im Gebet beschlossene Erinnerung an einen asymmetrischen Unterschied von seiner Fixierung auf den Unterschied zwischen einem explizit männlichen Gott und seinen Kindern zu lösen weiß, indem sie diesen Unterschied anders, nämlich als einen asymmetrischen Unterschied zwischen einer Mutter und ihrem Kind zur Sprache bringt. Es ist jedoch die Frage, ob hiermit nicht einfach nur ein patriarchales durch ein matriarchales Bild ersetzt werden würde - ein Vorgang, der der Intention Irigarays meines Erachtens keinesfalls gerecht würde. Als ein mich mehr überzeugendes anti-patriarchales und zugleich anti-matriarchales Moment des Gebets betrachte ich nämlich nicht die Rede von einem hilfreichen, liebevollen männlichen Gott und auch nicht die Rede von einer allmächtigen, sorgenden Mutter, sondern vielmehr die Struktur des Gebetes selbst, das heißt die Erinnerung an einen fundamentalen Unterschied, bei dem nicht zwei, sondern (mindestens) drei Faktoren eine Rolle spielen und bei dem durch das Denken einer unmöglichen Möglichkeit der tödlichen Alternative zwischen Nähe und Distanz ein Riegel vorgeschoben wird. Diese unmögliche Möglichkeit liegt bei Barth im Denken der Anrufung selbst als eines eigenständigen dritten Faktors zwischen dem sich erbarmenden Gott und dem empfangendem Menschenkind beschlossen.

Die Frage, die sich mir gegen Ende dieses Beitrages stellt, ist, ob es theologisch möglich ist, die Anrufung Gottes so zu gestalten, daß sie tatsächlich zu einer schönen und insbesondere auch zu einer zukunftsträchtigen, utopischen Erinnerung gerät. Ein erster Schritt für eine derartige Gestaltung des Gebets wäre womöglich, das Bild Gottes als Vater (aber auch das Bild Gottes als Mutter) theologisch so neu zu inszenieren, daß bei der Anrufung Gottes die Erinnerung an die ursprüngliche Szene erneut ins Leben gerufen wird. Mein Vorschlag ist in diesem Zusammenhang, hinsichtlich der im Gebet anzurufenden Instanz an ein biblisches Bild Gottes anzuknüpfen, in der die Sache, um die es geht, nicht ausgemerzt wird. Ich denke hierbei an das Bild und die Anrufung Gottes als 'Begleiter!'. Hiermit entspreche ich dem biblischen Immanuel-Namen Gottes: Ich werde mit Euch sein, wann immer ich mit Euch sein werde. Zudem referiere ich mit dieser biblisch möglichen Konkretisierung des ursprünglichen Vokativs an die ursprüngliche Szene im Bauch der Mutter: Die Plazenta kann nämlich durchaus als ein ursprünglicher Begleiter des Kindes betrachtet werden, ein Begleiter, der oder die selbst nach der Geburt in bestimmter Hinsicht noch begleitet.[35]

---

[35] Ich möchte an dieser Stelle auf die faszinierenden Forschungen P. Sloterdijks hinweisen. Sloterdijk untersucht im ersten Band seiner Sphären-Trilogie ausführlich die Rolle und die Bedeutung der Plazenta. Insbesondere in Kapitel 5 "Der Urbegleiter. Requiem für ein

Das biblische Bild des Begleiters erinnert auch darum an die ursprüngliche Szene im Bauch der Mutter, weil ein derartiger Begleiter weder 'fort' noch 'da' ist, sondern 'mit' und 'zwischen' uns. Zu guter Letzt möchte ich darauf hinweisen, daß auch Barth selbst in dem von mir zur Grundlage gewählten Text eine derartige Rede von Gott als 'Begleiter!' kennt. Dort spricht er nämlich von Gott als jemanden, der nicht nur für, sondern mit seinen Kindern und in Bezug auf das eigene Handeln der Kinder etwas tut. Aufgrund dieses mit-Sein Gottes nennt Barth Gott einen 'concursus'.[36] Meine vorläufige Schlußthese ist darum, daß die von Irigaray ins Leben gerufene Erinnerung an die Szene im Bauch der Mutter innerhalb der Theologie Barths als ein Sprechen der Kinder Gottes mit Gott als 'Begleiter!' oder anders gesagt als ein Sprechen mit Gott als 'Konkurrent!'(!) artikuliert werden kann. Es handelte sich hierbei um nicht weniger als um die utopische Erinnerung an eine Struktur des Begehrens jenseits jeglicher Herr-Knecht-Dialektik, bei der dem Denken eines dynamischen Zwischenraums zwischen 'Gott' und 'Mensch' bzw. dem gottmenschlichen Verhältnis als solchem Raum eingeräumt würde.

---

verworfenes Organ" spricht er von der Plazenta als einem prä-subjektiven 'mit' und vom Fötus als einem prä-subjektiven 'auch'. Vgl. P. Sloterdijk, "Blasen", in Id., *Sphären. Mikrospärologie*, Bd.I, (Frankfurt am Main: Suhrkamp, 1999³). Zur niederländischen feministischen Kritik an Sloterdijk vgl. G. van Ginneken, "Beelden van verbondenheid", in Hennecke/Reeling Brouwer, *Afdalingen*.
[36] Vgl. Barth, "Das christliche Leben", 169.

Authors

Kune Biezeveld
Kune Biezeveld is Lecturer in Systematic Theology and Professor of Feminist Theology at the University of Leiden (the Netherlands). She is the author of *Spreken over God als vader. Hoe kan het anders? [Speaking about God as a Father. How Else?]* (Baarn 1996), and co-editor of *Towards a Different Transcendence. Feminist Findings on Subjectivity, Religion and Values* (Bern 2001). Her current research is on the implications of monotheism for systematic theology.

Riet Bons-Storm
Riet Bons-Storm is Professor Emerita in Pastoral Theology and Women's Sudies at the University of Groningen (the Netherlands). She has published *The Incredible Woman. Listening to Women's Silences in Pastoral Care and Counseling* (Nashville, 1996) and *Kracht en Kruis. Pastoraat met Oudere Vrouwen* (Kampen 2000).

Mathilde van Dijk
Mathilde van Dijk is Lecturer in Church History and Women's Studies at the Faculty of Theology and Religious studies at the University of Groningen (the Netherlands). She works on biographies of men and women in the Later Middle Ages.

Grietje Dresen
Grietje Dresen is Lecturer in Moral Theology and Women's Studies at the Catholic University of Nijmegen (the Netherlands). She has published *Onschuldfantasieën. Offerzin en heilsverlangen in feminisme en mystiek* (Nijmegen 1990), her PhD thesis, and *Is dit mijn lichaam? Visioenen van het volmaakte lichaam in katholieke moraal en mystiek* (Nijmegen 1998). Her research is on gender aspects in the history of moral theology and, recently, on the concept of love (caritas) in the Christian tradition, interpreted against the background of a contemporary ethics of care.

Maaike de Haardt
Maaike de Haardt is Catharina Halkes Professor of Religion and Gender at the Catholic University of Nijmegen (the Netherlands) and Lecturer in Women's Studies in Theology at the Theological Faculty Tilburg. She wrote her PhD thesis on a feminist theology of death, *Dichter bij de dood. Feministisch-theologische aanzetten tot een theologie van de dood [Nearer to Death]* (Zoetermeer 1993) and co-edited the first book of the Dutch research programme, *Begin with the Body. Corporeality, Religion and Gender* (Leuven 1998). She is highly interested in the

relationship between systematic theology and everyday practices, art, and literature.

Susanne Hennecke

Susanne Hennecke works as Lecturer in Theological Genderstudies at the University of Utrecht (the Netherlands), especially in the field of the hermeneutical meaning of 'paradise' in the French philosophy of difference for the Theology of Karl Barth, Dietrich Bonhoeffer and Friedrich-Wilhelm Marquardt. She wrote her PhD thesis on Karl Barth and Luce Irigaray, *Der vergessene Schleier. Versuch eines theologische Gesprächs zwischen Luce Irigaray und Karl Barth* (Gütersloh 2001) and published " 'Nur ein Gott kann uns retten (?)' - die theologischen Implikationen poststrukturalistischer Subjektauffassung bei Luce Irigaray und Donna Haraway," in Andrea Günter (Hrsg.), *Feministische Theologie und postmodernes Denken. Zur theologischen Relevanz der Geschlechterdifferenz* (Stuttgart [ua] 1996).

Jacqueline Kool

Jacqueline Kool works as an independent trainer and advisor, partly in the theological field and partly in the disability movement. Her main interest is the connection between religion and physical health issues. Her book *Goed bedoeld. Levensbeschouwelijk kijken naar ziekte en handicap* is about to appear (Zoetermeer 2002). It presents a critical analysis of common religious views on differently abled persons and offers alternative ways of speaking about illness and disability in religious contexts.

Anne-Marie Korte

Anne-Marie Korte is Associate Professor in Theological Women's Studies at the Catholic Theological University in Utrecht (the Netherlands), and Honorary Professor in Theological Women's Studies at the Department of Theology, Utrecht University. She wrote a PhD thesis on the concept of faith in Mary Daly's writings: *Een passie voor transcendentie. Feminisme, theologie en moderniteit in het denken van Mary Daly* [A Passion for Transcendence. Feminism, Theology and Modernity in Mary Daly's Writings] (Kampen 1992) and currently works in the field of philosophical and theological anthropology. Recently she edited *Women and Miracle Stories. A Multidisciplinary Exploration* (Leiden 2001), and (together with Kristin De Troyer) *Wholly Woman, Holy Blood. A Feminist Critique on Purity and Impurity* (Harrisburg 2002).

Magda Misset-van de Weg

Magda Misset-van de Weg works as Research Scholar at the Catholic Theological University in Utrecht (the Netherlands). Her scholarly field is New Testament studies. She wrote the dissertation *Sara & Thecla. Representations of Women in 1 Peter and the Acts of Thecla* (Utrecht 1998). Her current project concerns the study of allusions to the Old Testament in the Fourth Gospel.

Inez van der Spek

Inez van der Spek is a scholar in theology and literature. She authored *Alien Plots. Female Subjectivity and the Divine in the light of James Tiptree's 'A Momentary Taste of Being'* (Liverpool 2000). Currently she is a grammar school teacher.

Anne Marijke Spijkerboer

Anne Marijke Spijkerboer is rector of the theological seminary of the 'Uniting Churches'. She wrote a PhD thesis on a hermeneutical study of Karl Barth and 1 Sam. 9 and 10, *'En zij vonden ze niet'. Storingen in de hermeneutiek aan de hand van Barth's exegese van 'de man Gods uit Juda' en van 'David en Saul'* (Kampen 1996). Her scholarly interests include the relationship between exegesis and art. She has published "Rembrandt und Hagar" in *Unless someone guide me. Festschrift for Karel Deurloo* (Amsterdam 2001), and "De koningen in Chauvigny" in G. Westra (red.), *Liturgisch Centrum. Taal in Schrift en eredienst. Opstellen voor Dirk Monshouwer* (Hilversum 2001).

Wissenschaftliche Paperbacks
Theologie

Michael J. Rainer (Red.)
"Dominus Iesus" – Anstößige Wahrheit oder anstößige Kirche?
Dokumente, Hintergründe, Standpunkte und Folgerungen
Die römische Erklärung "Dominus Iesus" berührt den Nerv der aktuellen Diskussion über den Stellenwert der Religionen in der heutigen Gesellschaft. Angesichts der Pluralität der Bekenntnisse soll der Anspruch der Wahrheit festgehalten werden.
Die Ausführungen über die "Einzigkeit und Heilsuniversalität Jesu Christi und der Kirche" werden in diesem Band dokumentiert und kommentiert. In der Perspektive der Fundamentaltheologie, historischer, ökumenischer und praktischer Theologie wird überprüft, inwieweit der in diesem Dokument formulierte Wahrheitsanspruch begründet ist und sich auswirkt. Das bleibende Problem der Ringparabel, Wahrheit nicht nur zu suchen, sondern auch zu verteidigen, stellt sich auf mehreren Ebenen:
Zwischen Gestalten und Bewahren: zur Hermeneutik von römisch-katholischen Dokumenten und ökumenischen Texten – "Sprengsatz für den Religionendialog"? Das Katholische und die Religionen im Zeitalter des Pluralismus – Wahrheitskern und/oder Konsens? Das Verhältnis der Katholischen Kirche zu den ökumenischen Kirchen – Chancen "messianischer Ökumene": die Beziehung zwischen Christen und Juden –
Der Band will durch Stellungnahmen und Erklärungen von innerhalb und außerhalb der Theologie zur Versachlichung beitragen und an Wahrheits- und Kirchenfragen Interessierten ermöglichen, das Dokument in größerem Zusammenhang zu erfassen. Das Grundlagenbuch zur aktuellen Debatte.
Bd. 9, 2. Aufl. 2001, 350 S., 20,90 €, br.,
ISBN 3-8258-5203-2

Michael J. Rainer (Red.)
Heil – Gerechtigkeit – Wahrheit
Grundthemen des Dialogs der Religionen und der Kirchen – mehr als ein Rückblick auf "Dominus Iesus". Mit Beiträgen von Michael Brumlik, Manfred Kock u. a.
Bd. 18, Herbst 2002, ca. 180 S., ca. 15,90 €, br.,
ISBN 3-8258-5588-0

Theologie: Forschung und Wissenschaft

Ulrich Lüke
Mensch – Natur – Gott
Naturwissenschaftliche Beiträge und theologische Erträge
Bd. 1, Herbst 2002, ca. 184 S., ca. 17,90 €, br.,
ISBN 3-8258-6006-x

Gabriel Alexiev
Definition des Christentums
Ansätze für eine neue Synthese zwischen Naturwissenschaft und systematischer Theologie
Eine wesentliche Führungsgröße im zwischenmenschlichen Gespräch ist die Eindeutigkeit der einschlägigen Begrifflichkeit, die erfahrungsgemäß durch möglichst klare und gültige Begriffsbestimmungen, also durch „Definitionen", zustande kommt.
Die vorliegende Arbeit bemüht sich unter Absehen konfessioneller Eigenheiten, wohl aber unter Einbezug naturwissenschaftlicher Ergebnisse (hier besonders der Biologie) um die Erarbeitung einer möglichst gültigen und klaren „Definition des Christentums".
Bd. 3, 2002, 112 S., 17,90 €, br., ISBN 3-8258-5896-0

Theologische Frauenforschung in Europa
herausgegeben vonProf. Dr. Hedwig Meyer-Wilmes (Nijmegen) und Prof. Dr. Marie-Theres Wacker (Münster)

Katharina von Kellenbach; Susanne Scholz (Hg.)
Zwischen-Räume
Deutsche feministische Theologinnen im Ausland. Mit Beiträgen von Teresa Berger, Elisabeth Gössmann, Elisabeth Schüssler-Fiorenza u. a.
In diesem Buch reflektieren im Ausland lebende deutsche und feministische Theologinnen die theologischen, politischen und soziokulturellen Bedeutungen ihrer multikulturellen Identität. Alle der in dieser Anthologie versammelten Autorinnen studierten zunächst evangelische oder katholische Theologie in Deutschland und setzten dann ihre Ausbildung und theologische Karriere in anderen Ländern (Chile, England, Japan, Philippinen, U.S.A.) fort. Das Buch versteht sich als Teil eines wachsenden Forschungsinteresses an "cultural criticism", in dem kulturelle, ethnische und religiöse Identität beleuchtet wird.
Die Beiträge sind theologisch-politisch gehalten

LIT Verlag Münster – Hamburg – Berlin – London
Grevener Str. 179 48159 Münster
Tel.: 0251 – 23 50 91 – Fax: 0251 – 23 19 72
e-Mail: vertrieb@lit-verlag.de – http://www.lit-verlag.de
Preise: unv. PE

und ziehen Persönliches zur Illustration heran. Sie bereichern die deutsche feministische und theologische Diskussion durch ihre multikulturelle Perspektive in zweierlei Hinsicht. Erstens erklären die Autorinnen nationale Eigenheiten, die in den im deutschen Umfeld entstandenen Theologien im Vergleich zu anderen Ländern vorhanden sind. Zweitens wollen sie bestimmte Grunderfahrungen von AusländerInnen und in komplexen Zusammenhängen lebenden Menschen für feministische Theorien und Theologien fruchtbar machen.
Bd. 1, 2000, 176 S., 20,90 €, br., ISBN 3-8258-4289-4

Anne Jensen; Maximilian Liebmann (Hg.)
Was verändert Feministische Theologie?
Interdisziplinäres Symposion zur Frauenforschung (Graz, Dezember 1999). Unter Mitarbeit von Christina Kölbl
Die Katholisch-Theologische Fakultät der Karl-Franzens-Universität Graz hat Frauenforschung zu einem ihrer Arbeitsschwerpunkte gemacht. Im Dezember 1999 veranstaltete sie in diesem Rahmen ein interdisziplinäres Symposion zu der Frage "Was verändert Feministische Theologie?" Der Blick war dabei in die Vergangenheit wie in die Zukunft gerichtet. Es sollten nicht nur die Ergebnisse feministisch-theologisch arbeitender Frauen vorgestellt werden, sondern es wurde auch ein Dialog mit Männern geführt, die sich für die Überwindung von Androzentrik und Sexismus in Wissenschaft, Kirche und Gesellschaft engagieren. Besonders im Blick war dabei das Theorie-Praxis-Verhältnis.
Der vorliegende Band dokumentiert dieses Symposion, dessen Gesamtleitung bei Prof. Dr. Anne Jensen lag. Die Beiträge stammen von Prof. Dr. Irmtraud Fischer, Prof. Dr. Hermann Häring, Bischöfin Maria Jepsen, Prof. Dr. Helga Kohler-Spiegel, Prof. Dr. Annette Kuhn, Prof. Dr. Hedwig Meyer Wilmes, Prof. Dr. Herta Nagl-Docekal, Prof. Dr. Michael Raske, Mag. Ingeborg Schrettle, Prof. Dr. Josef Wohlmuth.
Bd. 2, 2000, 232 S., 20,90 €, br., ISBN 3-8258-4616-4

Sonja Angelika Strube
"Wegen dieses Wortes..." – Feministische und nichtfeministische Exegese im Vergleich am Beispiel der Auslegungen zu Mk 7.24-30
Die Anzahl feministisch-exegetischer Publikationen nimmt stetig zu, die feministische Forschung differenziert sich aus und der Büchermarkt spiegelt ein nach wie vor reges Interesse an Frauengestalten der Bibel. Dies führt zur Frage nach dem "spezifisch Feministischen", nach dem Profil feministischer Exegese, der diese Arbeit nachgeht. Durch einen systematischen Vergleich feministischer und nichtfeministischer Auslegungen zur Geschichte von der syrophönizischen Frau (Mk 7,24 - 30) arbeitet die Autorin die Bandbreite und das besondere Profil feministischer Exegese heraus. Dabei zeigt sie auch überzeugend auf, dass nichtfeministische exegetische Studien und Interpretationen zahlreiche unausgesprochene und unreflektierte Voraussetzungen und Implikationen enthalten. Von besonderer Brisanz ist das Kapitel Fokus: Antijudaismus', das nachhaltig die Augen öffnet für latente antijudaistische Denkschemata der christlichen Bibelauslegung.
Bd. 3, 2000, 368 S., 25,90 €, br., ISBN 3-8258-4521-4

Anna Kiesow
Löwinnen von Juda
Frauen als Subjekte politischer Macht in der judäischen Königszeit
In bisherigen Untersuchungen zur politischen Geschichte und internen Organisation des königszeitlichen Juda wurde der Anteil von Frauen als zu vernachlässigende Größe betrachtet. Eine Monografie zum Thema fehlte.
Die vorliegende Arbeit will zur Schließung dieser Forschungslücke beitragen. Eingesetzt wird mit einem kurzen Überblick zu Leben und Arbeit von Frauen in dieser Epoche. Hierbei erfolgt erstmals eine systematische Zusammenstellung der bislang publizierten Frauensiegel. Danach werden Frauen am Jerusalemer Königshof in den Blick genommen. Lebten Frauen dort in "orientalischer Abgeschiedenheit" oder bewegen sie sich im "öffentlichen Raum"? Besonderer Diskussionsbedarf besteht im Fall des (hypothetischen) "Gebirah-Amtes", wonach es eine "weibliche" Leitungsfunktion am Jerusalemer Hof gegeben haben soll, besetzt meist mit der Mutter des jeweiligen Königs. Gesondert hiervon werden verschiedene alttestamentliche Nachrichten zu den politischen Aktivitäten der einzelnen Königsmütter untersucht.
Bd. 4, 2000, 224 S., 20,90 €, br., ISBN 3-8258-4653-9

Birgit Verstappen
Ekklesia des Lebens
Im Dialog mit Sallie McFague's Kosmologie und der Befreiungstheologie von Elisabeth Schüssler Fiorenza
Bd. 5, Herbst 2002, ca. 224 S., ca. 17,90 €, br., ISBN 3-8258-5304-7

Ida Raming
Priesteramt der Frau – Geschenk Gottes für eine erneuerte Kirche
Erweiterte Neuauflage von 'Der Ausschluß der Frau vom priesterlichen Amt' (1973) mit ausführlicher Bibliographie 1974 - 2001
Das Thema Frauenordination hat trotz der wiederholten amtskirchlichen Verlautbarungen gegen

LIT Verlag Münster – Hamburg – Berlin – London
Grevener Str. 179 48159 Münster
Tel.: 0251 – 23 50 91 – Fax: 0251 – 23 19 72
e-Mail: vertrieb@lit-verlag.de – http://www.lit-verlag.de
Preise: unv. PE

die Priesterweihe von Frauen in der römisch-katholischen Kirche nichts von seiner Aktualität verloren.
In dieser Situation des Ringens der weltweiten Frauenordinationsbewegung um Anerkennung der vollen kirchlichen Mitgliedschaftsrechte sowie der geistlichen Berufungen von Frauen bietet die vorliegende Veröffentlichung eine unersetzliche Orientierung. Sie macht ein international anerkanntes Pionier- und Standardwerk der Autorin wieder neu zugänglich. Im ersten rechtshistorischen Teil dieser Arbeit werden die mannigfaltigen Quellen (aus mittelalterlichen Rechtsbüchern, patristischen und biblischen Texten) aufgedeckt (c. 1024 CIC/1983). Der zweite (dogmatische) Teil beinhaltet eine kritische Auseinandersetzung mit der von der Kirchenleitung behaupteten Lehrmeinung, dass das männliche Geschlecht unabdingbare Voraussetzung für die Repräsentanz und Stellvertretung Christi im Priesteramt sei. Mit der seit Erscheinen des Erstdrucks dieses Werkes (1973) auf lehramtlichem und theologischem Gebiet vollzogenen Entwicklung, die durch eine ausführliche Bibliographie zum Thema Frauenordination dokumentiert wird, befassen sich einige ergänzende einschlägige Artikel im Anhang. In den USA wird gleichzeitig eine Neuauflage des Erstdrucks der amerikanischen Übersetzung (von 1976) vorbereitet.
Bd. 7, 2002, 328 S., 20,90 €, br., ISBN 3-8258-5579-1

Hedwig Meyer-Wilmes (Hg.)
Tango, Theologie und Kontext
Schritte zu einer Theologie des Alltags
In diesem Buch sind vier Studien zu einer Theologie des Alltags aus einer feministischen Perspektive versammelt. Die Autorinnen arbeiten als Theologinnen im Bereich von Ethik, systematischer Theologie und interkultureller Theologie in Nijmegen. Maaike de Haardt versucht, exemplarisch die Gottesfrage auf den Bereich von Essen zuzupassen, um die "Nahrung für die Seele" auch auf ihren körperlichen Nährwert hin auszubuchstabieren. Grietje Dresen untersucht im Alltag gebrauchte, zumeist unbewusst verwandte Sprichworte auf ihre ethische Handlungsrelevanz. Lieve Troch untersucht die "Zwischenräume" gelebter Frauenspiritualität innerhalb der Ambivalenzen einer globalisierten Welt. Hedwig Meyer-Wilmes beschäftigt sich mit Erinnerung als identitätsstiftendem Faktor an Gedenkstätten und im Tango, um den Umschlag von einer "Hermeneutik der Zeit" (Schüssler Fiorenz, Metz) zu einer Hermeneutik des Raumes zu skizzieren. Allen Studien gemeinsam ist die Verortung der christlichen Religion in den Vollzügen des Alltags.
Bd. 8, Herbst 2002, ca. 120 S., ca. 12,90 €, br., ISBN 3-8258-5708-5

Anne Jensen
Gottes selbstbewusste Töchter
Frauenemanzipation im frühen Christentum?
2. Auflage mit aktualisierendem Nachtrag
Bd. 9, Herbst 2002, ca. 560 S., ca. 30,90 €, br., ISBN 3-8258-5960-6

Studien zur christlichen Gesellschaftsethik

Karl Gabriel; Werner Krämer (Hrsg.)
Kirchen im gesellschaftlichen Konflikt
Der Konsultationsprozeß und das Sozialwort *Für eine Zukunft in Solidarität und Gerechtigkeit*
Bd. 1, 2. Aufl. Herbst 2002, 304 S., 15,90 €, br., ISBN 3-8258-3491-3

Heiner Ludwig; Karl Gabriel (Hg.)
Gesellschaftliche Integration durch Arbeit
Über die Zukunftsfähigkeit sozialkatholischer Traditionen von Arbeit und Demokratie am Ende der Industriegesellschaft
Bd. 2, 2000, 336 S., 17,90 €, br., ISBN 3-8258-4609-1

Werner Krämer; Karl Gabriel; Norbert Zöller (Hg.)
Neoliberalismus als Leitbild für kirchliche Innovationsprozesse?
Arbeitgeberin Kirche unter Marktdruck
Bd. 3, 2001, 232 S., 15,90 €, br., ISBN 3-8258-4730-6

Werner Krämer
Geschichte und Ethik der Arbeit
Bd. 4, Herbst 2002, ca. 270 S., ca. 15,90 €, br., ISBN 3-8258-4762-4

Timotheus Yu
Eine globale Umweltbewegung? – Die Kirchen im konziliaren Prozess
Bd. 5, 2001, 232 S., 15,90 €, br., ISBN 3-8258-4174-x

Oswald von Nell-Breuning
Grundzüge der Börsenmoral
Reprint der Ausgabe von 1928. Mit einer Einführung von Friedhelm Hengsbach und Bernhard Emunds
Bd. 6, 2002, 256 S., 17,90 €, br., ISBN 3-8258-5485-x

LIT Verlag Münster – Hamburg – Berlin – London
Grevener Str. 179 48159 Münster
Tel.: 0251 – 23 50 91 – Fax: 0251 – 23 19 72
e-Mail: vertrieb@lit-verlag.de – http://www.lit-verlag.de

Preise: unv. PE